The Blue Hour of the Day

BOOKS BY LORNA CROZIER

POETRY
Inside Is the Sky (1976)
Crow's Black Joy (1979)
Humans and Other Beasts (1980)
No Longer Two People (with Patrick Lane) (1981)
The Weather (1983)
The Garden Going On Without Us (1985)
Angels of Flesh, Angels of Silence (1988)
Inventing the Hawk (1992)
Everything Arrives at the Light (1995)
A Saving Grace (1996)
What the Living Won't Let Go (1999)
Apocrypha of Light (2002)
Bones in Their Wings: Ghazals (2003)
Whetstone (2005)
The Blue Hour of the Day: Selected Poems (2007)

ANTHOLOGIES
A Sudden Radiance (with Gary Hyland) (1987)
Breathing Fire (with Patrick Lane) (1995)
Desire in Seven Voices (2000)
Addicted: Notes from the Belly of the Beast (with Patrick Lane) (2001)
Breathing Fire 2 (with Patrick Lane) (2004)

The Blue Hour of the Day

SELECTED POEMS

LORNA CROZIER

McCLELLAND & STEWART

Library and Archives Canada Cataloguing in Publication

Crozier, Lorna, 1948-
The blue hour of the day : selected poems / Lorna Crozier.

Includes index.
ISBN 978-0-7710-2468-9

I. Title.

PS8555.R72B68 2007   C811'.54   C2006-905766-4

We acknowledge the financial support of the Government of Canada through the Book Publishing Industry Development Program and that of the Government of Ontario through the Ontario Media Development Corporation's Ontario Book Initiative. We further acknowledge the support of the Canada Council for the Arts and the Ontario Arts Council for our publishing program.

Typeset in Garamond by M&S, Toronto
Printed and bound in Canada

This book is printed on acid-free paper that is 100% recycled, ancient-forest friendly (100% post-consumer recycled).

McClelland & Stewart Ltd.
75 Sherbourne Street
Toronto, Ontario
M5A 2P9
www.mcclelland.com

1 2 3 4 5   11 10 09 08 07

For my mother, Margaret Crozier,
born May 19, 1918; died August 19, 2006,
my shining light.

Wait for me. I am coming across the grass
and through the stones. The eyes
of the animals and birds are upon me.
I am walking with my strength.
See, I am almost there.
If you listen you can hear me.
My mouth is open and I am singing.

– Patrick Lane

CONTENTS

ANGELS OF FLESH, ANGELS OF SILENCE

INVENTING THE HAWK

APOCRYPHA OF LIGHT

WHETSTONE

THE GARDEN GOING ON WITHOUT US

TAUTOLOGIES OF SUMMER

Every morning there are sparrows
and rhubarb leaves. Somewhere
a heron mimics shadows

while desire moves
just below the surface.
In spite of pain

desire repeats itself
again and again
like the snake who

looking for its lost skin
traces its shape in the sand
simply by moving forward.

Zero is the one we didn't understand
at school. Multiplied by anything
it remains nothing.

When I ask my friend
the mathematician who studies rhetoric
if zero is a number, he says *yes*
and I feel great relief.

If it were a landscape
it would be a desert.
If it had anything to do
with anatomy, it would be
a mouth, a missing limb,
a lost organ.

   ø

Zero worms its way
      between one and one
and changes everything.
It slips inside the alphabet.
It is the vowel on a mute tongue,
the pupil in a blind man's eye,
the image
    of the face
he holds on his fingertips.

   ø

When you look up
from the bottom of a dry well
zero is what you see,
the terrible blue of it.

It is the rope
you knot around your throat
when your heels itch for wings.

Icarus understood zero
as he caught the smell
of burning feathers
and fell into the sea.

Ø

If you roll zero down a hill
it will grow,
swallow the towns, the farms,
the people at their tables
playing tic-tac-toe.

Ø

When the Cree chiefs
signed the treaties on the plains
they wrote X
beside their names.

In English, X equals zero.

Ø

I ask my friend
the rhetorician who studies mathematics
What does zero mean and keep it simple.

He says *Zip.*

ø

Zero is the pornographer's number.
He orders it through the mail
under a false name. It is the number
of the last man on death row,
the number of the girl who jumps
three storeys to abort.

Zero starts and ends
at the same place. Some compare it
to driving across the Prairies all day
and feeling you've gone nowhere.

ø   ø   ø

In the beginning God made zero.

FORMS OF INNOCENCE

The girl can tell you exactly
where and when her innocence
took flight,
how it soared from the window
beating its wings
high above the stubble field.

A strange shape for innocence
when you think of Leda
but this girl insists
it was a swan, black
not white as you might expect.
From its head no bigger than her fist
a beak blossomed red as if wings
pumped blood up the long neck
to where the bird split the sky.

She watched this through the windshield,
lying on her back, the boy's breath
breaking above her in waves, the swan's
dark flight across the snow so beautiful
she groaned and the boy groaned with her,
not understanding the sound she made.

When she tells this story now, she says
though it was winter, she knows the swan
made it all the way to Stanley Park,
a place she's never been, just seen
in the room where no one
ever touches anything

in the book her mother keeps
open on the coffee table,
one black swan swimming
endless circles among the white.

THE PHOTOGRAPH I KEEP OF THEM

He on a big Indian motorcycle
and she in the sidecar.

It is before my brother
and long before I demanded
my own space in her belly.

Behind them the prairie
tells its spare story of drought.

They tell no stories.
Not how they feel
about each other
or the strange landscape
that makes them small.

I can write down only this
for sure:
　　　　　they have left the farm,
　　　　　they are going somewhere.

WILD GEESE

The wild geese fly
the same pathways
they have followed for centuries.

There is comfort in this
though they are not the same
geese my mother listened to
when she was young.

Perhaps I first heard them
inside her
as she watched their wings
eclipse the moon, their call
the first sound – separate
from the soft, aquatic
whispers of the womb.

And my sadness is her sadness
passed through generations
like distance and direction
and the longing
for the nesting ground.

THE CHILD WHO WALKS BACKWARDS

My next-door neighbour tells me
her child runs into things.
Cupboard corners and doorknobs
have pounded their shapes
into his face. She says
he is bothered by dreams,
rises in sleep from his bed
to steal through the halls
and plummet like a wounded bird
down the flight of stairs.

This child who climbed my maple
with the sureness of a cat,
trips in his room, cracks
his skull on the bedpost,
smacks his cheeks on the floor.
When I ask about the burns
on the back of his knee,
his mother tells me
he walks backwards
into fireplace grates
or sits and stares at flames
while sparks burn stars in his skin.

Other children write their names
on the casts that hold
his small bones.
His mother tells me
he runs into things,

walks backwards,
breaks his leg
while she lies
sleeping.

from THE SEX LIVES OF VEGETABLES

CARROTS

Carrots are fucking
the earth. A permanent
erection, they push deeper
into the damp and dark.
All summer long
they try so hard to please.
Was it good for you,
was it good?

Perhaps because the earth won't answer
they keep on trying.
While you stroll through the garden
thinking *carrot cake,*
carrots and onions in beef stew,
carrot pudding with caramel sauce,
they are fucking their brains out
in the hottest part of the afternoon.

CABBAGES

Long-living and slow,
content to dream in the sun,
heads tucked in, cabbages
ignore the caress of the
cabbage butterfly, the soft
sliding belly of the worm.

You know it's crazy
but they lie so still,
so self-contained, you imagine them
laying eggs
in the earth's dark pockets,
expect one morning they'll be gone,
dragging themselves
to the creek behind the house,

making their way
with great deliberation
to the sea.

LETTUCE

Raised for one thing
and one thing only,
lettuce is a courtesan
in her salad days.
Under her fancy crinolines
her narrow feet are bound.

CAULIFLOWER

The garden's pale brain,
it knows the secret
lives of all the vegetables,
holds their fantasies,
their green libidos,
in its fleshy lobes.

ONIONS

The onion loves the onion.
It hugs its many layers,
saying *O, O, O,*
each vowel smaller
than the last.

Some say it has no heart.
It doesn't need one.
It surrounds itself,
feels whole. Primordial.
First among vegetables.

If Eve had bitten it
instead of the apple,
how different
Paradise.

POTATOES

No one knows
what potatoes do.
Quiet and secretive
they stick together.
So many under one roof
there is talk of incest.

The pale, dumb faces,
the blank expressions.
Potato dumplings.
Potato pancakes.
Potato head.

In dark cellars
they reach across the potato bin
to hold one another
in their thin white arms.

CUCUMBERS

Cucumbers hide
                in a leafy camouflage,
popping out
when you least expect
like flashers in the park.

The truth is,
they all have an anal
fixation. Watch it
when you bend to pick them.

BRUSSELS SPROUTS

Brussels sprouts are Siamese
twins joined at the spine.
If you ask one out
you have to take the lot.
Do you have a sister?
sends them into giggling fits.

They all wear matching
sweater sets and sunglasses,
the reflecting kind,
so they see themselves
                    looking back
from the flat surface
of each other's eyes.

PEAS

Peas never liked any of it.
They make you suffer for the sweet
burst of green in the mouth. Remember
the hours of shelling on the front steps,
the ping into the basin? Your mother
bribing you with lemonade to keep you there,
popping them open with your thumbs.

Your tongue finds them clitoral
as it slides up the pod.
Peas are not amused.
They have spent all their lives
keeping their knees together.

PUMPKINS

Pumpkins are the garden's
huge guffaw.
             Toothy grins
splitting their cheeks
long before
you carve a face.

They roll on the ground
holding their sides,
deep belly laughter
rising in waves slapping
drum-barrel chests
like water in a bucket.

They are laughing
                  the last laugh
the ludicrous genital
tug and pull of things

laughing with the moon-mad
melons
         spilling like breasts
from the earth's burst buttons.

Delight in the small,
those that inhabit
only a corner of the mind,
the ones shaped by wind
and a season: a slip of
grass, the nameless flower
that offers its scent
to a small wind.

Delight in the silent,
the ones that change shape
soundlessly as moons:
the fossil golden bee
caught in amber, the bone
transmuted to stone, the
chrysalis of the gypsy moth.

Delight in flesh
that does not turn to
word, the ones without
voice or master. The old dog
who denies name, moves
arthritic legs to whatever
you choose to call him.

Weary of men, of words
carved even in the penis
bones of bears, delight
in the small, the silent
whose language lies

in their doing and their
undoing, those who turn
to stone to bone to wing
without a shout of praise
find their perfect form
become imago –

GLOVES

The gardeners, old country and tired,
plant their worn and loamy leather gloves,
the tannin good for growing
like soot, grass clippings, the ground
hooves of horses. Imagine all those
gloves stripped of flesh and bone
buried deep in the earth. Hollow fingers
slightly bent, an abacus of leather
knuckles, cracked palms – lifelines gone mad.
One glove holds the roots of a rose
like a tangle of veins. In another
a striped beetle builds a world from everything
the hand has touched. A star-nosed mole,
blind and dreamy, makes of one
a hammock for its noon-day naps.
Other gloves pass memories like prize squash
from hand to hand: the year of the bad frost,
the wind storm that pulled up the radishes,
the tomato blight. These are the ones
that want to go back to the hoe and trowel,
the sweat white on their palms
when the work was done,
the shed where they hung for years
from a nail like caught bats.

IN MOONLIGHT

Something moves
just beyond the mind's
clumsy fingers.

It has to do with seeds.
The earth's insomnia.
The garden going on
without us

needing no one
to watch it

not even the moon.

THE FLOWERS OF GEORGIA O'KEEFE

The nasturtium with its round leaves
sucks the bee inside, becomes an O'Keefe
blossom hung on the wall of the sky.
Light spills from each petal, gathers
at the soft, sweet centre. There sits
Sigmund Freud where he's always wanted
to be, whispering secret words as the bee
fills its sacks with pollen.

Georgia O'Keefe walks her dog
through the mesas where everything blooms.
Somewhere a painting begins.
It makes its first strokes across the canvas,
flowers open their mouths, bees mount stamens.
Freud checks his pocket watch, wonders
what his wife will make for dinner,
whispers *shit, cunt, fuck*, the bee
drowning in pollen. In the desert
Georgia watches the dome of a skull
rising like a moon over the horizon.
Her dog sleeps among succulents. Roses
lift his eyes to heaven.

Freud dreams himself inside a flower,
red and redolent with light.
Somewhere his wife is singing
but he doesn't hear. Too many
flowers in his garden. Too many bees
drunk on pollen. The blooms are hysterical.
They make his head hurt.

ANGELS OF FLESH, ANGELS OF SILENCE

FEAR OF SNAKES

The snake can separate itself
from its shadow, move on ribbons of light,
taste the air, the morning and the evening,
the darkness at the heart of things. I remember
when my fear of snakes left for good,
it fell behind me like an old skin. In Swift Current
the boys found a huge snake and chased me
down the alleys, Larry Moen carrying it like a green torch,
the others yelling, *Drop it down her back*, my terror
of its sliding in the runnel of my spine (Larry,
the one who touched the inside of my legs on the swing,
an older boy we knew we shouldn't get close to
with our little dresses, our soft skin), my brother
saying, *Let her go*, and I crouched behind the caraganas,
watched Larry nail the snake to a telephone pole.
It twisted on twin points of light, unable to crawl
out of its pain, its mouth opening, the red
tongue tasting its own terror, I loved it then,
that snake. The boys standing there with their stupid hands
dangling from their wrists, the beautiful green
mouth opening, a terrible dark O
no one could hear.

Hidden by trees, not deliberately,
wanting to be alone, I watch a man
not far below me drive a stoneboat
to a hollow in the earth, heave something heavy,
something the size of a full-grown pig
over the edge. Whatever it is gleams
like an animal without any skin.
He leaves without seeing me and I wonder why
I feel such relief. There's nothing to fear.
It's mid-morning. I can hear a tractor
in the neighbouring field, a magpie,
wind in the dry grass. Part of me
wants to walk down that hill, look
over the edge, see what's there.
Part of me stays in shadow,
watches the magpie fall from the branches,
disturb the swarm of flies that lifts
the shape of whatever it is into the air.

FATHERS, UNCLES, OLD FRIENDS OF THE FAMILY

Uncle Peter always told me
to wash my hands before breakfast
because I didn't know where they'd been
in the night   what they'd touched

                and his hands
lifted me from the paddling pool,
young seal   all wet and giggly,
his farmer's hands
soft in the towel,
my mother's
youngest brother
                pulling aside
my swimsuit.

Then there's the father
                of my friend
who did it to her
till she ran away from home.
On his seventieth birthday
she visits with the grandchild
he's never seen
and before she can pour their tea,
he reaches out,
                grabs her breast,
then cries   says he can't help himself
and she cries too,
what's there to say to him now?

One is always
the best friend of the family.
He makes her a fishing rod
from a bamboo pole
and with hooks   with bait,
rows her to the middle of the lake.
Shh, shh, I won't hurt you
                                        shhhh.

Years later
                    your flesh crawling,
you try not to turn away
when someone you love lays a hand on you.

Where did he touch you?

            Here   and here,
those places no one ever named.

ANGEL OF INFINITY

When she first touched the angel
her fingers burned
though the angel was invisible,
so much time and space,
so much light. The second time

the angel took shape
under the apple tree. The cat
watched the wings
                    surprise the air,
each feather so pure and well-defined
the woman tried to count them
to keep her mind on something real.

What do you ask of the Angel
of Infinity?
More room for your children, more
time, more time.

The cat seemed undisturbed.
He bunted his head
against the angel's legs
as if this were an ordinary guest
with cats of her own
in whatever house she lived in.

The woman felt comfort in this
and in seeing the wind
that lifted her hair
move the angel's feathers

so the air was filled with rustling
softer than the stir of leaves.

Maybe that was the blessing:
the cat purring in the shadow
of the angel's wings,
the apples on fire
                    in their usual way
in the apple tree

the wind
            touching everything
at the same time

IF A POEM COULD WALK

It would have paws, not feet,
four of them
to sink into the moss
when humans blunder up the path.

Or hooves, small ones,
leaving half-moons in the sand.
Something to make you stop
                              and wonder
what kind of animal this is,
where it came from, where it's going.

It draws nearest when you are most alone.
You lay red plums on your blanket,
a glass of cool cider, two sugar cubes,

knowing it is tame and wild –
the perfect animal –
knowing it will stop for nothing
as it walks
                    with its four new legs
right off the page

What I remember best about Rome
is the middle-aged woman
we saw on the path near
the Baths of Caracalla,
sitting in the rain
with her legs straight out,
one elbow leaning on a suitcase,
a plastic kerchief on her head.
A car stopped and a man
leaned out the window, said something
in Italian. She wouldn't look at him,
just shook her head, *no, no,* the cars
honking behind him and he pulled away.

She looked solid and respectable,
middle-class. I wondered
what kind of life
she was walking out of,
what was worse than these streets,
this pouring rain.

A block past,
we looked back, saw the car again,
the man rolling down his window,
the woman shouting now, *No!*
We smiled at that,
not knowing then we would leave each other
just as absurdly, three years later,
in a different country,
in the rain.

Right now I am the man in the Colville painting
staring at the Pacific. Behind me on a wooden table
that took months to build, dot by dot,
a Browning automatic. For the last time
I am watching a wave as it curls on itself,
rolling over and over. I've lost my breasts,
the curve of my waist and hips. I fit into
my new pants neatly, into my close-cropped
head floating above the painter's panel.
My other body lies somewhere else, perhaps
in a room that begins now. A woman and a dog,
she indistinct, but every hair on the animal
palpably there. Perhaps a mouth begins to open
on her left breast where the bullet
speaks its one clipped syllable. Right now
I am the man looking at the ocean. Inside
the head I've placed above my torso,
one thought turns over and over and won't go
away, the wave curling indifferently a precise
distance from the gun and table, a ruler
carved into its surface, inch by inch,
as if everything were measurable:
death, time, intent.
My new acrylic body about to move.

NOTHING MISSING

Mother and I wait for my father
who has gone into the labyrinth of rooms
where life and death dance like angels
on the tip of the doctor's tongue.
His cancer's been gone fifteen years
so we relax a bit, flip through magazines.
In the corner on TV young, firm women
bend, stretch, say *Don't stop now!*
There's nothing wrong with those bodies,
nothing missing.

I tell Mom about my friend Mary
who's just lost her breast,
about the purple scar stretching
like a run-on sentence across her chest.
Mom talks about a woman she knows
who lost both years ago
but found the solution to foam falsies
that didn't sway when you walked
or give when you touched them.
Bird seed, she says, *Frieda Yuricks
uses bird seed stuffed in cotton.
I guess it works real good.*

Later after Mom and Dad are on the road home,
the check-up good for another year,
Mary and I laugh over a bottle of wine.
She imagines stuffing her bra with bird seeds,
wonders what she'd do if she went swimming.
Wouldn't the seeds swell?

No need for bust developers here.
From 32 to 42 in fifteen easy minutes.
And what of sprouting?
Green tendrils
crawling up her cleavage.

I imagine Mary sitting in a park
surrounded by sparrows and chickadees,
the brave ones lighting
on her hair, her arms,
her soft, full breasts.

This morning, a heaviness to everything.
Even the crow is having trouble
lifting the air above its wings. The light
is heavy, the wind in the branches, the
silence between one thought and the next.
It is the feeling that follows
a long afternoon sleep in a strange house,
remember as a child, every object
solid and unfamiliar, holding you there,
alone and not quite human. Watching
the wings of the crow lift and fall,
I think of you, wonder if you sleep
long into the afternoon in another's bed.
I remember your story about the gopher
you shot and shot with a BB gun,
you cold and young, with no regrets.
The gopher pumped so full of pellets
it couldn't run, but dragged its belly
across the grass. That kind of heaviness.
The one the heart knows, its small gut
full of lead.

WITHOUT HANDS

*(In memory of Victor Jara, the Chilean musician whose hands were
smashed by the military to stop him from playing his guitar and singing
for his fellow prisoners in the Santiago stadium. Along with thousands
of others, he was tortured and finally killed there in September 1973.)*

All the machines in the world
stop. The textile machines, the paper machines,
the machines in the mines turning stones to fire.
Without hands to touch them, spoons, forks and knives
forget their names and uses, the baby is not bathed,
bread rises on the stove, overflows the bowl.
Without hands the looms
stop. The music
                stops.
The plums turn sweet and sticky and gather flies.

Without hands
                without those beautiful conjunctions,
those translators of skin, bone, hair,
two eyes go blind
two pale hounds sniffing ahead and doubling back
to tell us
          of hot and cold or the silk of roses after rain
are lost
             two terns feeling the air in every feather
are shot down.

Without hands my father doesn't plant potatoes
row on row, build a house for wrens,
or carry me

from the car to bed
when I pretend I'm sleeping.
On wash-days my mother doesn't hang clothes
on the line, she doesn't turn the pages of a book
and read out loud,
or teach me how to lace my shoes.

Without hands my small grandmother
doesn't pluck the chicken for our Sunday meal
or every evening, before she goes to sleep,
brush and brush her long white hair.

I like the kid who wrote on his first-year
history paper: "The Holy land is sorta like
Christ's Home Town."

He must have been from a town
with a Pool grain elevator, a Chinese café,
and one main street no one bothered to name.
One of those places you leave
but want to come back to.
A place where your friends return
for the high school reunion (there were only six
in your graduating class), where you fall in love again
with your grade-nine sweetheart and marry her
and it works.

One of those places you dream about
when you're stuck in the city on a muggy day
and the desert you have to cross to get there
keeps growing.

Not that it's perfect,
not that it doesn't have its share of wife-beating,
racism, and down-right human greed.
But Christ would've liked the town
this kid's from. Maybe it's even got a name
like *Manyberries*, *Porcupine Plain*, or *Paradise Hill*.

MOTHER AND I, WALKING

Father is gone again,
the streets empty.
Everyone is inside,
listening to radios
in the warm glow of their stoves.

The cold cries under our boots.
We wade through wind. It pushes
snow under my scarf and collar,
up the sleeves of my jacket.

Mother opens her old muskrat coat,
pulls me inside.
Her scent wraps around me.
The back of my head presses
into the warm rise of her belly.

When I lower my eyes, I see
our feet, mine between hers,
the tracks of one animal
crossing the open,
strange and nocturnal,
moving toward home.

A long line of black ants
moves across the sand, so many
they carve a trail. So many
if you step on one, the line
will not break. It is time
tracking itself. It is one
vast mind moving forward.

Ant after ant, each bears
an egg, a round white syllable.
Somewhere they are stringing them
together. Somewhere under the earth
they are spelling it out.

from THE PENIS POEMS

POEM FOR SIGMUND

It's a funny thing,
a brontosaurus with a long neck
and pea-sized brain, only room
for one thought and that's
not extinction. It's lucky
its mouth is vertical
and not the other way
or we'd see it
smiling like a Cheshire cat.
(Hard to get in the mood
with that grin in your mind.)
No wonder I feel fond of it,
its simple trust of me
as my hands slide down your belly,
the way it jumps up
like a drawing in a child's pop-up book,
expecting me
to say "Hi!
Surprised to see you,"
expecting tenderness
from these envious woman's hands.

PENIS/BIRD

There's an Indian story
about a boy who desires a girl
he can't have. She sleeps
in innocence, surrounded
by brothers and sisters,
her parents a hair's breath away.

The boy's penis grows wings,
it flies through the smoke hole
and straight to the girl
as if her lap were full
of breadcrumbs and berries.

I love that story, the penis with wings
more believable than a swan, somehow.
And here, the girl wanted it,
found pleasure
stroking this strange bird
that came from nowhere,
that sang so sweetly
and nested between her thighs,

the breath of her family
close around her,
warming her naked skin.

I like to think of that bird-penis
winging its way back to the body,
a little worse for wear
like a tattered crow

with some feathers missing,
maybe enjoying flight
more than it should,
the boy anxiously
watching the sky.

OSIRIS

Isis, a trinity of
mother, sister, lover,
sailed around the known world
and gathered up his parts,
the head, limbs and organs,
Osiris,
pieced together like a broken cup.
All that was missing was his penis.

How different our world would be
if she had left him so.

But she made one out of clay,
rolled it between her palms
the way we roll cookie dough,
sang it to life
between his thighs.

Was she tempted, the clay
wet with her spittle,
to shape it differently,

to make a rose,
a fish, a six-pointed star?

To make an owl,
a crescent moon, a second
pair of eyes,

to carve with a paring knife
another heart.

THEIR SMELL

Some smell like root cellars,
potatoes and crabapples
devouring themselves,
turning soft and brown inside. Some
of morel mushrooms in a paper bag,
the smell of earth
under a mound of damp leaves,
rosemary, marigolds, dead roses.

Some smell like geranium leaves,
like burnt stubble
when the smoke's so thick
it changes the light. Others,
the hands of a Chinese cook,
a bale of hay covered with snow,
old-fashioned hair oil. Some
of rancid butter or a fridge
when it goes crazy,
growing its blue, green, and black
gardens of mould. Some smell
like anchovies, others balsam poplar,
high-bush cranberries, dusty feathers,
a mouse's nest
in the pocket of an old coat bought at a rummage sale.

Some have a smell
you can't put your finger on,
like the scent of fear other animals pick up
and those high-pitched sounds

we never hear,
     what our bodies know
but can't put words to,
subliminal,
and most persuasive.

MALE THRUST

I can take no pleasure from serious reading . . . that lacks a strong male thrust.
   — Anthony Burgess

This poem bends its knees
and moves its groin.
It does the Dirty Dog
at parties. It pushes
against cloth, against
the page. It pokes
between the lines.
It breathes deeply,
closes its one eye
and wets its lips.
It writes lewd words
in the margins.
Wherever you are reading —
on the bus, at home
in your favourite chair,
in the library —
it flips open its coat
and flashes.
It backs the librarian
against the wall,
it comes
all over the stacks,
over *A Clockwork Orange*,
over *The Naked and the Dead*,
over *A Golden Treasury of Verse*,
over *Sexus*, *Nexus*, and *Plexus*.

This poem won't stop.
Even when you close the book
you can hear it
making obscene sounds,
smacking its lips,
completely in love
with itself.

INVENTING THE HAWK

The woman who undresses in the dark
with the curtains open. Slowly
she twists her hands around her back,
unhooks her bra, slides her panties
over her hips and down her legs.
No one can see her.
There is more light outside than in her room.
But she stands at the window naked as if
the moon were a mirror held in night's hands.
It is the colour of her breasts
when they are full of milk,
it is dimpled like her thighs,
her tired belly, it waxes and wanes.
She tries to hold it in her arms,
imagines wading into it,
all its roundness one tranquil sea.

On the street below her a man
in a red farmer's cap pulls a rusty wagon
full of empty bottles down the sidewalk,
the wheels rattling. She wants to show him
the moon, its calm indifference
on a summer evening when all her children
are asleep, when her husband kneels on a bed
in another house, entering a woman
from behind, so he can watch himself
disappear into the flesh,
his hands on her buttocks,
round and glistening with sweat.

The woman who undresses in the dark,
stands at the window, turns on the light.
This is what it looks like, she says,
this pale celestial body, faceless
as the moon is faceless, coldly luminescent.
You can stare at it forever
and never burn your eyes.

On the day named for the animals,
the tortoises crawl out of the soup vats
all across France, leaving herb-scented tracks
across the polished floors. Out of the poachers'
bags and through the restaurant windows
the quail fly, land on the linen tablecloths
and gather the speckled eggs to their breasts.
Foxes reclaim their silver coats
from the storage vaults, chew off the buttons
and slip into their smooth cold skins.
The elephants pull on their feet,
reassemble their long luminous tusks
earring by ivory earring, bead by bead.
One by one they claim what is theirs
and vanish
with the Sabre Tooth, the Dodo Bird,
the Dire Wolf. Only the animals
man has tamed or broken
remain, less
beautiful than they once hàd been,
for all that is wild
has gone out of them, even
the Appaloosa in the bluegrass meadow
eats only the hay thrown over the fence
and will not run.

ON THE SEVENTH DAY

On the first day God said,
Let there be light.
And there was light.
On the second day
God said, *Let there be light,*
and there was more light.

What are you doing? asked God's wife,
knowing he was the dreamy sort.
You created light yesterday.

I forgot, God said. *What can I do
about it now?*

Nothing, said his wife.
But pay attention!
And in a huff she left
to do the many chores
a wife must do in the vast
though dustless rooms of heaven.

On the third day God said,
Let there be light. And
on the fourth and fifth
(his wife off visiting his mother).

When she returned there was only
the sixth day left. The light
was so blinding, so dazzling
God had to stretch and stretch the sky to hold it

and the sky took up all the room –
it was bigger than anything
even God could imagine.
Quick, his wife said,
make something to stand on!
God cried, *Let there be earth!*
and a thin line of soil
nudged against the sky like a run-over snake
bearing all the blue in the world on its back.

On the seventh day God rested
as he always did. Well, *rest*
wasn't exactly the right word,
his wife had to admit.
On the seventh day God
went into his study
and wrote in his journal
in huge curlicues and loops
and large crosses on the *t*'s,
changing all the facts, of course,
even creating Woman
from a Man's rib, imagine that!
But why be upset? she thought.
Who's going to believe it?

Anyway, she had her work to do.
Everything he'd forgotten
she had to create
with only a day left to do it.
Leaf by leaf,
paw by paw, two by two,
and now nothing
could be immortal
as in the original plan.

Go out and multiply, yes,
she'd have to say it,
but there was too little room
for life without end,
forever and ever,
on that thin spit of earth
under that huge prairie sky.

NEWS FLASH FROM THE FASHION MAGAZINES

Breasts are back!
You can see them everywhere.
On movie screens, in restaurants,
at baseball games. You can feel them
bump against you in the subway
like friendly spaniels.
Big as melons they bob
behind grocery carts,
they pout under denim.
Breasts are back!
They won't stay locked up.
They shrink the space
in elevators, they leap
out of jogging bras,
find their own way
down the road, running
hand in hand. They wave
at you from buses,
swaying around corners
and swinging back. Oh,
how they move! Graceful
ballerinas, a *pas de deux*.
They rise and fall
under your grandmother's floral apron,
they flutter under your daughter's
t-shirt, small shy sparrows
learning to fly.
Breasts are back. On the beach
nipples peek from bikinis
as if they were eyes, wide open,

wanting to watch the sea.
Sailors rise from the Atlantic,
clutching their Mae Wests
for breasts are back.

But wait! Not just any breasts.
A breast should not be able to support
a pencil underneath it.
A breast must fit into a champagne glass,
not the beer mug you raise
to your mouth on a hot summer day.
A breast must have nipples
no bigger than a dime.
A breast must be hairless,
not even one or two small hairs
for your lover to remove
with his teeth. A breast must bear
no stretch marks, must be smooth
as alabaster, luminous as pearls.

Enough of that!
Let's stand up for breasts
any size, any colour,
breasts shaped like kiwi fruit,
like mandolins, like pouter pigeons,
breasts playful and shameless as puppies.
Breasts that pop buttons,
breasts with rose tattoos.
Let's give them the vote.
Let's make them mayor for the day.
Let's remember our old secret
loyalties, the first words
they placed in our mouths,

the sweet warm vowels
of our mother's milk
urging us toward our lives
before we even knew our names.
Breasts are back, let's shout it,
and they're here to stay!

GETTING PREGNANT

You can't get pregnant
if it's your first time.

You can't get pregnant
if you do it standing up,
if you don't French kiss,
if you pretend
you won't let him
but just can't stop.

You can't get pregnant
if you go to the bathroom
right after,
if you ride a horse
bareback, if you jump
up and down on one leg,
if you lie in the snow
till your bum feels numb,
if you do it in the shower,
if you eat garlic,
if you wear a girdle,
if it's only your second time.

You can't get pregnant
if he keeps his socks on,
if he's captain of the football team,
if he says he loves you,
if he comes quickly,

if you don't come at all,
if it's only your third time.
You can't get pregnant
if he tells you
you won't.

When I met you it was as if
I was living in a house by the sea.
Waves sprayed the windows,
slapped the wooden steps.
Yet I opened the door
and a white horse stood there.
He walked through the rooms,
swinging his head from side to side,
his hooves leaving half moons
of sand on the floor.

Make what you will of this. This was
the most natural thing I've ever done,
opening the door, moving aside
for the horse to come in.

Not that you were he. He was simply
a horse, nothing more,
the gentle kind that pulls a wagon
or drags seaweed from the shore,
ankles feathered, great hooves wide as platters.

He wasn't you,
that didn't matter. He looked at me
and we knew each other. That night
I wanted to live. I wanted
to live in a house where the door
swings on hinges smooth as the sea
and a white horse stands,
waiting for a sign.
Come in, I said.

And that was the start of it,
the horse, the light, the electric air.
Somewhere you were walking toward me,
the door to my life swinging open,
the sea, the sea and its riderless horse
waiting to come in.

I have no children and he has five,
three of them grown up, two with their mother.
It didn't matter when I was thirty and we met.
There'll be no children, he said, the first night
we slept together and I didn't care,
thought we wouldn't last anyway,
those terrible fights,
he and I struggling to be the first
to pack, the first one out the door.
Once I made it to the car before him,
locked him out. He jumped on the hood,
then kicked the headlights in.
Our friends said we'd kill each other
before the year was through.

Now it's ten years later.
Neither of us wants to leave.
We are at home with one another,
we are each other's home,
the voice in the doorway,
calling *Come in, come in,
it's growing dark.*

Still, I'm often asked if I have children.

Sometimes I answer yes.
Sometimes we have so much
we make another person.
I can feel her in the night
slip between us, tell my dreams

how she spent her day. *Good night,*
she says, *good night, little mother,*
and leaves before I waken.
Across the lawns she dances
in her white, white dress,
her dream hair flying.

She didn't believe the words
when she first heard them, that blue
bodiless sound entering her ear.
But now something was in the air,
a sense of waiting as if
the hawk itself were there
just beyond the light, blinded
by a fine-stitched leather hood
she must take apart with her fingers.
Already she had its voice,
the scream that rose from her belly
echoed in the dark inverted
canyon of her skull.

She built its wings, feather by feather,
the russet smoothness of its head,
the bead-bright eyes,
in that moment between sleep and waking.

Was she the only one
who could remember them,
who knew their shape and colours, the way
they could tilt the world with a list of wings?
Perhaps it was her reason for living
so long in this hard place
of wind and sky, the stunted trees
reciting their litany of loss
outside her window.

Elsewhere surely someone was drawing
gophers and mice out of the air.
Maybe that was also her job,
so clearly she could see them.
She'd have to lie here forever,
dreaming hair after hair,
summoning the paws (her own heart
turning timid, her nostrils twitching).

Then she would cause the seeds
in their endless variety – the ones
floating light as breath,
the ones with burrs and spears
that caught in her socks
when she was a child,
the radiant, uninvented blades of grass.

from THAT RARE, RANDOM DESCENT

ANGEL OF BEES

The honeycomb
that is the mind
storing things

crammed with sweetness,
eggs about to hatch –
the slow thoughts

growing wings and legs,
humming memory's
five seasons, dancing

in the brain's blue light,
each turn and tumble
full of consequence,

distance and desire.
Dangerous to disturb
this hive, inventing clover.

How the mind wants
to be free of you,
move with the swarm,

ascend in the shape
of a blossoming tree –
your head on the pillow

emptied of scent and colour,
winter's cold indifference
moving in.

PLATO'S ANGEL

It thinks the world
into being
with its huge mind,
its pure intelligence.

On the curve
of its crystal
skull
you see yourself,
you see your shadow.

One of you
will put on shoes,
will walk into the world.

The wheat ripples in the wind
like muscles under the skin
of a great cat.

Never have the fields
been so beautiful, so dangerous.
The beards of wheat flick back and forth,
even when the air is still.

In the long dry heat everything awaits
the gazelle-footed touch of the rain.

The horse has been standing
so long in the snow,
the side facing the wind
is white, the other,
black.

The white horse
walks off with the wind.

The black doesn't know
it is only
an absence
cut out of snow.

Now anything could walk
right through it
and disappear.

ANGEL OF NUMBERS

In heaven
the season for mathematics
is winter. Chalk falls
from the blackboards,
covers the earth.

The angel who invented
arithmetic
is trying to get rid of zero.

She erases and erases
the boards
then starts again

assigning to the numbers
already in the air
their own lost stars
to live on,
their own dark infinity
to name.

THE DEAD ANGELS

The angels lie down
in the field. That delicate
rustling is not the wind
playing the thin pipes of wheat,
but the angels' feathers,
their dead wings.

You can't see them,
but listen
when you check your crops,
the wheat so golden
it seems to float above the ground.

What a beautiful
sad sound they make,
all those feathers
remembering the wind.

FACTS ABOUT MY FATHER

1

He's five foot eight.
He has a large nose and thick grey hair.
He chews his nails to the quick.

2

He's skinny but he didn't used to be.
His hands and arms were huge from working hard, from shovelling grain in the elevators for a dollar a day, from digging sewers for the City with a back-hoe, from digging trenches in the oil fields. When I was a kid, he won all the arm-wrestling matches at the Healey Hotel. I wanted my arms to be as hairy and powerful as his.

3

He calls himself Irish and he's proud of it, though he's third-generation Canadian, his father moving from Ontario to Saskatchewan, settling on a farm near a town called Success.

4

He wasn't smart in school, quit in grade eight to help on the farm. His brains were in his hands, he could fix anything, his fingers knew exactly what to do.

He was famous for two things in the area where he grew up. He was the best driver for miles around Success, could drive to town through any kind of gumbo in his father's Model T. He was the district killer, shot dogs and horses for the neighbours without batting an eye, took pride in that, still likes to tell those stories.

6

He played the fiddle at country dances. Loved Wilf Carter's "Blue Canadian Rockies" and "Strawberry Roan." He married Peggy Ford, who loved to dance. She lived across the road on the farm with the big alkali lake where everyone used to swim. He didn't like to swim, didn't like to walk, didn't like to do anything that didn't connect him with a machine. As a kid he even rode his bicycle from the back door to the outhouse.

7

He has flat feet. That's why he lost the farm. He couldn't get in the army so his mother asked him to move to town. That way his younger brother, Orville, would be the only man around and wouldn't get drafted. He and Mom moved into a cook-car abandoned by the railroad in Success, which was already failing, the stores shutting down, the Chinaman moving away. When his mother died she left everything to Orville and Orville kept it all.

8

The Christmas of '41, just after my brother was born, there was no money. He shot a coyote, sold the hide for $5, and bought gifts for everyone. It was the first and last time he spent money on presents.

9

He wasn't there when I was born. He was betting on the horses at the Gull Lake Sports Day. The first time he held me, Mom was mad, he was hungover, his hands shaking.

10

He got throat cancer in 1969, had cigarettes smuggled into the Grey Nuns hospital, smoked a pack of Export A's a day, got well.

11

He caught his right hand in a lawn mower he was repairing, severed the first joints of three fingers. He smashed his left hand between the steel doors of a freight elevator. I was standing beside him. I fainted.

12

He had his gall bladder removed when he was sixty-four. The morning after the operation he pulled out the tubes from his arm and walked to the Legion for a beer.

13

He bought a speedboat when he and Mom were broke. He roared across Duncaren Dam, drunk, in a storm, leaping the waves. The boat finally tipped and he fell in with his clothes and rubber boots on. He can't swim, but he made it to the surface, the boat circling like a shark. Somehow he got in, made it home, didn't tell anyone till years later.

14

He buys hot goods in the bars and sells them for a profit. He cheated his son-in-law when he sold him a car. One time he came home with a rug he bought at an auction sale. When he unrolled it on the living-room linoleum, there was a hole in the middle, big enough to poke your head through. He rolled it up, tied it with a string and took it back, sold it to a Mennonite for twenty dollars more.

15

He collects ballpoint pens with names written on them, like "Ashdown's Hardware," "Ham Motors," "The Venice Café." He puts them in the bottom drawer on his side of the dresser.

One of them has a drawing of two minks fucking. As a kid I wasn't supposed to know it was there.

16

He never came to the plays I was in, never watched my brother play hockey. He was drunk at my grade-twelve graduation (I was the valedictorian), stayed out the night before and arrived home just as Mom and I were leaving for the gym. He couldn't tie his shoes. Beside the principal at the head table, he fell asleep, his head nodding over the plate of ham, scalloped potatoes, and jellied salad.

17

He uses the word *Bohunk* and the phrase *Jew him down*. One morning out of the blue he told me he'd rather kill me than have me marry a Catholic.

18

He owns the pool tables in the beer parlour at the Legion. Every Saturday morning he cleans the felt and collects his quarters, rolling them in strips of brown paper at the breakfast table. Though he's got cataracts and can't raise his arms above his head (it was all the arm wrestling, my mother says), no one can beat him playing pool. The young guys wait to challenge him after he's had a few beer, but he only gets better. His eyes seem to clear and maybe he forgets how old he is.

His favourite breakfast is Cream of Wheat. His favourite supper is roast chicken with mashed potatoes. His favourite bread is store-bought white though Mom bakes her own. His favourite shirt has snap-buttons and two pockets, one for cigarettes, one for pens. His favourite car is an El Camino painted bronze with razor-thin black stripes. Young guys stop him on the street and ask if it's for sale. His favourite story is how he picked up a semi-trailer from the factory in Windsor years ago, drove it through Detroit and all the way to Swift Current without stopping for a sleep. His favourite TV program used to be "Don Messer's Jubilee." He'd always say *Look at old Charlie dance.*

20

He doesn't have a favourite book. The only thing he reads is *The Swift Current Sun.* He follows the lines with the one good finger on his right hand, the nail bitten to the quick, and reads everything three times. I don't know how much he understands.

REPETITIONS FOR MY MOTHER

I want my mother to live forever,
I want her to continue baking bread,
hang the washing on the line, scrub
the floors for the lawyers in our town.
I want her fingers red with cold
or white with water. I want her
out of bed every holiday at six
to stuff the turkey, I want her to cut
the brittle rhubarb into pieces, to can
the crabapples, to grind the leftover roast
for shepherd's pie. I want her to grab me
and shake me out of my boots when I come home
late from school, I want her to lick her fingers
and wipe the dirt from my face. I want her to
put her large breast into my mouth,
I want her to tell me I am pretty, I am sweet,
I am the apple of her eye. I want her to knit and knit
long scarves of wool to wrap us in like
winding sheets all winter through. I want her
to sing with her terrible voice that rose above
the voices in the choir, to sing so loud
my head is full of her. I want her to carry
her weariness like a box of gifts up those stairs
to the room where I wait. Sleep, I will croon
at the edge of her bed, sleep, for tomorrow is
a holiday. Her hands will move in dream, breaking
and breaking bread. Not pain, not sorrow or old age
will make my mother weep. But the sting of onions

she must slice at six a.m., the bird forever
thawing in the kitchen sink, naked and white,
I want so much emptiness
for her to fill.

CANADA DAY PARADE

Two days later and I've turned the parade
into a story I tell over drinks. Start with
my favourite part, the band from Cabri,
the whole town marching, children
barely bigger than their horns,
old men and women keeping time. Then,
riding bareback, four Lions' Ladies
in fake leather fringes,
faces streaked with warpaint, not one
real Indian in the whole parade.
Finally the Oilman's Float, a long
flatbed truck with a pumping machine,
a boy holding a sign saying "Future Oilman,"
beside him a girl, the "Future Oilman's Wife."
I tell my friends it was as if I'd stumbled
into a movie set in the fifties, that simple
stupid time when everyone was so unaware.

That's my story about the parade,
three parts to the narrative,
a cast of characters, a summing up.
I don't mention my father
sitting beside me in a wheelchair.
Out of hospital for the day.
My mother putting him in diapers.
In the fifties he wouldn't have been
here beside us but somewhere down the street,
alone and cocky, drunk or about to be.
Or he'd have been racing his speedboat
at Duncaren Dam, the waves

lifting him and banging him down,
a violence he could understand,
that same dumb force raging inside him.
I don't describe my father
in his winter jacket, his legs covered
with a blanket in the hot light
bouncing off the pavement,
the smell of ammonia rising from his lap.

The day after the parade mom called
to say she saw us on TV.
When the camera panned the street
it stopped at us. "Not your dad," she said,
"they just caught the corner of his blanket."
As if he wasn't there.
As if he'd disappeared,
his boat flying through the air,
the engine stalled,
the blades of his propeller
stopped.

THE MEMORIAL WALL

When they built the wall
they had no idea the living would leave
so much stuff underneath the names.
They didn't know the dead had so many
strange requests, didn't know there'd be
so many pilgrims in a country with satellite TV.
The man who cleans up along the wall
can't wait to tell his wife after work each day.
You wouldn't believe what he picks up!
Flowers, letters, photographs, even a Coors,
okay, but a baby carriage full of human hair,
a stuffed alligator, a Lionel electric
train, its cars heaped high with wishbones.
They had to build a warehouse to store
everything that piled up, like so much merchandise,
as if the dead still need a shopping mall.
In a ledger each item is carefully described
by a retired bus conductor who used to classify
butterflies in his spare time. He records
the object's height and weight, the exact
place it was found, then lays it on a metal shelf.
He doesn't note its name or use, its possible intent.
One of the painters hired to coat the building
battleship grey, a young man who'd come
from Montana to find his brother's name,
paints the side door lapis lazuli
because he likes the sound of it. He doesn't know
the dead can walk through any kind of blue
as easily as air. At night when all the staff have gone,
when the pilgrims pile in buses, cars, and trains,

one after another the dead rattle down the aisles
with grocery carts to claim the one thing
they cannot leave behind: a baseball bat,
a red roller skate, a doll that says *Kiss me, honey*,
when you turn her upside down.

LAST TESTAMENTS

The cancer began in her tonsils,
she'd say it with a smile
almost expecting to be teased
for such a serious disease rooting
in that childish place.
She remembered her son at four
when he'd had his out, the way
he'd looked at her while the nurse
slid the cold thermometer up his bum.
She carried on as usual, cleaned the house,
fried a chicken for her husband
every Sunday, cutting the breast
in four pieces, the wings in two.
The morning of the day she died
she took him down the basement,
showed him how to separate
the clothes, set the dials,
how to hang his shirts and pants
so the creases would fall out.

               *

The man with a worn-out heart,
sold his tools so his wife
wouldn't be left with that part of him
to deal with. How he had loved them
in his hands, each so perfectly designed
to fit the palm; the wheels,
bits, and teeth made for one specific use.

On the empty walls of the garage
hung the shapes of wrenches, saws, and drills.
Years ago he'd traced around them row on row
so he'd know where to hang each one,
know what his neighbour had borrowed
and failed to return. From his pocket
he removed a black felt pen
and in the corner on a board painted white,
he drew the perfect outline of a man.

*

Before she walked into the river
and didn't come back,
the woman who couldn't remember
the day of the week
or the faces of her children,
made a list of all the men
she'd ever loved,
left it for her husband by the coffee pot,
his name on the bottom,
underlined twice
for emphasis.

WHY I LOVE PUMPKINS

Because they roll into town on the backs of trucks
with a loud, orange
crash –
tomatoes, apples, and melons
moving from the market stalls
to make way for their huge invasion.

Because the grocers pile them row on row
with the same skill that builds stone fences.

Because this fall for the first time, living
as I now do farther south, I saw
a whole field, pumpkins tumbling
to the horizon and doubling back,
and I had to stop the car to stare
as if I'd come upon a herd of deer.

Because they are more accurate than calendars or clocks.

Because of the grin some mother or father
carves for a child. The nose,
the triangular eyes that look at you
as if they know your face.

Because a candle flickers inside their heads
like memory
striking its paper matches and blowing them out.

Because they are the last
of autumn's light, the last to ripen,

an explosion, a contradiction of
colour in the colourless fields.

Because their flowers are deep yellow,
because their five-lobed leaves resemble hearts,
because *pumpkinseed* is also
the name of a fresh-water
fish resembling perch and the name of a type
of sailing boat.
Because you can therefore travel on a pumpkinseed
across any kind of water, or holding it to your ear,
hear the secrets of the sea.

Because the *OED* says, "A single pumpkin could furnish
a fortnight's pottage."

Because they are not a vegetable
for the delicate, the weak-hearted.
When you knock on their doors, someone
might answer, beckon you inside.

Because they are moons defeated by gravity,

hugging the earth in their orbits, as we do,
dust to dust. Because in soups and pies
and thick slices of pumpkin bread,

we taste what they know of time.

Because of the small distances
they travel on their trailing vines.

Because they float just above the earth
like lighted buoys marking the safest entrance
to the harbour.

Because the deer, born in the spring,
return to the pumpkin fields
after the harvest
and are lost,
though they nibble with their soft mouths
the broken shells left on the ground
and slowly
find their way.

Because the first snow falls,
the first snow falls,
into the huge silence
the pumpkins leave
in the fields.

THE CONSOLATION OF HORSES

The consolation of horses
in the meadow, yes, you console
though rarely am I near you.
You come to the fence (truth is
I almost fear you) out of fog or snow,
stretching long chestnut throats
for oats rattled in the pail,
grass pulled by the handfuls,
and sometimes you come only for the word *horse*
sung in the ear, first nominative and last
in the vast, ungulate kingdom
where the eye is more beautiful
because horses have walked through it.

In the stalls of the barn
hung with hoarfrost, harnesses, and bells,
your breath so tall above me
is a small consolation.
And when I ride the wide arc of your ribs
as I did as a child on a dappled, creamy mare
whose big bleached bones
now dazzle the meadow, you
find the latent heart of
wood, grass, and stone,
hoof by thudding hoof.
For you everything is movement,
everything is sound.

When you lower your great head,
graze so close to the ground,

you hear what lies beneath it,
the grey horses of the dead
moving from one darkness to another,
hoofbeats soft and slow
as though they walked on snow
without falling through.

EVERYTHING ARRIVES AT THE LIGHT

During drought, wind in the corn stalks
makes the sound of rain. It is comforting
to sit there, and startling to come upon
a wild delphinium in the aspen grove,
a shock of blue, almost pain.
My niece didn't understand the laughter
that followed the scattering of my father's ashes.
Or the place, the desolation –
an alkali lake edged with muck and salt,
no trees to speak of.
It sat at the bottom of the hill
my mother's family used as a garbage dump,
husks of cars and broken whisky bottles,
old combines waiting for a phantom crop.
Patrick found a rusted chain, two feet long,
with a hook on either end. Called a Come-Along,
he said. My brother and he had brought shovels
to dig up prickly pears for their gardens.
Mom thought it silly – with all their spines
they're pernicious on the prairies.
Not a plant anyone should grow at home.
She wanted to take nothing back,
nor did I,
though bits of my father remained
beneath my fingernails. The next summer
on the Coast, Patrick hung a Japanese lantern
from the chain, hooked the other end
over a branch of our cherry tree. At night
we sometimes light a candle, the lantern's filigree
designed a thousand years ago to keep a flame

alive in the strongest wind or rain.
Just after sunset at ripening time
the candle flame is not as bright
as the few globes of cherries
the birds have left,
though it gives their red an extra glow.

PHOTOGRAPH, NOT OF ME OR LITTLE BILLIE, CIRCA 1953

My mother stands with her bowling team,
she and three neighbour ladies
all in dresses, nothing fancy,
unless it's her buttons
black and shaped like pansies, later
my favourite in the button jar.
If you look at me, then back
at the four young women
who bowl every Wednesday afternoon,
you'll have a hard time seeing
a resemblance, picking out
my mother. Her face
is softer, in photographs
her smile tentative, uncertain,
as if she were back in a one-room school
and had raised her hand
without an answer.
Her dark hair falls in waves,
for all morning around the house
steel clips have gripped her hair,
all that metal making her head
look like some wonderful machine
for inventing electricity.
Like the others she's wearing
black two-inch heels and stockings
(though you can't see) with a seam.
Soon they'll put on bowling shoes,
each choosing one size smaller
than what they need because the number's
stitched in red on the back,

right where everyone can see.
This is my mother's only outing,
Wednesday afternoon, the bowling alley
four blocks from home. It's the beginning
of the fifties. My father's working
at the horseplant, my older brother,
the hockey star, is at school,
and I, too young to be at home
alone, am already obsessed
with the invisible.
Told to sit quiet on the wooden bench,
an orange pop in my hand,
I'm looking far down the bowling alley
past my mother and her team,
trying to catch sight
of the little man who lives
inside the darkness at the end of the lanes.
My mother said he sits on a shelf
as in a closet or a cave
behind the bowling pins
and his name is Little Billie.
When my mother wets her palms,
dabs them on the rag
and throws her last ball,
its echo rolling
down that long hardwood floor,
the pins explode
and he drops down,
flips them all upright
fast but not impatiently,
bent nearly double,
barely seen. He disappears,
balls roll and crash,

then there he is,
just outside the photograph,
waiting in the dark
to set things right.

Because we are mostly
made of water and water
calls to water
like the ocean to the river,
the river to the stream,
there was a time when
children fell into wells.

It was a time of farms
across the grasslands,
ancient lakes
that lay beneath them,
and a faith in things
invisible, be it water
never seen or something
trembling in the air.

We are born to fall
and children fell,
some surviving
to tell the tale,
pulled from the well's
dark throat,
wet and blind with terror
like a calf
torn from the womb
with ropes.

Others diminished into ghosts,
rode the bucket up

and when you drank
became the cold shimmer
in your cup, the metallic
undertaste of nails
some boy had carried
in his pocket
or the silver locket
that held a small girl's
dreams.

In those days people
spoke to horses,
voices soft as bearded
wheat; music lived
inside a stone. Not to say
it was good, that falling,
but who could stop it?

We are made
of mostly water
and water calls to water
through centuries of reason
children fall
light and slender
as the rain.

The most beautiful
is the woman behind the camera,
the one who is making
the three children smile. Years later
they'll laugh at the photograph,
the funny hair, the bony knees,
show their adult friends
how sweet they looked
in their Sunday dresses white as wings.

No one will remember the way
the woman looked. Now
as she composes sun and shadow,
the children across the lawn
are as separate from her body
as they'll ever be.

If she could see herself
she'd wonder
what has brought her here –
the ordinary house, the narrow garden,
the lilacs, literal and magical,
insisting their scent into the air.

Everything at this moment
conspires
to make her invisible

at the touch of her finger
her three small daughters

turning into memory
turning into light
and the other side of light

where the brightness
she is
        disappears.

Beautiful, ethereal, like a child
imagined for a play, Dominic
born premature five years ago
still has the look of someone
not ready for this world.

Just before his parents
and their two guests
sit down for dinner,
he places his hands
on the thin woman's belly, says
You are going to have a baby.
The adults laugh.
She has three and, at forty-five,
wants no more.

Like a midget clairvoyant
he walks around the table,
looks her husband in the eye.
Soon you are going to die.
Someone tries to make a joke.
There is nervous laughter.
Mommy, when you and Daddy die,
I'm going to build a house out of your bones
and there I'll raise my children.

He speaks precisely
and with a slight English accent;
white Namibian, he's a boy who's travelled
an ocean and a continent to be here.

After dinner, the man and woman
who began their drive home
with smiles and teasing
now shout at each other.
Who's the father? he demands for the third time.
He's had a vasectomy and she is angry
he won't believe the baby's his
(that is, *if* she's pregnant).
Soon I'll be dead anyway, he says,
I guess it doesn't matter.

In his room Dominic lights birthday candles
to place in his mother's skull
where her eyes used to be.
She is calling from downstairs.
Do you have your pyjamas on?
I'm coming up at the count of three.

Dominic tucks his children inside
his mother's head. The rubber mouse named Mimi,
the velvet kangaroo with a penny in its pouch,
the armadillo no bigger than a walnut shell.
One. Two. Three! Dominic stares through
the small round windows at his babies
in their beds. *Sleep,* he says, and breathes
his warm breath over them. *Sleep.*
Bone houses are so cold.

It was the wild ones you loved best,
the boys who sat surly at the front
where every teacher moved them,
the ones who finished midterms
first, who showed up late,
then never showed at all.

Under the glare of outdoor lights
you watched them bang
their hard bodies against the boards,
gloves and sticks flying.
In the cold they looked back at you
through stitched and swollen eyes,
smiled crookedly to hide
their missing teeth,
breathed through noses broken
in a game or pool-hall fight.
There was always someone older,
a fist and grin
they just couldn't walk away from,
there was always some girl, watching.

They were the first boys you knew
who owned a car, who rolled
a thin white paper, who talked
out of the side of their mouths,
cigarettes burning.
You watched them fall
quick and bright and beautiful
off the highest diving boards,

you watched them disappear
then throw themselves on top of you
till you thought you'd drown.

Oh, they were cool and mean,
but sometimes they treated you
with such extravagant tenderness,
giving you a rhinestone broach
they'd nicked from Woolworth's,
a fuzzy pink angora, giving up
their jackets on an autumn night
to keep you warm. How you loved
to move inside the shape of them,
the smell of sweat and leather
kissing your skin. For months
you wore their hockey rings
wound with gauze and tape
as if one day
you'd need to bind a wound.

The wild boys had the fastest
tongues, the dirtiest jokes,
and told anyone who'd listen
what they'd done to a girl
the night before
though in the narrow darkness
of a car or on a blanket
by the dam where eels slid
just beneath the surface, you knew
you did it to each other
and the words they said were sweet.

The boys you loved
knew everything, guided your mouth
and hands, showed you what you really
wanted from this life. Now,
it is their brokenness
you long to touch, the parts
they left behind or lost

as they learned too soon
too many years ago
what it took and took
to be a man.

I KNOW I'M NOT SUPPOSED TO SAY IT, BUT

I miss the smokers, the heavy drinkers
though my eyes burn when someone lights
a cigarette. I miss the poet who drank
a bottle of gin a day and talked to his
parrot in bird-vowels of squeaks and squawks,
its eyes following his big gentle hands
stumbling through the air. I miss the post-coital
smoke of my lover as he raised two fingers
that smelled of me to his mouth and inhaled
again and again. I miss the whisky priest who danced
wet in his robes in the fountain below the Spanish Steps,
holding a gelato high above his head and
never dropping it. I miss the tin tobacco can
of my sixty-cigarette-a-day mother-in-law who insisted
she didn't inhale. I miss my father who asked me
to smuggle a case of beer into the cancer ward,
who dragged his intravenous stand to the dungeon
smoking room five times a day. I miss the artist
in Zagreb who for over an hour in the bar
tried to touch the mole on my left shoulder
and always overshot his mark, his yellow-stained
finger jabbing the air. I miss the beautiful
woman who drank with Dylan Thomas. After three
scotch on ice, she tossed her head all night,
throwing back the long hair she didn't have anymore.
I miss the smokers, the heavy drinkers,
the ones who walked naked through parties,
covered with the host's shaving cream, the ones
who pushed dill pickles into their ears,
who played the harmonica with their noses,

who could aim a smoke ring to settle like a halo
over someone's blessed head. I miss them on the couch
where I covered them with the extra blanket,
where I took the glowing ember from between their fingers
I miss climbing the stairs to bed, draped in their silky
cape of smoke, their singing and jubilation, the small
bonfires of their bodies burning through
what little was left of the night.

When he finally showed himself
he was a bird with ragged wings
and black crow feet. He landed
on her window sill, then hopped to the floor,
wings clattering like TV antennae
lowered from the roof and taken
to the nuisance grounds.
On one foot two toes were missing
and his chest was plucked bare,
goose-pimpled skin raw and scabby.
When he saw the look on her face,
he began to whine. "You think
I can help the way I look?
I like going where I'm not wanted?"
The woman felt sorry for him
till she remembered who he was.
"Shoo," she said, "Shoo."
He limped toward her.
"I'll call the dog."
Death stopped. He coughed and coughed,
chest heaving as if his heart
were breaking out. "I don't feel well,"
he said. "I don't need all this trouble."
He hopped twice, his tail dragging
like a dirty broom across linoleum.
At the bedside table he raised
her cup of spittle, drank it down.
He unwound the bandages
from her throat and wiped his brow.
This close up, there was something

in his yellow eyes she found appealing.
They never blinked,
never closed, never had a chance
to stop looking at the world.
She threw back the covers and sat
on the bed for the first time in days.
Death put his wing around her
like an old-fashioned gentleman
offering his cape because
the night was cool. He said,
"It's not so bad, where we're going,
but you'll have to carry me a while.
My feet aren't what they used to be."
The woman felt her last
breath leave her body,
it hovered in the air between them,
then she stood and picked up Death.
He was light and suddenly no bigger
than a sparrow. If he spoke
she could no longer hear him.
He trembled in her hand,
the only warm thing against her flesh –
it was so cold. "It's okay,"
she tried to tell him.
"I won't hurt you."
She placed him gently in her mouth.
Her tongue seemed to be missing
and the inside of one cheek.
As she floated to the window
she was careful not to break
his small wings with her teeth.

NOAH'S WIFE

Of all the animals it was the snails
I loved best. There was beauty in the others,
the foxes' flaming tails, the eyes
of owls, pools of pure light
where I would have bathed if not
for all the water lapping,
my mind an island of eroding sand.

The salamanders, too, with their grace.
Their fingers seemed to stroke green
music from the air. Cats were my familiars,
perhaps too close for me
to remember my earthly delight
in the small hairs inside their ears
like the ones that guided bees into
the foxglove blooms drowning in my garden.

After a week at sea the air smelled
of rotting pomegranate and banana,
the autumn scent of hay, waste that grew
on wooden planks like strange
misshapen mushrooms slick with flies.

When I watched from the deck
almost all I had loved swept away,
it was not my husband
but the snails who comforted me. Each
came aboard with its house intact,
its room devoid of altars, of reminiscence,
the small things a boy might save
to remind him of the earth.

Like a woman the snail tucked itself
inside its shadow, slid on silence,
whatever it said to its mate no one could hear
nor the cries when they came together
on the underside of leaves.

As the ark sailed on my strange imagining,
and dove after dove fell from the sky,
I built my shell: one door, one window, stairs
leading nowhere because there'd been no stars
for days. Rain hammered the waves,
shattered the faces that stared at me
with the eyes of dolphins.
I began to see my husband's penis
as a snail's silver horn. Without words
I welcomed it under the eye of his angry god
whose spittle had drowned the world.

When my husband slept I slipped into
my own domed emptiness
and for no reason I could understand,
I licked the snails one by one
and placed them on his eyelids,
living coins.

THE END OF LOVE

I can phone him any time, he says,
though most mornings he's in the garden.
The days are sunny now, mid-July,
and there's weeding to be done. I'm sick
with worry and a thousand miles away.
He says he's getting better, the infection
in his eyes is clearing up though he forgot
his allergy to sulpha. Now he can see
well enough to weed between the lupines.
When I hang up, not home for a week
or more, weariness washes over me.
The way I feel is like the end of love
when you're the one who's been jilted
and nothing you can say or do will stop
what's going on. On top of that,
the cat is home from the vet's,
a tube sticking from his stomach.
My stoic love with troubled eyes
pushes food into him three times a day
with a syringe. The cat has begun to bite.
I've written on a stone and buried it
in a potato field so I won't think
about them any more. For a week I have to
find a way to keep on going. At the end of love
everything around you seems so tender,
so absolute. When the red-crested
chipping sparrow throws back his head and sings
outside my window, his whole body
trembles inside the song.

I love your feet. Father Phillip can't
believe it, tucked inside his socks
just delivered from the laundryroom
this note, *I love your feet*, then
three *x*'s, double *o*'s. Halfway across
the grounds to tell the Abbot,
he thinks better of it, remembers
an hour ago when he'd squealed on
Brother Harold, the disgusting
butt floating in the toilet bowl,
the Abbot saying, "Lighten up,"
as if they were teenagers
or part of a commercial for selling cigarettes.
I love your feet. Could it be Agnes
the laundry woman who laughs too loud
and slaps him on the back as if he were choking
though he hasn't choked in years,
forty chews a mouthful and lots of tea.
I love your feet. Could it be the young
pony-tailed novitiate who picks weeds
from the roadside and calls them flowers,
who replaces turnips with columbines
in the old monks' garden, carrots with lupines
taller than the chapel candle stand?
Is it the reflexologist who drives from the city
once a week on the Abbot's invitation,
bounces around the grounds without a bra
and pounds the brothers' soles with wooden hammers?
I love your feet. Yesterday, his turn to do the dishes,
the cook reached in the sink to grab a pot

and touched his hand beneath the bubbles.
Sure it was deliberate, he'd jumped
as if she'd thrown an eel into the water,
fleshy and electric. Someone loves his feet.
Could that someone know he wears socks
in the shower, and in winter nights,
the sheets so short, wears socks to bed?
Could they know when he lived alone
before the abbey, he married each pair
with a safety pin so the machine wouldn't
swallow one and leave a single
he couldn't match? *I love your feet.*
After vespers he makes himself
look at them, naked on the bed,
innocent and pale, like something on its way
to being something else. The vein
that runs from toe to ankle could be
a fat blue worm, in another's eyes,
the river of Jerusalem. *I love your feet.*
He waits for laundry day with dread,
with sweet anticipation,
the way the chubby, hopeful boy he was
drew a line through each square
on the Wheat Pool calendar
and walked the dirt road to the mailbox
once, twice, three times a day,
fingers trembling when he lowered the flag
and opened the little door, expecting
the secret kit from Charles Atlas.
I love your feet. Three *x*'s, double *o*'s.
Maybe he should pin a note
inside his dirty socks, but what to say?
He walks more lightly about the abbey

as if on water, raises his robes
a little higher when he climbs the stairs,
stands with one foot slightly forward
like the beautiful David poised in stone.
When he finds Brother Harold's cigarettes
forgotten beside the cookie tin,
he tucks a note inside the pack,
I love your mouth. Already he is planning
what to slip in the pocket of the Abbot's
clean pyjamas, what to write in pencil
on the cotton gloves of the novitiate
whose fingers green from gardening
smell like flowers
even when the season's done.

FALLING IN LOVE

The worst thing about
a horse bite is the horse

can't change his mind,
can't open his mouth,

release the flesh
until his jaws clamp shut.

Once the pain starts
you know it has to

get worse before
it stops.

I'm the one you've fucked
across the continent,
sometimes in the back seat
of your Fairlane Ford,
sometimes in the basements
of your friends. I always left
before breakfast while you
flirted with the wife
and fried the bacon,
your fingerprints
and smoke all over me.

I first met you in Winnipeg.
Wearing my mother's fur
over my naked skin,
my breasts sweet as apricots.
I called you *Mister*
when you drove me home,
your poems
singing in my head.

Off the 401
in the dashboard light
I showed you my scribbler
where I'd written you
in pencil and kissed
the pages red. You put
my hand in your lap
under the wheel, said,
This one's for you.

The radio was playing
"It's a Heartbreak"
Bonnie Tyler's throat
full of Grand Marnier and come.
I was chewing Certs so hard
I cracked a tooth. See,
I never got it fixed.

A year ago in Montreal
you snorted my skin
like uncut coke
until your nostrils bled.
Weeks before, knowing
you'd be in town,
I wore designer jeans
in the bathtub
so they'd be tight enough
to peel off
the way you'd strip
a peach.

Okanagan's a word
I've become familiar with.
I wash my hair in the smell
of pears and apples,
wear a t-shirt
that says *Cherryland*
so you'll think
it's my first time
when I close my eyes
and moan.

The night your wife walked in,
in Calgary, me naked on your lap
in the chair we'd bucked
across the kitchen,
you said I was the one
who started it and we'd
just met. I left my clothes,
even my new boots behind,
and ran into the street,
wet with you and cold.
A boy lent me his hockey sweater
to cover up. All I had
to do was jack him off
and he gave me a lift,
the face of an Indian
on my chest and back.

That afternoon in Halifax
we made it
on a fishing boat,
legs alive with scales,
your face red as a lobster
when you came.
Who smells of fish? I said
and laughed, the wooden
traps jumping around us.

Now I'm waiting at Mile Zero,
my yellow slicker
a lantern in the rain.
I can feel you moving
toward me like a cowboy
in a paperback, his horse
smelling home.

Admit it. You just can't
stay away – I'm the music
in your mouth, your love
of cunt and whisky,
my whole body fits you
like a lambskin glove,
oh Mister, where do we go
from here?

The only way to tell you is to write
this down, our lives a journal
with notes about the weather, perhaps
a grocery list and appointments never kept
because the sparrows sing for seeds
in our apple tree, and the spider
at the centre of her web demands
your poet's eye to hold her still.

You are fifty-five today. I must find
as many ways to tell you, as many places
on your body for my tongue to touch.
Last spring, our first on the Coast,
you said you'd never had a better birthday
and wondered why. You'd been working
in the garden, turning the damp earth.
On the prairies it would still be frozen
nine feet down. For a body to be buried,
the ground is set on fire, bundles of straw smoking.
Birthdays always bring the old deaths back.

From the window, I watch you digging
in one of the sweaters you'll wear
till the wool is worn thin and I insist
on putting it away. I save each one
as if your mother who knitted them
wanted what little warmth is left
to make something smaller, a sweater
for the boy who curled inside her belly
as she waited in the spring for the pale
buds of fingers to unfurl and bloom.

Earlier in bed, your hands cold from the soil,
I wept after I cried out, not knowing why.
Fifteen years together and some days
there's such pleasure in our bodies
as they move through the seasons, far
from the beauty they were born to. Now
they shine like parchment, worn by fingers,
by the spittle on the thumb as we turn
a page. We read each other, nearsightedly,
hands and tongues and even toes find where
the skin gives way. Since I cannot say
it right, for you today I must try

to keep this journal. Write:
March 26, and a little cold.
Write: Overnight the plum tree
has become one blossom. Write:
The days are getting longer
because my lover in the garden
turns and turns the earth.

A SAVING GRACE

A Saving Grace *is a tribute and response to Sinclair Ross's novel* As For Me and My House. *Set in Saskatchewan during the Dirty Thirties, that infamous decade of drought and Depression, the novel is narrated by a character the reader knows only as Mrs. Bentley, the wife of a small-town preacher who wants to be an artist, and who has lost his faith. The poems in* A Saving Grace *are told in the voice of a re-imagined Mrs. Bentley. I follow Ross's plot, but I've taken liberties with the story, incorporating some of my parents' experiences and inventing new characters who I hope are emblematic of that time.*

A MAN AND A WOMAN

Wind blows from the west.
In a double bed a man and woman
lie side by side, pretending sleep.
Breathe in, breathe out.
When he feels me move, he rolls over,
turns his face to the wall.
Why don't I tell him it's okay?
I know he's awake, I can't
touch him, can't speak.
My hand would have to separate
from my body to reach for him.
A country lies between us, a prairie
winter, years and years of drought.
When did it begin?
Wind blows from the west.
Surely even in this dusty room,
this marriage bed,
the small rain down will rain.

TWO ETERNAL THINGS

Early summer, the land wanting
colour – sienna, gamboge,
burnt umber – Philip says,
making a joke of it,
he'll paint a thistle
against a rock.

Two eternal things
in this godforsaken place:
rock – what the drought
cannot destroy,
thistle – what the grasshoppers
will not eat.

Call it *Hope*, I say.
Despair, he replies.

COUNTRY DWELLER

Paul, the school teacher
who drops by to see us
now and then, tells me
pagan means *country dweller* –
that's where we've gone wrong.
We've tried to tame the wild gods
and make them one.

Maybe even Philip
could believe in them.
A horse god. Among the reeds
and rushes, a wind god.
In aspen leaves, a god of light.

The smallest, the most slender
is the god of rain.

I tell Paul she must be
female, a four-legged animal
with soft paws and swishing tail
for that's what we hear
when she comes near us
for her green communion
with the grass.

DUST

Rags stuffed under the doors,
around the windows
as if they were wounds
that needed staunching

yet the dust
settles everywhere,
on my skin, my hair, inside
my sleeves and collar.
I feel old, used up,
something found
in the back of a cupboard.

I cover the water crock
with a tea towel
embroidered with a *B*,
turn the dinner plates
face down on the table.
When we lift them
two moons glow
on the gritty cloth

and in the mornings when we rise,
the shape of our heads
remains on the pillowslips
as if we leave behind
the part of us
that keeps on dreaming.

THE KIND OF WOMAN

Yesterday they found Emma Humphreys
at the bottom of the dry well
on the neighbour's farm. Mrs. Bird
says there's no way she could have
fallen in. It was deliberate.
She threw herself and the baby
into the darkness and lay there
for three days until Rusty Howes
lowered a lantern on a rope
to take a look inside.
Just a hunch, he said.

When he saw her there,
the baby still and white as wax,
he didn't know if the kindest thing
was to walk away. But his brothers
eased him down, hand over hand,
to bring her up, still alive,
saying nothing, a dead
look in her eyes.
Her husband took her home.

He seems a decent man
but what goes on in houses
when no one's there
but family? A man,
a baby and his wife.

Dr. Bird said it was amazing
nothing was broken.

The church women at Mrs. Finley's
over tea wondered what kind of woman
would do a thing like that?
I wish I'd said the kind of woman
like you, like me

but I changed the subject
to next Sunday's hymns, afraid
if I talked of her, the darkness
she found more comforting than light,
I'd say too much. Who knows
what makes a woman leap
into a well with her baby,
lie there for three days –
that small death in her arms –

and not call out,
not call out,
for her own good reason
not wanting to be found.

SKINNING HORSES

No one wants to do what Alex does.
It's horses he's after, the dead
who starved in winter pastures,
their hides worth three bucks each.

Only Paul will sit with him,
his wife and daughters in the pew
just behind the organ.
The true outcasts in this town
though few will talk to Dong,
Woo Chow, or Ephraim, unless
there's business to be done.

Early mornings when I'm out walking
I've seen him with his team and wagon
creaking through the countryside.
El Greco wants to follow but I grab him
by the scruff of his neck
and wait for them to pass.

I try not to imagine his hands,
the slick work they do
to keep his family clothed and fed,
that stench all around him.
They say it's soaked into his flesh,
it's on his wife and children,
but there's never been a man
with cleaner hands.

I've heard he scrubs each day
with a brush soaked in vanilla
bought from the Watkins man in bulk.
That's what I smell at the organ,
a faint whiff around his family
like when I bake a custard or a cake.

Now when I measure a teaspoon of vanilla
I can't help but see
those huge flayed bodies
and the bloody muzzles of the farm dogs
who follow Alex and his wagon
like gulls that swoop and dive behind a plow.

NOT THE MUSIC

Not the music.
It is this other thing
I keep from all of them
that matters, inviolable.

I scratch in my journals,
a mouse rummaging through cupboards,
nibbling on a crust of bread, apple skins,
chewing the edges of photographs, the small
details of a life. I hoard and save,
place one thing inside another
inside the next.

Start with the prairie, then Horizon
and inside it our house,
the kitchen, the table where I sit
with my journal, and inside it
everything I write – dust, moths,
wind speaking in whispers
across the page,
the absence of rain,
forgiveness –
everything shrinking
to the smallest
thinnest letter,
I.

JOE LAWSON'S WIFE

The woman who pounded on our door
came out of the wind, hair wild,
voice thin and broken. Philip
drove with Dr. Bird beside him,
I sat in the back with her,
Joe Lawson's wife, both of us silent
and staring straight ahead
though there was nothing to see
in those two beams of light. How
to comfort? When we got to the barn,
Philip was awkward with the rope.
The doctor pushed him aside,
climbed the milking-stool
the man had kicked away
and cut him down. Joe Lawson,
though it was hard to call
what hung in the barn
that name – the rope had cut into his neck,
his face blue and bloated.

I kept my eyes on his hands.
They were what you noticed
when you first saw Joe. Big, solid hands,
as much a part of the land as the stones
ice heaves from the earth every spring.

It was a minister they needed
not the doctor, but Philip hung back.
Dr. Bird was the one who told me
Take her to the house and make some tea.

She wouldn't leave,
but covered her man with a blanket
that smelled of horse, then sat
in the dirty straw, his swollen head
in her lap. By then her sister had arrived
and the neighbour with a wagon.
The sun was rising, its splinters
from the cracks in the walls
falling all around her.

At last she let the men
carry the body from the barn
but still wouldn't go.

She pulled the wooden stool
to the stall and milked the cow,
its udder heavy, barn cats
coming out of nowhere at the sound.

There was no pail,
milk streamed out and hit the ground,
pooled around her feet,
the cats licking and mewling.
Her sister stood helplessly beside her
and motioned us away.
There was nothing to do but go,
above her head Philip mumbling
something I couldn't hear.

At home, he clung to me
as if his feet were swinging through the air
and it was I that held him up.
How to comfort. We bring so little

to each other. Later, after we had slept
he went into his study and I followed,
watched him from the door.
So upset, he left it open.

He tore the drawings he had sketched
last Sunday, his parishioners
as he had seen them from the pulpit – all
alike, his pencil strokes relentless,
pinning them and their piety to the pews.

Everything would change for us
if he could draw
that woman on her stool, her simple
act of courage – or was it resignation?
The shadow of her husband still
swaying from the rafters,
milk puddling at her feet
and between the cracks,
the sun's bright nails pounding through.

JUDITH

It's taken me this long to write it:
Judith. A strong biblical name
for such a girl. I should say
woman, Miss Judith West.

   I am my beloved's, and my beloved is mine.

That night I moved through my fever
as if it were a house; remember
the game you played as a child?
Lying on your back in bed you stared
till the ceiling became the floor.
You stepped over a ledge
through the doorway, circled
the lightbulb, stem tall as a tulip's.

   The beams of our house are of cedar
   and our rafters of fir.

That's where I was, on the ceiling,
looking down. They weren't in the woodshed,
as I said, in that smell of dog
and kindling, but in the kitchen,
everything scrubbed and shining and
reflecting light. It made it worse somehow,
in my kitchen. He sat naked on a chair.
She straddled him.

   He feedeth among the lilies.

I seemed to float above their heads
though I could clearly see
the swell and blaze of her buttocks
and hear him groan.

I am my beloved's
and his desire is towards me.

My whole body ached
not with the pain of fever but
a deeper hurt, less centred.
If I'd been a different woman
I would have screamed, raked my nails
down her back.

Who is she that looketh forth
as the morning, fair as the moon,
clear as the sun, and terrible
as an army with banners?

I moved my legs and arms
like an underwater swimmer
and made it to our bed. The dog,
hearing them, scratched at the door,
whimpering. Or was it me?

This is my beloved,
and this is my friend,
O daughters of Jerusalem.

In the morning I thought
I made the whole thing up,
But Philip was too kind to me.

His left hand should be under my head
and his right hand should embrace me.

And when he left
to buy something special
for my breakfast, I climbed out of bed,
stumbled through the kitchen
to the door. On hands and knees,
I followed with my fingers
the dog's claw tracks in the wood,
an exegesis white as scars,
and I saw everything again
as I had seen it –

    his belly bright ivory,
    his legs pillars of marble
    set upon sockets of fine gold,
    this is my beloved

the marrow in my bones aching.

If her family had been better off
she'd have gone to Saskatoon
"to visit an aunt." That's what
they called it then, aunt or no.
Here I've heard the locals say,
"She's gone visiting a Model T,"
because it probably happened
in the back seat.
Judith's family was dirt poor.
Nothing for her to do
but go back to the farm,
pretending she was ill.

No one guessed the father
though every name in town
came up except the preacher's.
I sent Philip to the farm –
I'm not sure why,
gave him a sack of oranges,
insisting he tell her
they were a gift from me.
I packed them in hay
so they wouldn't bruise.
I wanted them
round and hard and sweet.

That morning when I watched him
ride away, I wished he'd leave for good,
do something brave and true for once.
Then I panicked at the thought.
Who am I if not Mrs. Bentley?

When he returned, I asked him how she was.
Don't send oranges again, he said.
She wept and wept in the kitchen chair,
holding one in each hand.

After supper, before he could go
to his study, close the door,
I said, We'll help her out.
We'll take her baby. (I couldn't bear
the joy flickering across his face.)
It's the Christian thing to do.
Poor Philip who has tasted
the waters of Paradise,
the sip small and brief.
If she is a fruit full and ripening,
I am a gourd with hard
and bitter seeds.

PAUL

I made him promise
not to say a word.
And I wrote nothing down.

I wanted it to be
unreadable.

He met me underneath
the trestle, in the coulee's dip.
Both of us were clumsy, he
from inexperience, I guess,
me too long out of use.

This is the funny part –
Paul, the philologist,
was very good with his tongue.

When I came
there was no roar of
a train overhead, no
jealous husband on the ties
looking down. *Paul*,
I said out loud,
twice, so I wouldn't
trick myself
and he felt good inside me,
as good as   any man

though afterwards
we couldn't look at each other.

I walked through town
my blouse buttoned wrong
and didn't know it
till Philip undid the buttons,
did them up again,
under the cotton my skin burning.

I was peeling potatoes
at the kitchen sink.
When he touched me
the knife slipped –
flames spilling from my finger.
I burnt my mouth with its heat.

MRS. BENTLEY

I've walked through this story
in housedresses and splay-
footed rubbers. Mousy hair
without curls. Philip never drew
a convenient portrait
for me to comment on,
a hasty sketch. I could have said,
though his hand is flawless,
this does not resemble me.
That's my high forehead
and the way I purse my lips
but he's placed my eyes
far apart. I look in two directions.
The right one stares at you,
follows you as you move.
The left, my prairie eye,
gazes at what lies just over
where the lines converge.
No portraits exist, no photographs
and little self-description.
And nowhere in these pages
can you find my name.
Gladys, Louise, Madeline?
I fancy Margaret though in the country
everyone would call her Peg.
We're left with Mrs.
Bentley, dowdy, frumpy, plain.
Don't you wonder what Philip
called me as we lay together,
my flesh warmed by his hands,

the taste of me on his tongue,
as if there were no better sound
in all the world,
my name, my name!

WHAT THE LIVING WON'T LET GO

THE NIGHT OF MY CONCEPTION I

Waiting six years
since my brother drifted from my touch.
I have almost forgotten his smell,
forgotten how we moved together,
water over water, breath riding breath
into the emptiness of blue.

It is the night of my arrival.
My father sits on the couch,
throws a ball for the bull terrier
they've called Patsy.
Behind him my mother bends,
unfastens her stockings.
They slide down her legs
with the sound of sunlight
slipping through the petal of a peony.
Soon he will turn to her.

These are the two
I love and will love
no matter what they do to me
or to each other.
This is my brother's house.

He has opened a window in his room,
the night hot and sticky.
He is trying not to hear
through the wall that keeps him
from the huge bed
they won't let him sleep in any more.

Lightly as a moth I slip
through the screen. He feels
a breeze lifting his hair.
It is me, breathing over him,
savouring his smell,
dusting my small hands
across his forehead
till my mother cries that cry
and I must go.

Months later when he leans
over my crib
he will see it in my eyes,
the way I look at him
as if I know
what he's forgotten

and the first
of the many times
he'll deny me
will begin.

THE NIGHT OF MY CONCEPTION 2

Mist in the fields. Inside it,
a rabbit and a wishing stone.

A man and woman lie in their own
whiteness, the brief balsam of the flesh.

Her hair is darker than I've seen it,
his less thin. When I look closer

the mist thickens, but I glimpse
the round gleam of his buttocks

and one of her breasts, from under him,
fallen a little to the side.

Its nipple is a rose quartz
polished by his tongue,

a stone for several wishes.
I am less corporeal than water,

than the rabbit, smaller
than a child's footprint on a page.

Soon the man and woman will make
a space for me between them.

Sweet Jesus, he cries,
and I'm the one who answers.

Smaller than a barley pearl,
I curl inside her longing.

It is my voice
singing when she comes.

THOMAS HARDY'S HEART

My name is Jude. I am the cat who swallowed
Thomas Hardy's heart. I snatched it
from the bowl in my mistress's kitchen
and leapt through the window to the woods.

She was his sister.
What was she going to do with it?
Stuff it with veal and breadcrumbs?
Soak it in cider and serve it with the funeral meats?

It pumped a trail across the sill
and then the paving stones,
pounding out its life. I believe
she'll never get over it,
such screams and shrieking, her face
drunk with tears.

Plump as a rat and slippery,
he would have said *the deadest thing*
– it was the strangest thing
I've ever eaten. In the mouth it was sweet;
in the belly, all wormwood and rue.

Better than a tongue, a bitter heart
speaks truly. I had nine lives.
Now I've ten.

At night my mistress walks the woods,
bare trees flecked with candlelight,
a pulse that flickers in her hand.

Twice no one dies.
I've eaten nothing since.

In a plaintive voice she calls.
First *Jude*, then *Thomas*, then *Jude* again.
The warmth of her lap, the nest I made
from her hair spread across the pillow
like a pelt, no muscle underneath
so it was also a darkling stream.

What dreams I've had!
My hands are paws.
Was she the one who used to feed me
when I was young?

The sky is clear tonight –
out of the woods I don't know what to come to
or if I should at all

starlit in my loneliness and magic in my eyes.

ONE FOOT IN THE GRAVE

If my friend hadn't loved
the mole on the side of my right foot –
a beauty mark, she said –
would I have noticed when it twinned
to twice its size? A perfect heart
some child had cut from folded paper
then opened it and spread it flat.

Melanoma.

When I say the word out loud
vowels unfurl off my tongue,
petals on a flower I've never seen before –
mimosa, bougainvillaea. May 24, 1948,
the gardener's youngest daughter writes,
The melanoma blooms so lush this year
bees wake us every morning.

A wild sea shipwrecks me on Maui,
Bali, Melanoma – the lost misty isle
where the last of the lepers live.
Shy and ancient, one stares at me
with half a face through thick wet leaves.

Rare spices of the East –
melanoma, tamarind, cardamom –
worth their weight in gold.
A little goes a long way.

Melanoma, first name Carmen,
the famous middle-aged flamenco dancer
García Lorca applauded in Granada.
Five o'clock in the afternoon
in saffron candlelight
he could hear *duende*
in the pounding of her heels.

MILDRED

The panties I buy wear a sticker:
Inspected by Mildred.
All the pairs in my drawer
have passed through her hands
before I slip them on.

I've been buying this brand
for years because of Mildred.
What kind of trouble can I get into
wearing panties inspected
by Mildred? How can I not
keep my knees together, my
underwear clean?

The elastic still snaps
after countless washes,
the seams hold, the 100% cotton
hugs the hips and bum
because my panties have been
inspected by Mildred.

What will I do when she retires?
When her name is replaced
by Tonya or Charlotte,
some one who wears silk and lace
or nothing at all, someone who
doesn't know the first thing
about the tenacity of
the double-lined
cotton crotch?

I hope Mildred has medicare,
a dental plan, and wages
that match her labour.
I hope she works
in a factory full of windows,
in a comfortable chair,
pulling panties over her hands
like evening gloves and holding them
to the light with the close attention
of a woman candling eggs.

Hail to thee, sweet Mildred,
Mother of Cotton Panties,
immaculate and flawless,
for the blossoms of your labour,
for the blessings of your hands.

PACKING FOR THE FUTURE: INSTRUCTIONS

Take the thickest socks.
Wherever you're going
you'll have to walk.

There may be water.
There may be stones.
There may be high places
you cannot go without
the hope socks bring you,
the way they hold you
to the earth.

At least one pair must be new,
must be blue as a wish
hand-knit by your mother
in her sleep.

*

Take a leather satchel,
a velvet bag and an old tin box –
a salamander painted on the lid.

This is to carry that small thing
you cannot leave. Perhaps the key
you've kept though it doesn't fit
any lock you know,
the photograph that keeps you sane,
a ball of string to lead you out
though you can't walk back
into that light.

In your bag leave room for sadness,
leave room for another language.

There may be doors nailed shut.
There may be painted windows.
There may be signs that warn you
to be gone. Take the dream
you've been having since
you were a child, the one
with open fields and the wind
sounding.

*

Mistrust no one who offers you
water from a well, a songbird's feather,
something that's been mended twice.
Always travel lighter
than the heart.

WATCHING MY LOVER

I watch him hold his mother
as she vomits into a bowl.
After, he washes her face
with a wet cloth and we try
to remove her soiled gown
tied in the back with strings.

Unable to lift her
I pull the green cotton
from under the blankets, afraid
I'll tear her skin.
He removes the paper diaper.
No one has taught us
how to do this, what to say.
Everything's so fragile here
a breath could break you.

She covers her breasts with hands
bruised from tubes and needles,
turns her face away.
It's okay, Mom, he says.
Don't feel shy. I've undressed
dozens of women in my time.
In this room where my lover
bares his mother, we three laugh.

Later, I curl naked beside him
in our bed, listen to his sleeping,
breath by breath. So worn out
he burns with fever – the fires

his flesh lights to keep him
from the cold.

Though he has washed
I smell her on his skin
as if she has licked him
from head to toe
with her old woman's tongue
so everyone who lies with him
will know he's still
his mother's son.

THE OTHER WOMAN

Nearly twenty years ago and finally
I can think of her. She used to dial,
put the older of the two boys on the line.
Only four, *Daddy*, he'd say,
when are you coming home? till his father
clicked the receiver down. He'd left them
$10,000 and a yellow truck, came to me
with more than his pockets empty.

We struck out across the prairies,
wind roaring through the car, the road
hurtling us into the sky like a midway ride.
Every night a bottle of wine, a cheap motel,
we went so far we came back animal
and wild. No child could hold us.

The first time he visited his sons
she wore clothes he'd never seen before,
hair shampooed and newly permed.
Stay the night, she said, *save the price of a room.*
Home with me his hands stammered
down my belly in a language they'd forgotten,
one with several words for guilt and pain.
I almost lost him then.

Now it's she who phones
late at night, the boys grown up.
When I answer, she doesn't ask for him.
There's a silence, both of us breathing,
and I think of her mouth almost touching

the phone – as close as we have come.
Sometimes the next morning I keep quiet.
In twenty years I've never seen her face.

Nineteen seventy-eight, the end of summer
is a snapshot I never took –
the first time I see him with the boys.
In Okanagan Lake he holds around the waist
his younger son, pale legs kicking.
So beautiful together, it's an ache
I've carried since, something small and shining.
A stranger, from the shore I observe
the other boy thrash toward the raft.
She may be standing in the trees, invisible,
watching. She should have been.

If the child had been drowning,
if his father had turned to me
and the little one, free,
kicked into deeper water,
I couldn't have moved,
couldn't have saved them,
so fierce I was
holding on to my new life.

A KIND OF LOVE

You can see it
in my graduation photograph.
You're Daddy's little girl, he said,
his arm heavy around my shoulders,
his face too naked, a sloppy
smile sliding to one side.
I held him up. Mom tied his shoes.
His love made me ashamed.

Some days I felt protective,
his hangdog look at breakfast
when no one talked to him but me,
sugar spilling from his spoon.
Don't tell Mum, he'd say
on Sundays when he took me boating,
sunk his third empty in the lake.
At home, she fried a chicken
in case he didn't catch a fish,
waited and kept things warm.
Even so, he died too soon.

Now I wait for you as if
you've spent a summer afternoon
in waves of wind and sunlight. I know
you've hidden a bottle somewhere
upstairs in your room. So far
I've stopped myself from looking
though I can't find what to do.

More and more I'm Daddy's
little girl in peau de soi,
my first long dress, its false
sheen a wash of mauve.
When you lean into me
the same look's on your face
as in the photograph,
your smile's undone.

Among the other things
it could be named
this too is love, the kind
I'm most familiar with –
the weight I claim
I cannot bear and do,
and do.

from COUNTING THE DISTANCE

THE YOUNGER SISTER: TOO CLOSE TO THINGS

My sister's breasts were shy as fawns
and like a fawn they hushed you
when you glimpsed their sheen,
filled you with tenderness and wonder –
you had to touch them. We shared
the bath until her legs grew long,
her beauty made me stare. In spring
thick with run-off the creek bent
toward her, the willow in the yard
let down its hair to hide her from the sun.
Only she could calm our mother, her blue
eyes soothed as water smooths a stone.

Once, I saw her with a fox
in the coulee at the edge of town,
I'd swear she held its paw
and when she turned to look at me
her eyes flashed green. Sage
and mother's camphor were her smells.
They left a spoor the boys would follow,
startling her at night, their eyes
upon her – motionless –
as if they held her in a rifle scope,
trigger fingers taut, love too soft
a word for what they felt. Mornings
on the path below our window
I'd find some boy's silver slick
like the trail a snail will leave
in its slow slide across the grass.

The crow who woke us long before the light
left my sister gifts in the birdbath –
once, a sparrow's wing, a heron's foot,
the velvet body of a mole. Even then
I knew she came too close to things.
Nothing I could do would make her stop.

THE OLDER SISTER: HUNTER'S MOON

In the fall, red leaves
splattered the ground, the moon
bloody too, our father would return,
deer or antelope spread-eagled
on the car roof, its stare
the deadest thing I'd seen.
I disappeared while he sawed
and wrapped the flesh,
buried the head without its rack
behind the burning barrel.

It is said if you kill a buck
his wife will seduce you,
lead you through the grasslands
till you are lost. That fall
our father was distracted.
His gaze moved far beyond
what we could see, hills yellow
in the last of heat, silver where
wolf willow hugged the rills.

Our mother simpered at the table,
dipped her tongue in sugar.
Jumping up and down
she filled his plate till food
spilled over on the cloth.

Every afternoon she changed
into something finer, practised smiling
in the mirror above the kitchen sink.

She licked her lips so often
it became a habit she couldn't break.
His tires spitting gravel, she stood
at the window, the stiffness of new cotton
against her skin finally loosening
in the breeze that accompanies
the sun going down.

The antelope wife, her two daughters,
waited in the dusk, first frost
feathering the grass. Offering him
an easy silence we couldn't give
they led him through the hills,
the season of the trembling aspen,
our father lost forever from our lives.

THE BOY: THE ONLY WAY TO EXPLAIN IT

Our spaniel in heat,
Dad locked her in the shed.
He wanted purebred pups. He'd pay
a stud fee and make 200 bucks
a litter. In the middle of the night
the neighbour's lab
crashed through the window.
Head bloody, he humped our bitch.
Dad couldn't pull him off
without a risk to her. Months later
he drowned the mongrels in the creek.

I'd have shattered glass,
sliced my arms and chest on razor wire.
For hours as a kid I hid beneath her window,
came with every movement
behind the blind, her or her sister,
hard to tell.

A good man, a family man,
I'm still tinder to her touch.
When I'm inside her, she's not there.
That doesn't stop me, though little
pleasure's in it. Like going back
to the house where you grew up
and no one's home but sadness.

Too much red-eye and I'm rough.
I need to taste what's underneath her skin.
Midday when she walks by my store

and I'm waiting on a customer,
my wife beside me, making change,
I have to dig my elbows in my ribs
to keep from crying out. She wears
my hands beneath her skirt.

Nothing I do resembles a life
if she's not in it. Some nights,
my family sound asleep in the house
that holds them brick by brick,
I walk to the river and the river takes me in.
Like an older brother it drags me under
but it will not let me drown.

HIS WIFE: NO WORD CAN HOLD IT

The wife's the last,
but I knew from the start.
As a kid I watched him
hang around the edge of things
to catch a glimpse. Across the schoolyard
his long gaze bent around my friends and me
to stroke her face. I wanted
what it was she had. No word can hold it,
now or then. A bird must feel it
in its wings, a salmon rising.

Lately I follow him, drift to the edge
of town in my white nightgown,
sometimes a neighbour's sprinkler
forgotten on the grass, its *wish, wish, wish*
wetting my feet. Most nights this is
as far as I will go – I stare across the road
like a ghost who's lost her way,
watch the curtains at her window
suck in and out as if the house itself is breathing.
So much life in her and mine in pieces.

I could make him choose,
but what's the use? He married me
and she won't have him
longer than a night.

When he slides between our sheets
near morning, he believes he keeps
her scent a secret. How can he not sense

my knowing? I curl around him,
pretending sleep, pray her smell
will soak into my skin and
he will take me hard
without the gentleness he thinks I want.

THE MOTHER: WITHOUT BLESSING

One daughter's too good for me,
the other a whore. A married man
rolls in her stink. It's my house
they rut in, thinking I can't hear.
She used to care for me,
the spitting image, some would say.
When I cry out she threatens
to gag me in my bed.

The younger one won't visit
with her husband.
Sends us junk as if
we're worth as little.
Rugs braided from rags,
a piece of jewellery
that cheapens the skin.
I don't remember much
of them as children.

There was a man,
a satin dress
I can't get into.
It's there on the wall,
my face half-veiled, a funny
hat on my head.
How can so much happen
then be gone?

Once, I spoke in tongues.
Now words dissolve

like wafers in my mouth,
bland and thin,
without blessing.

THE OLDER SISTER: EVERYTHING YEARNS

Crow, what treasures you bring me.
Something made of bones and feathers,
something blind. One of the boys
who followed me as a child
comes to me at night, his rightful wife
drugged by his desire. He roots in me
for something he won't find,
his hands on either side of my head
so I must look at him and cannot drift away.
Though I'm sick to death of beauty
he says, *Look in my eyes.*
See how fine you are.

After a night of him and whisky, I walk
into light's brass fist, its knuckles
gleaming. My cheek splits and darkens,
my nose bleeds. Now my mother's
still and quiet as if I've strapped her
to the mattress the way a farmer tries
to rope the wind, chain it to a windmill
to keep it from his rows of seed.
Days I lived inside her.
No one has the right to pull you
through her eyes.

In me a man's been everywhere
a man can go. Not my father.
He gentled me. *Say fox,*
he said. My eyes turned green.
I can't remember what I knew –

it was larger than any telling
like the heron's story, like the heart's.
I tended her. So many years
I swore I'd leave, marry someone
who wouldn't stay. Still
I wear our mother's cotton,
her gabardine, the loose folds of her skin.
No one's burden but my own.

Everything yearns –
that stone in your hand,
that singular blade of grass.
Don't think it's only for the light.

APOCRYPHA OF LIGHT

APOCRYPHA OF LIGHT

On the first day, light said
Let there be God
        And there was God.
Light needed shape to move inside,
a likeness tawny and thick-maned.
It strode into the absence we call night
and what it tongued
sparked visible then glowed,
warmed by its golden spittle.

It splashed and rolled in water
till rivers and seas could not be parted
from its gleam. It lingered:
        on the hourglass
        of August pears; on blackbird,
        bear scat, calves' blood;
        on the hand of the beloved,
        its unlikely flare.

It went everywhere, glossed all
that waited to be seen. At last
it slipped into the farthest corner –
there, it stumbled. Stopped.
Hid its brightness and would not move.
What in the dark did it wish it hadn't found?

Not arbutus limbs, an otter's head
just above the sea; not orange pips,
fish fin, a panther's muscled plush.

Now you make a list of things.
Remember light's likeness, remember
this is the beginning of the first day.

THE ORIGIN OF THE SPECIES

. . . but the old man only said that it was pointless to speak of there being no horses in the world for God would not permit such a thing.
    —Cormac McCarthy, *All the Pretty Horses*

Drenched with dawn
eohippus, smaller than a fox,
walked out of chaos.

She struck the sand. Water
gushed from her hoofprint,
drops flying through the air

and where they fell
the sky came down to rest
and a thousand miracles of grass

meadowed the desert.
For centuries eohippus lived
satisfied and self-contained

then her legs and muzzle lengthened,
muscles pushed against
her withers, thickened her neck.

Now, ready for the wind
she made it lean and boneless,
its mane and tail visible

across the sky. Imagine
horse and wind
in the sun's warm pastures

before the fall. Imagine
the two of them alone
adrift in the absolute

beatitude of grass,
no insect biting,
no rope or bridle.

In the mornings of that lost
and long ago beginning,
nothing broken

or in need of breaking.

THE START OF THE BLUES

Leaving the garden, the snake
drags its old skin behind it
like a long smoky breath
trapped inside a saxophone,
the first saxophone
in the world.

Warts,
earwax, hic-
cups, the little
toe, wisdom
tooth.

A PROPHET IN HIS OWN COUNTRY

The gopher on his hind legs
is taut with holiness and fright.
Miniature and beardless,
he could be stoned or flooded out,
burnt alive in stubble fields,
martyr to children for a penny a tail.

How can you not believe an animal
who goes down headfirst
into darkness, into the ceaseless
pull of gravity beneath him?
What faith that takes!

I come to him with questions
because I love his ears, how perfectly
they fit, how flat they lie against his head.
They hear the inner and the outer
worlds: what rain says
underground. The stone's praise
for the sparrow's ankle bone.

Little earth-otter, little dusty Lazarus,
he vanishes, he rises. He won't tell us
what he's seen.

EVOLUTION IN MOONLIGHT

Always you come back to the moon:
old man, bull's horn, winter hare,
the thin body of an ancient god
placed there on the tongue.

What will you say then?
Stars are wasps dipped in silver.
They chew holes in the darkness
to build their paper nests.

What will you say then, that taste
dry and holy in your mouth?

Here it is moonlight.
You walk the garden paths,
your hands shiny as scales
as if you are only
on your way to being human,
still smelling of the sea.

What you've called a soul
hovers just beneath your skin.
Or has it left your body?
And now walks
beside you, bright-eyed
and feline, each paw placed
so carefully
on the rain-slicked grass, the way
a new god enters the world.

WHAT THE SNAKE BRINGS TO THE WORLD

Without the snake
there'd be no letter S.
No forked tongue and toil,
no pain and sin. No wonder
the snake's without shoulders.
What could bear such a weight!

The snake's responsible for everything
that slides and hisses, that moves
without feet or legs. The wind, for example.
The sea in its long sweeps to shore and out again.

The snake has done some good, then.
Even sin to the ordinary man
brings its pleasures. And without
the letter S traced belly-wise
outside the gates of Eden
we'd have to live
with the singular of everything:
sparrow, ear, heartbeat,
mercy, truth.

ORIGINAL SIN: THE FIRST WOMAN

We were mothers giving birth
to each other, or we were sisters,
our home the night's vast womb.
We orbited inside its silky
black cocoon. If Galileo had been
there with his telescope
and blasphemy, he would have named
our double brightness
and I wouldn't have been so lost.

My hand reached out
and to prove I was the first
the angels tied it with a strong red string,
the origin of scarlet as a curse.
I felt her grow beside me, her spirit curve
against my bones like cream inside a spoon.

We were one creature then,
four-legged, perhaps a fawn
whose hooves had not grown hard,
a calf so strange we would be kept
inside a jar. Then I counted fingers,
counted toes, and she looked back at me.

I, not Eve, brought pain into the birthing room.
I didn't want to leave her. I clung to the womb
with my nails and teeth, ripped night from day,
eternity from now.

That was my first argument with God.
The second: I wouldn't lie placid
as a hooked and fatty fish under Adam,
my wings pinned back. For punishment
God banished me and turned my sister into bone,
honed away everything she'd been
when we lay together among stars.

Some nights I wait at the edge of the garden –
how lush it is, how full of anguish.
Light and docile, she walks toward me,
a trail of creatures at her side.
Does she know I'm here? She's forgotten

my face, forgotten our one smell
as we wound around each other,
her fingers in my mouth, my hand
holding her heartbeat, a wounded wren
I cannot save from grief

THE SACRIFICE OF ISAAC

I bind my breasts with hide. Eat a jackal's heart
and ride in dust to the mountains of Moriah.
Three nights I sit with what they cannot see
beyond their fires. Though I'm close enough
to touch his cheek, I will my hands to stillness.
Before dawn, our last day on the road, a caravan
stutters by, heavy with its load like something
from the past. I am too old for them to trouble me
though a boy rides up, tips his goatskin
and offers me a drink. He drops his eyes
when I unveil my mouth, the darkness there.
I swallow his breath with water from his father's well,
mumble a blessing though I do not know
his gods, their indifference or their lust.
When the groan of wheels fades, I hear
my child's laugh ringing through the grass
like bells tied to the morning wind.
He is climbing. Bent double under wood,
he bears his fire upon his back.
I wait by a thicket, tufts of ram's wool
on the brambles, knife cold against my thigh,
until the altar's built, Isaac asking,
Father, where's the lamb?
then I step into the open, fists on fire,
above my swinging arm
the bare throat of my husband's
Lord opening in a flood of crimson light.

WHAT I GAVE YOU, TRULY

I am speaking from the other side
of the bramble bush, the side where nothing
grows but wheels and cogs and the loneliness
of exile on this earth. I am speaking
in the voice of thorns, the voice of wire,
though once I was a softness longed for
at the end of day, its vesper song,
mothering the weary. What I gave man
without a lie and truly, what I give you now
is Gravenstein, Spartan, Golden Delicious.
Eat this, I say, and your eyes open
as mine did then, all things innocent, unused,
my new man naked before me.
Remember that.
I give you the apple and you see
your lover for the first time, this wonder
repeated in the flesh. *Eat this*, chew
more sweetness before the bitter seeds,
the hard star at the core. I am speaking
in the voice of crow, the voice of rain. Stark naked
I am out here in the large and lovely dark,
the taste of you, the taste of apple in my mouth.

from THE DIVINE ANATOMY

GOD'S MOUTH

That prairie sky you rhapsodize
is one huge yawn. He's bored
with what you're doing here.

Like a tone-deaf kid
who's been told
he carries a tune in a sieve,
God mouths the words.

The animals of course
can hear him. Look at that dog
who stares into the night,
his ears on fire –

it's God's great singing.

HIS HANDS

So much ravelling
and unravelling,
the scrubbing of souls,
the peeling and plucking.

So much doing
and undoing,
the baking of bread
and the tearing apart
when the winged-ones gather.

UNTITLED

He claims in fact it's
the socket of an eye,
a second anus,
a prim pursed mouth
that talks to creatures
living neither up nor down
but in the middle kingdom.

He'd never say
it was a navel.

You can see why.

GOD'S HEART

It's tempting to say
he doesn't have one.

Otherwise,
what of the soft throats
of the lambs, the white
bulls – their startled blood?

That's to say nothing
of the other things
written inside
your book of grief.

Maybe his heart is thin,
maybe his heart is
made of hunger.

It comes into the world
as fox or goshawk,
or that winter tree
stripped clean of pity

branches bare of anything
that warms or blossoms
or makes them
break.

GOD'S BONES

His bones are light,
they are light walking,
light sitting
and standing still.

If he dies
you can't bury them.
Light slips out of
any darkness. In pine
it becomes the pine;
in oak it gathers in the grain.

If he dies
you cannot cremate them.
They are fleshed with fire,
fire-fattened.

Even the smallest bone
in his inner ear –
there's enough light
for the whole world
to read by.

from BOOK OF PRAISE

The titles are lines from Patrick Lane's book A Linen Crow,
A Caftan Magpie.

REMEMBER THE HEART. LITTLE MOLE.

My heart's as blind but sometimes
it's a winter hare. Soft-pawed and quick

it follows you in daylight and can't be
seen. You suspicious of sentiment,

its poverty and pride. Instead
you gave me a stone worn by water

so a chain slipped through.
It sat in the hollow of my throat

until I lost it. Remember the hare
invisible in snow, the little mole?

Star-nosed and dusty, he knows
at least two doorways to the light.

NOW WE ARE ANYONE. THIS COMING TO LOVE.

This grey brings no sustenance.
Only the dead attend to their gardens

under the snow. The sky's so low
it drapes across the fields –

an old woman's loosened hair.
That's what the wind untangles

and combs across the highways.
Weather takes a nasty turn –

wind chill, white-out, no
rum or candles in my survival kit

and I'm four storms
from seeing you.

GIVE YOURSELF THE LIGHT.

Night comes quickly
but the snow gives off so much shine

its not as dark as where you are,
the big trees leaning in.

TEACH ME THE STARS. THE WAY TO SUMMER.

Snow brings down constellations
without number.

No one names them.
What relief! Sinking in starlight,

I walk to the creek,
mouth stoppered with ice.

They call the water Wolverine
though I haven't seen the animal

or his tracks. Just the deer's,
silk-screened. Small moves

toward spring: their hoofprints,
the shape of maple seeds.

WELCOME WISE ONE. TELL ME A STORY.

Today the snow is indecisive,
says both *yes* and *no* to falling

yet it chalks just one side
of the elms – magnetic north.

You could throw away
your compass, get lost in me.

I live between two places
like these elms, their proper name

Siberian. Babushkas,
hidden icons white with flour. Poems

learned by heart and eaten with the gruel.
Mandelstam! You'd be so welcome.

In this catholic garden no one lights
the caraganas' candelabra. Native

to Siberia too, they're no strangers
to hard labour. All day long, thin-

barked and twisted,
they break the stony wind.

EXCELLENCE IN THE SMALL. TEARS FROZEN ON YOUR FACE.

Winter: *eat the little, talk a lot* –
that's magpie's definition.

Tears freeze on the cheeks and
never fall. This is cold, not sadness.

Somewhere warmer, Vallejo said
we must learn

a different way of weeping. For now,
the old way will have to do.

MY MOUTH BETWEEN YOUR LEGS. O FLESH!

I admit it – I licked your hand-
writing, words made flesh, my tongue

stained black as if I'd sucked
a licorice stick. Now your letter's

impossible to read. Like the magpie.
Like the heart. You can have

that scavenger. Noisy magus,
he grants me nothing

with a sweep of his tail.
I'm sick of this undoing,

greenless miles of snow,
the coyote's scat red with rosehips.

Right now I'd trade the open
and all my braggadocio about the cold

for the little dogs
in raincoats on Dallas Road.

THE GEESE IN THE SOUTH RAISE THEIR HEADS IN PRAISE.

Have they begun their journey
to the nesting grounds? If I could

I would warn them, too soon,
too soon. Is there nothing you can do?

Everything's still hard here
under the moon. Wind makes it swing

on hinges like a sign made out of tin.
Truly, I can hear it creaking.

The body also moves
before the beloved has prepared

the fires and feasting.
When I raise my head it is you

I praise, this waking into wind's
slow change of seasons,

wings lifting under the great
glittering belly of the Bear.

WHETSTONE

With all this sky to cross
how can Jesus find you? Surely
there's too much of it, even for one
who's called the Lord of Light. You try to find
the stone that speaks in tongues. The rooster
who's an angel with a useful job.
Sometimes wind leaves its footprints
on the water. Sometimes the dust's
a voice that rises when a car goes past.
A god is walking through the wheat fields,
you're sure of that. But it's not you he's come for.
There are coyotes to save, the wheat itself, short
and shriven, and the skunk who's about to eat
the poisoned egg. Let alone the egg, the song inside it.
The devil seems to have more focus; he believes
you deserve his full attention. If you hang your soul
on the line he's right there, especially if it's pinned
beside a good woman's laundry,
her cotton underwear so thin from all the washings,
light passes through it and is changed.

BEAUTY

It's not the antelope's
            golden leaps across the grasslands
but how she stops

drops to her knees at the barbed-wire fence
                              and crawls under
            then springs when she's on her feet again

So too with you. The beauty's in
            your fall, your startled
                        grace –

        everything
                turning on
the hinges of your neck, waist, and knees
                        how you bend –

SAND FROM THE GOBI DESERT

Sand from the Gobi Desert blows across Saskatchewan,
becomes the irritation in an eye. So say the scientists who
separate the smallest pollen from its wings of grit,
identify the origin and name. You have to wonder where
the dust from these fields ends up: Zimbabwe, Fiji,
on the row of shoes outside a mosque in Istanbul,
on the green rise of a belly in the Jade Museum in Angkor Wat?
And what of our breath, grey hair freed from a comb, the torn
    threads of shadows?
Just now the salt from a woman's tears settles finely its invisible kiss
on my upper lip. She's been crying in Paris on the street that means
Middle of the Day though it's night there, and she doesn't want
    the day to come.
Would it comfort her to know another, halfway round the world,
    can taste her grief?
Another would send her, if she could, the rare flakes of snow
falling here before the sunrise, snow that barely fleeces the brown
    back of what's
too dry to be a field of wheat, and winter's almost passed. Snow
    on her lashes.
What of apple blossoms, my father's ashes, small scraps of sadness
that slip out of reach? Is it comforting to know the wind
never travels empty? A sparrow in the Alhambra's arabesques
rides the laughter spilling from our kitchen, the smell of garlic
makes the dust delicious where and where it falls.

When Louis Armstrong left New Orleans for Chicago
at King Oliver's request, his mother
packed him a trout sandwich and no one met him
at the train, though he could blow his trumpet
and be heard across state lines. I don't know why,
but I love to think of that trout sandwich he carried
in his pocket and later ate, the wheels spinning him
into fame, though it took some years and at least
two women. When my dad and I went fishing
Mom laid roast chicken from the day before
between slices of store-bought white. Was there mayonnaise?
I don't remember, but in the boat, a few fish biting,
our fingers shone with butter as if we'd dipped our hands in fire
then treated them for burns. The sun was bright but weaker,
the afternoons so long I watched the hairs on my father's arms
turn gold. If I'd been called away by someone other than myself,
years later, that's what I'd have wanted, chicken on white bread,
and the thing that turned my breath and body into music.
Leaving home like Louis Armstrong – though there's no one like
    him –
and his trumpet. And the sandwich he saved until he reached
the outskirts of Chicago, savouring the Southern taste of what
his mother made him. Imagine those fingers, that mouth.

PRAYERS OF SNOW

Snow is a lesson in forgetting, a lesson in gravity,
a long loose sentence spiralling to the end of thought.
It prays to the young god robed in white, his ascent
a blizzard returning to the sky. It prays to the white-footed
mouse, the snowy owl, the varying hare and vole,
the cat with fur between his toes. It closes the gap
between drought and plenty, belief and blasphemy,
the ear and silence. It is a migration of birds
without eyes, without feet, who settle white in branches
on breasts and wings. When you stride through snow
in dreams or waking, you are a star-walker.
It prays to the soft fall of your boots.

WHAT COMES AFTER

I am my own big dog.
Walk, and I'm at the door,
eat, and I take what I offer,
lie down, and I curl on the floor,
my heavy head between my paws.

I don't need anything but this,
I don't think of what comes after.

I sing the way a dog sings,
I weep the way a dog weeps.
Every night at my feet
I am a big sack of sleep
stinking of me.

The air annunciates. It breathes a frosty haze
on my pants and jacket as if I'm growing fur.
Immeasurable, indifferent, now it can be touched
and tasted. It can be seen. Have I fallen through
to the other side of morning or risen above clouds?
This weight, this stillness: splendour thickening.
Down the road a dog barks. Someone walks toward me,
head and shoulders plumed with white. Father?
Lord of Winter? O Death! When his lips touch mine
they will be feathers. I don't know what to do.
I pray for wind, for sun, I pray for my father to speak
before he turns to crystals as he turned to ash.
In the visible around me hoarfrost
hallucinates a thousand shards of bone.

FORM

The chickadee
drops
to the middle
of the lily pad

makes it dip a little

just enough water
slips over the edge
for the bird
to bathe.

SHADOW

To lie on one side of a tree
then another, over rough or smooth.

To feel cool along one's whole body
lengthening without intent,
nothing getting in the way.

To give up on meaning.
To never wear out or mar.

To move by increments like
a beautiful equation, like the moon
ripening above the golden city.

To be doppelganger,
the soft underside of wings.
the part of cumulus that slides
thin promises of rain across the wheat.

To disappear. To be blue
simply because snow has fallen
and it's the blue hour of the day.

IT IS NIGHT

Wind turns back the sheets of the field.
What needs to sleep, sleeps there.
What needs to rest.

The door has fallen from the moon.
It floats in the slough, all knob and hinges.

Now the moon's so open
anything could walk right through.

Only the fox is travelling.
One minute he's a cat, the next a coyote.

Enough light to see by
yet my mouth lies in darkness.
What needs to sleep, sleeps there.
What needs to rest.

Outside my mind, the wind is reckoning.
Always there is something
to figure out.

ANONYMITY

The country of the dead keeps growing.
Is my father lost there, too? Nameless,
without schooling or belief, our love for him
worn thin. Do the animals he killed remember him?
The horses his neighbours couldn't shoot,
the dog who dragged her sack of guts
studded with gravel from the road to our door.

So many times, outside the house,
I refused to know him.
I'd turn my back on the slant-six Fairlane,
black and white, the muffler he installed
illegal even then, the roar in the street
not a teenage pal, but my Dad.

Now I want him behind the wheel again,
his colour back. Seventy-three and thundering
past the tall white houses of the dead,
louder than their strings and benedictions,
so they'll *have* to notice him, so they'll say out loud,
There he goes, and have to name him:
Emerson Crozier in his souped-up Ford.

SETTING

Light dozes into autumn and late afternoon.
The good dishes clean, the table set.
One place missing a spoon.

The crow's flown off with it.
He's laying his own meal on a black cloth.

Something you can chew on,
something you can spit out,
something you can share

with that part of you
you've given nothing to
all your life.

Ripple after ripple of lake-light
breaks on the sand and stays there.
The faraway has just passed through.
The day is small but it begins with so much
beauty, I am poured out like water.
A red squirrel stands upright on the woodpile,
clenches his paws on his chest and stares,
wanting me to choose. Maybe it was Jesus on the lake
in his fishing boat, the disciples pulling up their nets,
light from their faces and hands – *his* face, *his* hands –
what water carries to the shore, the hard gleam of heaven.
There should be music. Harps in the birches,
psalters and a drum. I dance on the sand,
twirl one way, then the other. The fire begins in my feet.
There should be baskets for the fish, there should be
hunger. That I can give you. I used to shine.

REBUTTAL TO THE HIGHER POWER

Think of all the names the unnamed could borrow –
  blue-eyed, fescue, little quaking –
if it had a mind to.
  You lie down in the pasture,

  the back of your head
pressing into green like a fieldstone
that's stayed in the same place
  since muscles of ice heaved it to the sun.

Beneath you grass stretches its roots
  farther than an arm and hand
can reach into water. They douse for darkness,
draw it up to meet the light, or is it light

the dark becomes on this other side
  where footsteps fall?
Through hollow stems, grass siphons
the can't-be-seen

  and sends it out ignited.
It's what gives the shine to everything
  that roots, inclines, or rises only inches.
Dirt, lichen, stone, their telluric under-glitter.

It's the gloriole of wild oats
in all the ditches, the nodding seedheads.
  The same nod as the birch bough's,
the rowboat on its tether,

the same nod –
        no – slightly different
as the crow's, as he hops stiff-kneed around
the roadkill. As if everything but you

knows the body's way of saying *yes*,
all afternoon
        the grass replying
                when the invisible asks.

DIVINING

The wind's low humming: how it turns
every leaf beneath the trees, swirls cilia of snow
so the snow hears too the warm earth stirring.

I try to listen in that way, the grace notes
on the underside of sound, what my mother wanted
to say, what my father wished he hadn't,
my brother's teasing, how it makes me
stumble still and think I'll fail.

The horizon was a line we couldn't hear
except when a jet traced it white across the sky
and that was rarer then. I'd know the poplar's
rush and sighs outside my childhood window
anywhere, but it's grown taller or it's gone.
It comes now in a different way
like the almost-sound of falling snow,
or the cry of my first lover.

They say hearing's the last to go. After sight,
taste, the loss of smell and touch, it's the rustle
of someone's hands turning you over in a bed,
dry wind through a screen, death's whisper.

The ear's a diviner, then. It witches sounds
like water from under clay, dipping
its bone-wands deep into the dark.

The exhaustion of flowers, midafternoon,
the stale sun's spill and stutter
across the lawn, a sprinkler lifting
its tired arc and letting it fall. All things
moving to an end. In the loveseat
under the apple tree I open
The Art of Memory and laugh
out loud when I forget the place
I stopped at yesterday. Soon
I'll go in, wake you from your nap
and start our supper, anything
the garden's greens have left to give,
lettuce and chard, that undertaste of
bitterness. We live with who we are and not
what we once wanted. Late August,
its weight on my shoulders, my hand
not on your skin. I turn back
the page and start again,
not sure if I've read
this part before.

BLIZZARD

Walking into wind, I lean into my mother's muskrat coat;
around the cuffs her wristbones have worn away the fur.

If we stood still we'd disappear. There's no up or down,
no houses with their windows lit. The only noise is wind

and what's inside us. When we get home my father
will be there or not. No one ever looks for us.

I could lie down and stay right here where snow is all
that happens, and silence isn't loneliness just cold

not talking. My mother tugs at me and won't let go.
Then stops to find her bearings. In our hoods of stars

we don't know if anyone will understand
the tongue we speak, so far we are from home.

Under the bridge the dead are gathering.
What happened to the ferryman,
his bag of coins, his pity? In all this traffic
how can they cross these girders of steel
and starlight? One of them hears a creaking.
It is you in your father's rowboat,
newly painted. Your lunch beside you
on the seat, in the bow that singer
who died young. He has spelled you
on this journey but now he begins
in Mandarin the version of Red River
he learned in exile in the fields
far from Beijing. Under the bridge,
hearing him, the dead, too, start singing
We will miss your bright eyes
and sweet smile, in at least
a dozen different tongues.

ACKNOWLEDGEMENTS

I want to thank the editors of the magazines in which these poems first appeared, as well as Donna Bennett, Jan Zwicky, and the inimitable and quick-eyed Molly Peacock, who worked with me on this selection. For their careful attention to my work, I owe much appreciation to Ellen Seligman, Anita Chong, and Heather Sangster. Over the years, the Saskatchewan Artists/Writers' Colony at St. Peter's Abbey has provided me with a hospitable place to work and the University of Victoria has supported me with travel grants and study leaves. My husband, Patrick Lane, continues to be an enthusiastic believer in my poems, a passionate gardener, a herder of cats, and a great cook. And finally I owe much to my mother, who, although she didn't always understand the poems, never failed to express her pride in me and her love. She died while I was pulling this collection together. I miss her terribly.

INDEX OF TITLES

HOW TO DO IT STANDING UP

The Friars Club GUIDE
TO BEING A COMIC, A CUT-UP, A CARD, OR A CLOWN

BARRY DOUGHERTY
FOREWORD BY "RICHARD PRYOR

Black Dog & Leventhal
Paperbacks

ISBN 1-57912-254-X

Library of Congress Cataloging-in-Publication Data

Dougherty, Barry.
How to do it standing up: the Friars Club guide to being a
cut-up, a card, or a clown / Barry Dougherty; foreword by
Richard Pryor.
    p.   cm. Includes index.
  ISBN 1-57912-254-X
  1. Stand-up comedy.   2. Comedy.   I. Friars Club (New
  York, N.Y.)   II. Title.

PN1969.C65 D685 2002   792.7—dc21

2002008098

Cover design and photo collage: Cindy Labreacht

Book design: Martin Lubin Graphic Design

Manufactured in the U.S.A.

PUBLISHED BY

Black Dog & Leventhal Publishers, Inc.
151 West 19th Street
New York, New York 10011

DISTRIBUTED BY

Workman Publishing Company
708 Broadway
New York, New York 10003

g f e d c b a

THIS BOOK IS DEDICATED
TO ANYONE WHO HAS
THE CHUTZPAH TO BE
FUNNY IN PUBLIC.

ACKNOWLEDGMENTS

My God, this book was a hell of a lot of fun to write. Since I'm still somewhat euphoric over the experience, I may as well show my appreciation to all those people who helped me along the way.

Many thanks to Jean Pierre Trebot, the Executive Director of the Friars Club. He's one of the few Frenchmen who realizes that Jerry Lewis isn't the only comedian out there—although, true to his heritage, he loves Jerry. Jean Pierre's continued support and unwavering trust in my ability to produce this book is truly appreciated, along with his allowing me to interview some of these comedians over lunch at the Friars Club. Thanks for the extra pounds, Jean Pierre.

The only reason this book exists at all is because of the comedic artists who do the impossible on a daily basis—bring laughter to millions. There is something to be said for standing alone on a stage and having the world laughing at your feet. Personally I'd prefer money at my feet, but then I'm not a comedian. I am indebted to them all for taking out the time to sit down, for a change, and talk one-on-one with me. They shared their memories and their expertise and I can't thank them enough for their candid recollections, heartwarming tales, and hilarious comments: Joy Behar, Richard Belzer, David Brenner, Red Buttons, Dick Capri, Anthony Clark, Pat Cooper, Norm Crosby, Phyllis Diller, Susie Essman, Jeff Foxworthy, Jim Gaffigan, Gilbert Gottfried, Shecky Greene, David Alan Grier, Carol Leifer, Samm Levine, Howie Mandel, Kevin Meaney, David Mishevitz, Freddie Roman, Jeffrey Ross, Rita Rudner, Neil Simon, Ryan Stiles, Jerry Stiller, Stewie Stone, Scott Thompson (Carrot Top), Lily Tomlin, and George Wallace.

I also extend my sincerest thanks to those equally talented people behind the comedy scene, some of whom opened the doors to their comedy clubs to let me in to experience the scene firsthand. They all weighed in with their own stories about the comedians who have touched their lives: Bernie Brillstein, Caroline Hirsch, Cary Hoffman, Rick Newman, and Mitzi Shore.

I can't begin to thank Richard Pryor for his contribution. He battles illness every day yet continues to fan the flames of humor. To Jennifer Lee Pryor I am indeed indebted for helping Richard be such an important part of this book. Her patience with my daily e-mails goes beyond sainthood.

A very special thank you to all of the comedians whom I have met at the Friars Club who have been the professors in my ongoing education on laughter.

I'll be honest, I have a bad memory, and I can't read my own handwriting, so a huge thanks to S. Joseph Begun for inventing the first consumer tape recorder. More importantly, I want to thank Alison Grambs, Michael Matuza, and Oscar Riba for transcribing hours and hours of my conversations with the comedic experts. They seem to be the only ones associated with this project who aren't laughing.

Thank you to Laura Ross, my editor, whose obsession with chickens frightens me just a bit, I admit. Without her lust for laughter this project would never have happened. To J. P. Leventhal, the head honcho at Black Dog & Leventhal, I also extend a hearty thank you for his never-ending quest to put humor on paper so it can spread beyond a comedy club.

A huge thank you to Eve Darcy Burhenne, who diligently and good-naturedly withstood my constant barrage of irritating questions in her quest to research every teeny detail that I put to her.

It's time to acknowledge my mother, Rita Dougherty, who's pissed that I haven't dedicated any books to her. But that's only because I'm waiting for one that doesn't have the "F" word in it. Thanks, Mom.

To all of the future comedians out there who are about to embark on an amazing journey—I wish you all the luck in the world. You're going to need it because it sounds just so horrific—although sorta fun!

—BARRY DOUGHERTY

THE CAST

JOY BEHAR

RICHARD BELZER

DAVID BRENNER

BERNIE BRILLSTEIN

RED BUTTONS

DICK CAPRI

CARROT TOP

ANTHONY CLARK

PAT COOPER

NORM CROSBY

PHYLLIS DILLER

SUSIE ESSMAN

JEFF FOXWORTHY

JIM GAFFIGAN

GILBERT GOTTFRIED

SHECKY GREENE

DAVID ALAN GRIER

CAROLINE HIRSCH
(CAROLINES COMEDY
CLUB)

CARY HOFFMAN
(STAND-UP NY)

CAROL LEIFER

SAMM LEVINE

HOWIE MANDEL

KEVIN MEANEY

DAVID MISHEVITZ

RICK NEWMAN
(CATCH A RISING
STAR)

FREDDIE ROMAN

JEFFREY ROSS

RITA RUDNER

MITZI SHORE

NEIL SIMON

RYAN STILES

JERRY STILLER

STEWIE STONE

LILY TOMLIN

GEORGE WALLACE

CONTENTS

1 STAND UP AND BE COUNTED ON FOR LAUGHS **16**

...The art of stand-up comedy from the stand-ups (who were sitting down at the time)

What the hell is stand-up comedy anyway? You'll discover that even "real" comedians are divided as to its origins—so you won't be finding the real answer to that question in this book. Try the *Encyclopedia Britannica* if you want academics...do they even publish that now that you can just Ask Jeeves on the Internet?

If you're curious about going into the laugh business, this chapter gives you some insight into the life of stand-up comedians, along with their commentaries on the business of laughter.

2 MAYBE IF I JUST STAND HERE THEY'LL ALL LEAVE **49**

...There's a first time for everything— even laughs

Everybody has to start somewhere. Whether it's at the dinner table regaling Aunt Sylvia and Uncle Morty, or cracking up your drinking buddies over beers, the natural comedian inevitably finds his or her way into the spotlight. Of course, sometimes the bulb blows and you end up asking how many nuns it takes to change it, in which case please just say, "Good night, Gracie." Others, however, shine brighter than the Hope Diamond and careers are born.

Whether it happens spontaneously on a dare or as a result of a lifetime of preparation, that first time can be a bitch. It can make or break a future stand-up comedian. Listen to firsthand accounts of comedians who lived to tell how their first time was a dream come true or of nightmarish proportions. The thing to remember is, they're all still here.

3 GOTTA GET A GIMMICK 101

...In case my jokes fail, my voice will still be heard

Be it a scratchy violin to punctuate that one-liner or a feather boa to accentuate the punch line, every comedian has a gimmick. They needn't be as pronounced as Andy Kaufman's phonograph playing the theme from *Mighty Mouse,* nor as in-your-face as Señor Wences' hand puppets, but today's stand-up comedians still need to stand out among their peers.

A gimmick can be as subtle as a shifty eye or an emphatic sneer or even a randy tête-à-tête with an audience member. Just make it your own. The comedians, in addition to describing their personal styles, shed light on how their voices are heard among the many and, of course, over the laughter.

4 IT WAS THE WORST OF TIMES 165

...And hurt like the dickens

Everyone, at one time or another, has a bad day, a worst moment, a time when he just wanted to crawl into a hole and pretend he was Jimmy Hoffa. Being naked with only your jokes to clothe you and audience laughter to keep you warm can quickly turn into a pneumonia-inducing gamble. Thankfully, comedians are a therapeutic bunch and find it cathartic to talk about their mishaps, mistakes, and mortifying moments.

Don't think of this chapter so much as laughing *with* the comedians but more as laughing *at* them—which is much funnier. They share their intimate tales of embarrassing woe, allowing others to learn from their mistakes—or maybe just have a good laugh at their expense.

While it may seem like these seasoned comedians just walk out on stage and casually enlighten and entertain audiences to apoplectic proportions with no forethought, there is oh so much more than meets the eye. For some, it might be akin to jumping out of a plane with no parachute, propelling their adrenaline to the heights necessary to garner laughs. For others, it's devouring newspapers for current events and topical targets of jest. In any case, they all have their personal preparations for laughter down pat.

Allow the experts to reveal their special techniques in their quest for laughs. Is that "K" sound really funnier than the "B" sound? Well, duh!

A guy walks out of a diner without leaving a tip. The waitress runs after him and says, "Hey, mister, what gives? Where's my tip?" And the guy says, "Oh, I'm sorry, here's your tip...wear less makeup!" It's all good. We all need a helping hand every once in a while to get started on whatever road we're about to head out on. While getting to a comedy club stage may not take as much practice as it does to get to Carnegie Hall, it still doesn't hurt to get some sage advice. Who better to get it from than those that spent time in the trenches? Here, they impart their words of wisdom to the neophyte comedian.

Listen up and hear what the masters of mirth have to say about this wacky biz called stand-up comedy.

FOREWORD

Comedy rules! Don't let anybody tell you otherwise, and there are no rules in stand-up comedy, which I really like. You can do anything you want and say anything that comes to mind—just so long as it's funny. If you ain't funny then get the fuck off the stage, it's that simple.

My first time in front of an audience I sat at the piano and improvised, using the three or four chords that I knew, sang whatever words came to mind and told some god-awful jokes. I tried to look cool as the sweat poured off me. The people didn't know if I was putting them on or just plain weird. But at the end of the night, the club owner told me, "You've got more nerve than anybody I've ever seen," so he let me come back—and a comedian was born.

It takes nerve to get up on that stage, alone, and stand there in front of a room full of strangers expecting you to make them laugh. Man, that's one tough gig. I learned this business by the skin of my ass. Every once in awhile, though, I got to hear some advice from other comics, like Bill Cosby, Redd Foxx, Woody Allen, George Carlin, and Sid Caesar. They all had their own styles and at first I ended up having their styles, too. That's just how this business is, you gotta work toward eventually finding your own voice. Mine got me in a lot of trouble sometimes, but it was all mine and nobody could take that away. As long as I made people laugh, they were gonna keep letting me speak anyway.

If you want to get into this business of stand-up comedy then you might as well find out what you're in for ahead of time. Everybody in this book has a story to tell, their highs, their lows…and you'll get a lot out of reading what they have to say. I didn't have a book like this when I was coming up, but it sure would have saved me a hell of a lot of grief if I knew what those other guys went through. Wouldn't have stopped me, of course, 'cause if being a comic is in your blood, it's never gonna leave. But at least I could have seen I wasn't the only one going through some strange shit. Not that it's all bad, most of it is downright fantastic. You'll read all about those times, too.

I think it's pretty cool that the Friars Club put this all together for you. They love comics. Believe it or not, I'm a Friar myself—that's right and I bet you thought they were just a bunch of old Jews. Do I look like I fit that category? They even gave me my own Roast. Robin Williams was the Roastmaster. I remember he said that it seemed strange to Roast somebody who did it to himself. I guess he had a point.

If you made it this far in your desire to be a stand-up comedian, then good luck to you, you're in for an interesting experience. Maybe if you play your cards right, we'll all watch you make it to the big time. If you fail, well, what can I tell you? Shit happens.

—RICHARD PRYOR

RICHARD PRYOR began his stand-up career in New York in the early '60s, bringing a new, hip humor to the venues he played. While his personal life became as newsworthy as his professional life he always stayed in top form among his legion of fans through films such as *Lady Sings the Blues, Bustin' Loose, Car Wash, Silver Streak,* and *Stir Crazy.* He received critical acclaim for his autobiographical film *Jo Jo Dancer, Your Life is Calling.* On television, his first appearance on *The Ed Sullivan Show* springboarded him into national prominence. He also appeared on TV in *The Richard Pryor Show* and *Pryor's Place.* Richard has made numerous guest spots on several shows including *Saturday Night Live.* He is the author of *Pryor Convictions,* an autobiography. Despite his health problems and his debilitating bout with MS, Richard continues to demonstrate that he is a survivor and is living proof that laughter is indeed the best medicine. The Friars Club roasted him in 1991.

INTRODUCTION

I'm going to let you in on a secret—I'm a wannabe. I want to be a stand-up comedian. It doesn't matter that I may not be funny nor is it an issue that I'm incapable of speaking in front of strangers without getting bug-eyed and tongue-tied. It doesn't even matter that I wasn't the class clown. What matters, is that I want to do it. I want to stand alone, on a stage, and make people laugh at jokes and comments that I said just for that purpose. Call it ego, call it the need for approval, call it an adrenaline rush—different people have different reasons, I suppose.

I've been around a lot of comedians but that osmosis thing doesn't really work. Standing next to them and talking about the weather doesn't cut it. But something interesting happened: The Friars Club had a roundtable discussion with a few comics of different generations talking about "the biz." They talked about their funny moments and shared their embarrassing ones. It was fascinating and I realized as they spoke that they thought they were just telling war stories but to me they were explaining how to be a comic.

I took it to another level. I thought, if I can gain a little knowledge of their craft by listening to just a few comedians talk about stand-up comedy, imagine speaking to a whole bunch of them about it with the sole purpose of my wanting to learn. So I did it—I met individually with some of the funniest people around. Young, old, those just starting out, and the well-seasoned pros, it was a great cross-section of talent. I asked them about their first time, their worst time, how they prepare, why they do this, and what they can tell me about my getting up there. They didn't hold back. They were insightful, passionate, enlightening, and yes, funny. I even hung out with some of them behind the scenes in theaters and comedy clubs, witnessing this unique world they've chosen to live within.

If you're expecting a thesis on the art of comedy here, you won't find it. Don't even think of it as a book at all. Think of it as conversations with comedians talking intimately about their dedication to a craft they love. If you've ever had that desire to make 'em laugh, then you're sure to discover a tidbit or two that will help make you a little less anxious when it's your time at the microphone. If the thought never entered your head to try stand-up, then just take a really cool ride with a group of fun people.

Enjoy the experience. You never know, you might be inspired to learn more about how to do it standing up!

—BARRY DOUGHERTY

photo by Richard Lewin

BARRY DOUGHERTY is the Editor of the Friars Club's magazine, the *Epistle*, profiling celebrities and covering their popular entertainment events. Since 1991, he has been writing jokes for the Friars legendary Roasts, and speeches for Testimonial Dinners. He is the author of *New York Friars Club Book of Roasts*. Barry also edited *The Friars Club Encyclopedia of Jokes* and is the co-author of *The Friars Club Bible of Jokes, Pokes, Roasts, and Toasts.*

CHAPTER 1

STAND UP AND BE COUNTED ON FOR LAUGHS

...The art of stand-up comedy from the stand-ups (who were sitting down at the time)

"A duck walks into a bar and says to the bartender, 'Hey, gimme a Brandy Alexander!'..." If you can finish that joke and elicit a smile, a chuckle, or a guffaw, then you have just passed the first test of stand-up comedy: make 'em laugh. Unfortunately, if you plan on making a career out of it there are a gazillion tests left, but it is certainly a formidable beginning. Oh, and don't ever tell that joke if people are paying money to hear you.

It is no secret that comedy is subjective, which explains why some people actually laughed at the humor in *Ishtar* while others weren't even aware it was a comedy. Fortunately, those involved in movie flops have a whole list of other people to blame when the laughs don't come—or worse, when they come in all of the wrong places. So, where actors may have that Key Grip to flog for their failure, the stand-up comedian has nothing standing between him or her and the deafening silence mourning the death of a punch line.

"A comedian is naked up there. A comedian lives or dies solely on his own, which is always so terrifying. I have the utmost respect, I think we all do, for anyone who can get up there and is brave enough to just let it fly," says Rick Newman, whose Catch a Rising Star comedy club in Manhattan showcased the superstars of stand-up.

Would you buy a kakemono without first doing a little research to find out what the hell a kakemono is? Doubtful. Well, we're not going to send you out to strut your comedy stuff until you get the poop on comedy from our pool of grand masters. (A kakemono, by the way, is an upright Japanese wall picture. Now get your mind out of the gutter and back on comedy. The only reason it is of any interest here is that it begins with "K"—a sound you'll find out later is funnier than, say, the "U.") Allow our professional comedians to step in and guide you along on the not always funny journey to laughter.

"Joey Bishop used to do a wonderful thing in his act," says Freddie Roman. "Someone asked him, 'How do you become a comedian?' and he said, 'Well, you get up in the morning and you fill your mouth with marbles. And everyday you take out one marble and finally, when you've lost all of your marbles, you're a comedian.'"

Rita Rudner is as concise about her art as she is in garnering laughs: "When you stop talking, the audience has to start laughing."

Gilbert Gottfried has cornered the market on low self-esteem: "Anything besides me. Anything that's not my act has a chance of being funny."

"Comedy is what makes you laugh. It's that simple," says Phyllis Diller. "You want something deep, I can't give it to you. If it makes you laugh, it's funny no matter what it is."

"Maybe it's sad and mundane turned inside out," says Jeff Foxworthy. "I guess I learned early on to trust the fact that if I did something, or my kids did it or my wife did it, then other people did it. That's kind of a leap of faith. I remember one night I was writing a set for Carson and I asked my wife, 'Is this funny? Why is it that women can lie down on the couch and take a nap with-

SAMM LEVINE started stand-up at the age of 13. He performed at many of his friends' bar mitzvahs, not to mention his own, before quickly moving onto the tougher crowds at comedy clubs—and being just as successful. Along with his stand-up career Samm was one of the stars of NBC's critically-acclaimed sitcom *Freaks and Geeks*, playing the character of Neal. He has also appeared on *Late Night with Conan O'Brien, Ed, Spin City, Just Shoot Me,* and *Yes, Dear.* He recently starred in the film *Not Another Teen Movie.*

out sticking their hand down the front of their pants?' And she said, 'You know what? You're gonna embarrass yourself if you say that. You're the only guy in the world that lays on the couch with his hand stuck down his pants.' I started thinking, well, surely I'm not the only one, and usually I take her advice but on that one I'm like, no. I went out on Carson that night and told the joke and every woman in the place turned around and elbowed the guy with her and I was like, 'Oh, thank you, God!'"

Samm Levine started doing stand-up comedy at the age of thirteen. Now, a mere seven years later, he is an expert. "Comedy, oh my gosh, so many definitions. Comedy to me means something funny, it's just that simple. Does it make you laugh, does it tickle your fancy, does it make you chuckle, does it make you giggle? Is it something you can think about two months from now and look back on it and just start laughing? To me, anything that has that power is good comedy. There's also bad comedy, unintentional comedy. William Shatner is the king of unintentional comedy and that, in my opinion, can sometimes be the funniest comedy."

Howie Mandel weighs in with his thoughts on who in the crowd can become a stand-up comedian and who should probably just go through life as an audience member. "Why is one person the life of the party and the next person isn't? Why is one person someone everybody wants to hang out with and the next person, everybody ignores? Why is one person important? It's about presentation. In life we all have a style of presentation, whatever we do, we're all performing. The performance works better for some people than it does for others and therein lies the luck, I believe, of whether you have mass appeal or not."

Mass appeal is what you want to have if you're going to pull off this comedy thing successfully. Bernie Brillstein, a talent manager of some of the biggest names in comedy as well as a successful producer, notes, "Comedians, stand-ups especially, are exceedingly bright, exceedingly well read, exceedingly opinionated; most of them are penurious; many of them are promiscuous; and they don't walk to the same drummer as everyone else." Such traits make one wonder why stand-ups aren't all brain surgeons. "Because we all have ADD, that's why," says Joy Behar. "We all are television freaks and we all were cutups in school. I mean, just because you're smart doesn't mean you're studious."

They may not be Einsteins in the academic sense, but Rick Newman describes their studies on a more human scale. "I think a comedian has to be able to be on top of everything that's going on, whether it's socially or in a relationship or politically. A comedian should be, certainly in this day and age, very well read. Take someone like Richard Belzer—Richard reads newspapers from all over the world on a daily basis. At any given time, when he's called on for some sort of corporate function or to do something for Comedy Central, Showtime, or HBO, he's able to do it because he does stay on top of things. But he's just one example. I think a comedian has to be aware of everything that's going on in every aspect of everyone's life and in the world."

If you're considering going into this stand-up biz then you might want to consider giving your therapist notice that you won't be needing him or her anymore. As Newman acknowledges, "They seem to have a dark side. I think very often it's the dark side—slash—light side that gives the work that execution, that exclamation mark. The comedian's life, in general, is a tough life. It's a wonderful way to make a living, because there's a certain amount of therapy that each and every one of them is able to experience by being up on stage. It's cleansing. There are many who go to therapy and there are many who don't have to go to therapy because they're able to get up and talk about things and get that adoration and that laughter and that acknowledgment. There are many friends of mine, male and female comedians, who have said that it saves them. Not only do they get paid for their art, but it saves them the expense of having to go to therapy at the same time. It's really the truth."

A therapeutic result doesn't negate their being funny, which is a key element in this business. Just ask Norm Crosby: "A comic is somebody who starts out being funny with his family, funny in school with his schoolmates, funny in his local pool room with his friends until enough people say, 'Hey, you ought to be a comedian.' Comedy is inborn. I don't think anybody can go to school and learn to be a comedian because comedians have a certain insight. Comedians see humor in things that the average person wouldn't. Comedians have a flair, an ability, a talent, whatever you want to call it, that's instinctive. When something happens, they see the humorous aspect of it. They see something that could be potentially a joke, a line, or something that they can add to their act. Even as an amateur, even before you become a professional, you can do that because to my mind, a comedian is somebody, not who memorizes a set, rote routine and goes out and recites it. That's what certain guys that we call mechanics do—they learn a routine and they recite it. They might have the best timing in the world and the best delivery, but they're not humorous because it's not coming from their mind, it's coming from their mouth.

"That's the difference. It's not coming from the inside, it's a surface thing. I think that that gift to be humorous is what separates the men from the boys. If you think about the great comedians, you're talking about the people who have been in the business for thirty or forty years and have always been in demand and productive. It's a natural gift for humor that the average person does not have. That's what I mean when I say, you can't learn to become a comedian."

Getting back to Brillstein's assessment of the brightest and the best, apparently David Brenner has an addendum. "You left out one word, most 'neurotic.' One of the best examples, of course, is Richard Lewis who is one of my best friends in this whole world. What's so unbelievable about him is that he is exactly the same way in life, even more so, than he is on the tube. I mean, he is a madman who doesn't have to be institutionalized. He's like that crazy person in the asylum, except he's not in the asylum and the best thing about it is that he's probably the most caring human being with the biggest heart of anyone I know. He's so psychotic. He talks openly about it, and he wrote a book about his psychiatrist.

"We were both doing a tour of television shows so we got together in New York. I went up to his suite overlooking Central Park. After about five minutes he mentioned he had been at his psychiatrist's. I said, 'You know, Richard, you and I have been friends for seventeen years now, and how many times a week do you go to ...' Like a minimum of twice a week he goes to the psychiatrist's. I said, 'You're just as crazy today as you were the day I met you. Don't you think that if you had a toothache, and after seventeen years you still had the toothache, you might think there was either something wrong with your dentist or something wrong with you? Wouldn't you think, 'this doesn't work?' And he looked at me, bewildered, like, 'What are you talking about?' I realized he didn't get it. He had no clue and I said, 'Aw, forget it. Forget it. So what do you want to do? Get lunch?'

"Sometimes when comedians get together they can be the most boring. The worst show to do, and I always turn these shows down, are TV shows with a panel of comedians discussing comedy. There is nothing more boring than a panel of comedians discussing comedy. There's nothing funny about the discussion. If they're telling war stories, that's one thing, but then they're

SHECKY GREENE has headlined all of the top Las Vegas casinos and lounges. His appearances have earned him numerous awards including the Las Vegas Entertainment Award, and the Jimmy Durante Award for Best Comedian. While he claims to shun movie and television appearances for bookings in the best stand-up venues, he has still amassed such film credits as *Splash, Mel Brooks' History of the World Part I* and *Tony Rome.* On television, he has been seen on *Laverne and Shirley, The A-Team,* and *Northern Exposure* as well as guest host on *The Tonight Show* with Johnny Carson.

always trying to one-up each other. I will never do these shows. Never!

"Comedians are basically serious. I get together with Steve Landesberg and Richard Lewis and some of the guys I started with and we'll spend time talking about world affairs and some personal stuff, but mostly world affairs. We never talk about show business. You get singers together, all they talk about is singing and songs. You get actors together, all they talk about is acting. You get comedians together, we talk about life—and it's so much more interesting."

Shecky Greene equals Comedy, it's as simple as that. "It's really funny because at the beginning of my career I worked some places that wouldn't use the name Shecky. I worked a place in Milwaukee and the guy, he was a Greek guy, said, 'What's your real name?' I said, 'Fred Sheldon Greenfield.' He said, 'Okay, you're Freddie Greene from now on.' For a long time I worked there and I was Freddie Greene. Then when I went to different places people would say to me, 'Why do you use that name [Shecky], and what does it mean?' Well, that name was given to me by my brother when I was one or two years old and it just stuck. I went all through school with it and it's caught on as far as being synonymous with comedy. I hear a lot of people say, 'You're not a Shecky

Greene ... No, you're not a Shecky.' On the *Today Show*, Katie Couric says that all the time. I wish I was working as much as my name!

"I think it's good. It says in the dictionary some-place that 'Shecky' stands for comedy and I think that's nice. But on the Internet now, I found out a lot of people are using my name. They're using Shecky Greene, they're using Shecky—Shecky Club, Shecky this, Shecky that. I haven't done anything about it. I had a lawyer who said, 'Let's sue,' but in California you sue about everything. In California if you just walk down the street and you see an accident, you sue."

That was Shecky on being a Shecky, but on the intel-ligent breed of comics, Mr. Greene says, "I think we're very analytical and analyzing, if that's what makes some-body bright. There are so many things happening in the world and the world is changing so fast, there's so much material. I still can't do calculus and I never did algebra too good either, you know, and English, I'm still working on prepositions." But *funny* he can do, no problem.

To Jim Gaffigan, comedians are out of this world. "I think of comedians as aliens on this planet. We're aliens and our home ship is stand-up comedy clubs or on the road or at some diner at four in the morning. But every now and then you'll see a comedian with his kid or his wife and you kind of look at him like, 'You got them fooled huh? You've infiltrated. I know you're an alien, you know you're an alien, but you're pulling this off and congratulations. But I know you're an alien.'" Just keep him the hell away from comet Hale-Bop.

"Historically, the court jester was the only one who could make fun of the king," says Susie Essman. "In a certain way, we're needed as the thorn in the side of society. Because somehow when you say something and it's funny, it's more acceptable. When somebody's laugh-ing, there's a window, there's an opening there to stick something in, some new ideas or some new thought or something."

Richard Belzer has no problem making fun of the king, the queen, Mother Theresa, whomever ... "I just feel it's the role of the comic to define what's on everyone's mind but articulated in a way that causes a moment of surprise that engenders laughter. Nobody knows why people laugh. It's a mystery, and it's just fortunate that a handful of people in any culture have the ability to make people laugh. To me it's very mysterious, hard to define.

"It's a whole different thing making strangers laugh, and I think a lot of people who are told they're funny by their friends and family who then try stand-up are sobered up pretty quick. It's very hard to make the transition from a familiar surrounding and the support of people who know you to total strangers who are usually drinking. When I emceed at Catch a Rising Star, I was amazed at some of the people who were almost masochistic and would keep on. I mean, you cringe and it's sad, but some people just have to learn for themselves. I would never say to anyone, 'Don't quit your day job,' 'cause stand-up is the most difficult thing in show business. It takes a certain kind of bravery. In some cases it's madness, but in other cases it's true bravery to do it. There were some people I would've said, 'You should give this shit up,' but they persisted and they became good. That was a lesson for me. You never say to anyone, 'You're fuckin' terrible,' because there were some people who were really bad who went on at two in the morning and eventually they got better and better. That was a lesson in reality."

David Brenner concurs that there are people who try way too hard to become comedians. "Oh, painful? It's like having a root canal when you're sitting there!" Caroline Hirsch, owner of Manhattan's famous comedy club, Carolines on Broadway, echoes the feelings stirred up by those open mikers. "It's painful, you have to sit and watch it. I know they can't do it in front of a mirror, but it's just painful." And Rick Newman's take is, "It's the loudest, fucking silence I have ever heard. You can hear the beads of sweat; the flop sweat just rolling down the back of their neck. Your heart wrenches for them, you cringe into your seat and go, 'Oh, my God, this poor person.'" Cary Hoffman, who manages comedians and television writers and owns Stand-Up NY, a club in Manhattan, says, "It's part of our lifestyle. In our club there are people not making a living who are still coming

COMEDY CRIMES

One of the few crimes people can get away with is joke stealing. Oh, some have tried to put a copyright on a good punch line, but for the most part it is more of an occupational hazard than a call to arms. Maybe comedians should just pray their jokes are so bad that nobody wants them.

FREDDIE ROMAN

"There's no secret that the king of that was Berle. He was known as the 'Thief of Bad Gags.' Even late in his life, at the Friars Roasts. Ten, twelve years ago, Dick Capri did five jokes, a huge hit, and at the next Roast, Berle did every one of those jokes. Nobody got mad at Milton. It was almost like a compliment to you that the greatest stand-up of all time thought enough of your material to steal it, which is stupid really. That's the attitude, guys would look at each other and say, didn't Capri do that last year?"

DICK CAPRI

"A lot of guys steal jokes from me. I'll do a three-minute routine and they'll take the best joke out of that routine and do it as a one-liner. It does bother me. Comics hate that. They're stealing your blood."

PHYLLIS DILLER

"I am appalled sometimes when I hear a joke that I'm using and somebody else is using it too. In the old days, it was frequently a joke I had bought, which means I thought I owned it and then I realized that these assholes had written it down and sent it to me. I don't want to steal even a line. There are about five lines that Dangerfield and I have in common, but I'm sure they're public domain. And we use them in different ways."
Bring up Berle and Diller gives her hearty signature laugh,

"Oh, [Bob] Hope is still mad at that. Honest to God. Happened back on Broadway in vaudeville. These old guys, boy, they won't let go."

STEWIE STONE

"We all stole, it was part of life. You take a stock joke and you bleed it into your life and you try to camouflage it."

RED BUTTONS

"I'm experiencing that right now. I have people out there doing my stuff all over the place, some of them friends of mine, and some of them not even comedians—singers are doing some of my best stuff. People come back and tell me, 'Red, you know who is doing four, five pages of your lines?' They tell me who and I'm half shocked, hurt, I don't know ... just disappointed, I guess.

"It's more of a disappointment in that they don't understand the origin of it. Nobody knows that I sat there and sweated over that material for some Roast that I did somewhere, and you feel like you're being mugged and raped when people do that. If you get in front of a really sophisticated audience they'll know, 'Hey, that's Red Buttons' ... because my style or the material that I do is so clearly defined. I mean, who else is doing 'Never Got A Dinner' or 'I Was There,' the two big routines that I'm into now and have been for quite some while. These are definitely Red Buttons." (You can experience some of Red's famous—not to mention *hilarious*—routines on page 68. Don't worry, we didn't steal them, he gave us his permission—honest.)

RYAN STILES

"Any comic who tells you that he didn't steal some stuff to start off is probably lying."

back doing amateur shows—a bullet, a stake in the heart couldn't stop them, they want it so badly."

Speaking of pain, "My dentist, who is a wonderful man, thinks he's funny, thinks he's a comic," says Pat Cooper. "I tell him, 'Look, I don't tell you how to drill teeth, don't come and give me comedy.' He says, 'Well, I got people who say I'm funny.' I say, 'Yeah, you're funny in a parlor. Get up there in front of four hundred, five hundred people and you do twenty-five or thirty minutes and keep the audience laughing....' You're not singing Cole Porter over and over and over. Frank Sinatra could sing the same songs until he died, and he did. All these singers, what are they gonna say, 'Well, I'll do George Gershwin or I'll do Rodgers and Hart.' We don't have that. With television you gotta keep changing your material or you gotta have a great attitude so that people say, 'I just wanna hear you talk.'"

It seems that for many comedians, those comedy/ tragedy masks work in tandem. Just ask George Wallace. "Oppressive times, that's what comedy comes from. That's exactly what it is. If we didn't have tragedies, we wouldn't have comedies. We were hit with tragedy in New York City on 9/11, this was completely different for us comedians. I mean, we were down four months. Nobody wanted to even go on stage. This was a different tragedy. A month after it happened I was doing jokes like, 'Anybody who's been in this country less than a year with a visa from any country with a history of terrorism or anything, y'all got to go home. This is America, you've been here for a party, the party's over, you all got to go home. We love you, but right now, you got to go home. Fifty years, we'll think about it, we'll let you come back. But right now, y'all got to go home.' Time is always the essence of everything.

"Feelings of pride, depression, being held down, held back, bad situations, slavery, even for the Jews, there was one person who went beside some overseer's back and made somebody smile. That's what comedy comes from."

Cary Hoffman sees comedy as a formula: "Comedy is tragedy plus time. All of a sudden someone dies in a horrible accident, like Princess Diana, and in six months a comic is on stage making a joke about it."

Tragedy comes up a lot among these funny people and Stewie Stone keeps the flow going. "Comedy is the opposite of tragedy. Comedy is different things to different people. Charlie Chaplin was the funniest man who ever lived, but basically he subscribed to the cruelest form of comedy because he was always hitting the big guy with the cane. Or, take the guy falling on a banana peel. There's cruel comedy, which everybody laughs at, the pie in the face, the other guy's discomfort."

David Alan Grier is a Yale man, which means that he knows a lot of stuff: "A lot of times comedy comes from sources of pain, awkwardness—you talk about your life growing up, trying to fit in, an outsider's view of the world. On the flip side it can be the common man's view of the world. One of the things that draws people in on a very general level is sitting in the audience going, 'Oh, I know what that's like.' When you talk about work or your career or your home life, your wife and kids or your girlfriend or learning to drive, you tap into a common experience. A common, shared, nightmarish experience or joyous experience, but told from a different perspective."

Funny bone doctor Jerry Stiller is in. "I always felt that comedy was a way of alleviating pain. Anyone who can make you laugh is taking you off some bad track. He or she is like a healer. Anyone who can do that is really a doctor of some sort. The beauty of it all is that when people laugh, total strangers become a single family. At that moment, there is some kind of unconscious binding of souls.

"When I go to see a show it takes me back to the Depression, when there was lots of sadness. I was a kid who went to see radio shows with Fred Allen or Eddie Cantor. The people who came into those studios were hungry for something. The comedians were masters at changing those feelings of sadness in an instant."

Caroline Hirsch has seen so many comedians come through her doors that she could have a doctorate in the subject. "There is a reason why people sit in a room and laugh at a joke, it's just common experience. It's this community that forms. That's why people respond, because they are all in the same boat. It's the reason things are funny. It's talking about tragedy and having the same experience. Take any situation in life, explain the situation, and get somebody to go, 'Oh, yeah, that, yeah, we did it.' There's a release that happens and when things are funny and people laugh, there's also an emotional release from the tragedy."

Bernie Brillstein sees deeper meaning behind the laughter. "You're drawn to comedy because you're angry. I've represented comedians and funny shows and funny things all my life. All I was doing was compensating for my anger, which I turned toward comedy. The first time I saw Lenny Bruce at Carnegie Hall, the thing I was most amazed at—other than that he was just great and my best friend—was that everything he said on stage, we had said to one another whispering. It was our sense of humor, but instead of localized, it was in front of four thousand people.

"I can do humor sitting here, or among six people at dinner, or if I get on a roll, I can probably do it in front of a few people I don't know. That doesn't make me able to do what they do. They can go out and do the same material they've done, maybe adding some stuff, maybe not, and kill. If you look at most comedians, fat or thin or tall, look at their legs, they're like football player legs, they're all strong."

"I grew up in a family that was really very supportive of me," says Joy Behar, who has her own opinion on the comedian as an angry, tragic, neurotic individual. "A lot of people say to me, 'Oh, she became a comedian because she was abused or she had a difficult childhood,' but I subscribe to the Mel Brooks position which is, I was so adored, I just kept looking for bigger houses to adore me. That's another way that people get into the industry. If you come from an abusive background a lot of the behavior is very compensatory, then I don't think you do very well, because you probably have a lot of anxiety even when you're doing well. One comedian told me that he's only happy when he's on stage. Come on, that's only twenty minutes a day, if you can get a set! Get some Prozac."

Joy's right, enough with the morose comedians, time to change the topic. How about comedy club life? That ought to cheer things up a bit. "It's very hard," says Jeff Foxworthy. Then again, maybe not so cheery. Even so, we'll hear Jeff out. "Somebody asked me a couple of years ago, 'If you knew then what you know now would you have quit your job to try this?' I said, 'No, but sometimes ignorance is bliss.' I had no idea how hard it was or how few people made it doing this. All I knew was, 'Hey I'm hanging out at this club in Georgia and there's a hundred and fifty pictures on the wall' and after a year I was like, 'well I know kind of where I stand in this pack of a hundred and fifty.' Then I would go to Cleveland and there would be a different hundred and fifty and then I would go to New York and there was a different five hundred, and in Chicago there was a different ... and I'm like, 'Oh shit! There's a lot of people doing this.' I think I read somewhere, one time in the mid '80s, there were like five or six thousand people doing stand-up. Well, out of that five or six thousand how many made it? Half a dozen, a dozen, that's not very good odds, so yeah, looking back I'm like, 'Shit, I wouldn't take those odds again.'

"I always worked at it and I think that that's probably a common denominator. When I started, the big dogs in the clubs were Leno and Seinfeld and Larry Miller and Tim Allen, and those people worked at it, they worked hard at it. It was the ones that thought it was a 'let's get drunk every night and see how many waitresses we can bring back to the comedy condo'—those people didn't make it. So I worked at it, not only in the number of shows I did, but I was always trying to write. I was always trying to get to new places. I thought from day one, the bottom is going to fall out of this comedy club thing and I want to be above that fallout line when half of these people go away. Let me go play in Detroit so when the bottom falls out and I call the club in Detroit, they know who I am."

For Rita Rudner the club life was a good experience.

RITA RUDNER is one of the most ethereal comedians on today's comedy circuit. Her soft-spoken humor has led to sold-out club appearances across America as well as in Europe and Australia. She has appeared on *The Tonight Show, Late Night with David Letterman, Comic Relief,* and her own HBO special *One Night Stand.* Prior to becoming a major comedy star, Rita appeared on Broadway as a dancer in *Annie, Follies,* and *Mack and Mabel,* among others. Rita co-wrote and co-starred in the film *Peter's Friends.* She holds the distinction of being the first female to perform in the capacity of a Roaster at a Friars Club Roast.

"There's no backstage, there's just the bar and I loved it, it was wonderful. I would always bring my notebooks and when I was starting out I would always hang out with people like Ronnie Shakes, who was a wonderful comedy writer, or I wouldn't say I tried jokes out with Gilbert [Gottfried], but other people—Bill Maher—and we'd sit there and we'd say, 'Is this funny? Is this funny? Is this a joke?' I love that, that was one of my favorite bits."

Once and for all Rita answers the question, was the movie *Punchline* at all reflective of the scene? "Whoever wrote that had never been a stand-up comedian or been to a comedy club because that was totally unrelated to anything that happens." Susie Essman backs up Rita's claim. "No, nothing like the movie *Punchline.* You don't have lockers."

"They love doing stand-up," notes Caroline Hirsch. "They just want to be on stage. Jerry Seinfeld once told me, 'It's that sixty minutes of control that I have over my audience. It's amazing. It's control. I'm here, you're all focused on me now, and you will pay attention to what I'm doing.'"

Richard Belzer says, "There were times when I would do three shows a night, which is fuckin' torture, 'cause by the third show, doing a bit's like, 'Didn't I do this? Did I do this in this show?' You go through that while you're talking, you're having this debate while you're doing a bit. So sometimes I would leave something out 'cause I thought I had done it in the show, but I hadn't, I had done it in the previous show. I don't recommend three shows to anybody."

For Kevin Meaney the clubs were a transitional experience. "When I first started off it was, 'I can get free beer.' Then there were the drug years—everybody would be doing drugs, it was a lot of fun. Then you get away from that, you grow up and you go, 'I still want to do this, but I don't want all this other baggage.' Then you gotta leave that behind and in the process you lose a lot of your friends 'cause they're still into that. Then you get married and you have children. It's not that dramatic this lifestyle: You go out, you do the show and you go home. When you were single it was different because then you would want to pick up women and go out all night and party. It really lends itself to that darker side of being a night owl and sleeping all day. It can be fun.

"But that's just when you first start off. I don't think Dom Irerra is there at midnight waiting to go on, but I'm sure that some guy who's just starting off that's been in the business like maybe two or three years, I'm sure that midnight spot means a lot to him. Most likely he's young, he's not married, he doesn't have a family to care for. For me, the wife and the baby came after I was somewhat successful, when I could afford not to go to the clubs. I could go up to Santa Rosa for a night and make enough money to support my family. I don't live to go to a club and hang out there, unless I want to do a set. I don't really need to go to a club to work on new material, I go out and get paid to do a show."

Some comedians do use the comedy clubs for breaking in new material. Cary Hoffman is an eyewitness from his Stand-Up NY perch. "The first time that Robin Williams was ever here, my wife and I were running this club almost by ourselves, with four waitresses and one guy downstairs. I didn't know about the showcase comedy system, where comedy stars come in to work out. So I was standing at the front desk and he came in and I didn't know why he was here. I said, 'Hello Mr. Williams, would you like to have a seat?' and he walked back to the bar. One of the comics saw him and said to me, 'He wants to go on.' I said, 'No he doesn't. It's Robin Williams, I can't pay him, he's gonna charge a hundred thousand dollars.' He said, 'No, he'll go on for nothing.' 'You're kidding?' So I walked over to him and I said, 'Would you like to go on stage?' He said to me, 'Only if it's okay.' I said, 'Are you kidding? Of course it's okay.'

"So I ran back, we had a signal light when the comic's time was over, and I began to flash frantically to get rid of the comic who had just gotten on stage. I was flashing him off and I felt a hand behind me and it was Robin, saying, 'Why don't we let him finish?' I said, 'Oh, that's a great idea.' I said to the emcee, 'Robin Williams wants to go on.' It's sold out, it's a Saturday night, there's a hundred and eighty people in there and he says, 'Ladies and gentlemen, we have a surprise tonight, we have Robin Williams.' The personality of this emcee, he had said a lot of things that weren't true as part of his act so why would they believe him? Robin and I are standing in the back and I'm fucking embarrassed because nobody's turning around. They're going, 'Yeah, yeah,' there was no response at all. Robin knew exactly what to do, he started walking right to the stage and then some people just started to turn around and the shock, they started to stomp their feet. It didn't come out in laughter or applause initially, but it was like thunder when they finally recognized him. My landlord, who used to live in the building, called down, 'What's going on down there, have you turned it into a disco?'

"He went on stage and they wouldn't stop applauding and yelling. He couldn't open his mouth sometimes because they were screaming so much, like the Beatles at Shea Stadium. He did about ninety minutes and he did an incredible show. Then he came off and he said, 'Can I come in again?' I said, 'Yeah, I don't know what we do about money.' He said to me, 'You do nothing about money.' I said, 'Oh, that's good, 'cause there's no way ...'

and he's been coming in for years and years. He'll come in any night he wants, always unannounced. His manager doesn't trust me, he thinks that I would spread the word if I had advanced notice—and he's absolutely right."

Samm Levine may not have hung out, drinking and drugging with the other comics during his comedy club gigs, but he does have his own observations on that damn light. "If the light is flashing, a sniper is gonna kill you in thirty seconds. The light is the club owner, it's his way of telling you, 'Alright buddy you're done.' Either you're doing terribly and they don't want you to sink any further, or you're killing and you have given no respect at all to the other comics who have to perform that night, and you want to eat up all the time you can.

"If you were given fifteen minutes and you're on there for twenty-eight, that light will be solid, they won't blink it anymore, they'll give you a solid light. In fact, in some cases, I've even seen the manager walk behind the audience and take a flashlight and start flicking it to the comic to make sure they see it. A lot of comics I know will deliberately not look up at the light if they see it flashing, so the manager will be unsure as to whether or not they see it, even though they clearly do, with their peripheral vision.

"If a guy plays the club regularly and he's a sure thing and he's always gonna bring the house down, the manager probably won't yell at him. But most of the time the comic will just make up an excuse for himself when he gets off. 'Sorry man, I ran away with it.'"

Speaking on behalf of those who actually turn on that light, Rick Newman admits, "Well, you need to, a comedian can get lost in his act. You're on a roll and you're having a great time up there, and very often, unintentionally, you go over the allotted amount of time. We've got another act we gotta get on. So I give them the light when they have about two minutes to go. A comedian doesn't want people to see him looking at his watch."

What about that act that you're about to follow? You know, the one that just brought the house down and you're up next? According to Newman, "Yeah, most comedians don't want to do that. You need something to

RICK NEWMAN is the founder and owner of the New York comedy club, Catch a Rising Star, affectionately known as Catch. Joy Behar, Andy Kaufman, Freddie Prinze, Chris Rock, Ray Romano, Janeane Garofalo, Jerry Seinfeld, and Robin Williams, among so many others all stood up at Catch and worked their stand-up magic. Rick, in his capacity of talent scout, has also nurtured and managed the careers of comedians such as Richard Belzer.

bring the audience down, calm them down a little bit afterwards. That's why the balancing of the show is sometimes very important. You could take someone like Mario Cantone, he gets so fuckin' funny, you gotta calm them down afterwards 'cause it's tough to balance."

"It was fun," says Carol Leifer of her days in the trenches. "It's exciting to be in a nightclub when you're twenty-two and twenty-three years old. It was really thrilling for me. I always tell people that are interested in going into stand-up comedy, 'If you're deterred by hanging out and waiting to go on and all that goes with it, it's really maybe not for you, because it comes along with the territory."

Mitzi Shore, owner of The Comedy Store in LA, saw many comics barreling through her doors, but if pressed she'll cop to one standout stand-up—Richard Pryor. "Richard was our King Solomon. When he needed the stage, and we needed to survive, he was there."

Freddie Roman's training ground wasn't the comedy clubs of today, but he's kept up with the scene. "I go to the clubs and I love a lot of the young people. They are having a much harder time getting started than I did. We were in beautiful resorts where we got paid to be bad. They will stay 'til one in the morning with three drunks left, begging to go on. No money, rejection, and yet they do it, night after night, so that someday they'll go on at ten thirty to a room full of people. That's the progression today, it's murderously hard.

"There's an innate jealousy if somebody hits. My generation, yes, there was jealousy. Why did he get the jobs in Baltimore, Detroit, and Pittsburgh and I didn't? But there was a camaraderie. The drive today is the sit-com situation. It's much harder now because there are literally thousands of people trying to become comedians. In the '50s, if there were five hundred in the whole country, that was a lot. So there were a lot more chances to make it then than now. Yes, those who have made it have made it tremendously, but for that net list of names, there are twelve hundred you're never gonna see."

Ryan Stiles' stand-up these days is focused on the improvisational aspect of the art, but he still paid his dues in comedy clubs. "Well, it's really competitive. I grew up in Canada with a great bunch of guys, we would help each other out. We'd watch each other's acts and make suggestions, and see how we could get a better line or get a better laugh somewhere. But when I came down here and started doing it, it wasn't like that at all. In Canada I was working with all guys that I knew, here it was just really, really, really competitive. That's another difference about improv, you don't find that. I actually do laugh at my fellow performers more in improv than I do in stand-up. We have a better time, a much better time. I probably would have gotten an ulcer if I kept doing stand-up."

Rick Newman has seen comedy club life from the inside. "It is always amazing to me, the underlying camaraderie that they have. Although it's competitive, they really, really have this camaraderie and respect for each other. Especially when it was really a big deal to do *The Tonight Show*, we'd have the television at the bar and everyone came out and was pulling for that first appearance on *The Tonight Show*. Even though it was competitive, and it is competitive, they really have that underlying association, club, if you will, of their own."

For Susie Essman the experience has been … well, she'll tell you: "Some of it is a lot of fun. You're with your colleagues and you're having fun and comics have their own language. Comics understand each other in a

FREDDIE ROMAN

Freddie Roman is the president of the Friars Club. He began his career in the infamous Catskills mountain resorts, which served as the catalyst for his highly successful Broadway production, *Catskills on Broadway*. As the creator, producer, and star, Freddie offered a nostalgic and laugh-packed salute to the upstate New York region whose hotels spawned scores of America's foremost performers, writers, and directors. Freddie's television work includes NBC's *Stark Raving Mad,* MTV's *The Big Room,* Comedy Central's Friars Club Roasts, PBS's *Now That's Funny,* and several appearances on *The Tonight Show*. He also co-starred with Maureen Stapleton in the film *Sweet Lorraine*. Freddie spends forty weeks a year touring with his unique brand of humor.

To the young men out here tonight, the prostate gland is a gland that's in your body from the day you were born. It doesn't bother you—fifty, sixty somewhere around there. But it will bother you. I get up sometimes now five, six times a night. The other night I got up at four-thirty in the morning. I walk in and I stood there—waiting; finally I look down, I said, "Hey, this was your idea." My wife said, "Who are you talking to?" I said, "No one you would remember." I pee like a stutterer talks. And that's what happens.

I am now sixty-four years of age and I'm going through my mid-life crisis. I want to grow old, young. Ten years ago I went for hair-transplants because it made me look younger. Six hours I sat in a plastic surgeon's chair, I came home, I said to my wife, "My rear end is killing me." She said, "I thought they took the hair from the back of your neck?"

I'm dieting again. Those of you that have seen me over the years, you know that I'm always dieting. I'm trying to get back to my original weight, seven pounds, four ounces. It's very hard. I'm only dieting now because four months ago I went to the doctor and he told me a word that thirty years ago nobody had ever heard: cholesterol. So I took a cholesterol test and my number came back 9-1-1.

Anytime a new diet came out I was the first to try it. I love them all. The Beverly Hills diet. The first day, all the pineapple you can eat and two bananas. The second day, after you climb down from the tree, all of the papaya you could eat. The third day, mango. The fourth day, guava and kiwi. You have to go to Borneo to buy this junk. The fifth day, watermelon. The sixth day, figs and prunes. Now the seventh day, you buy three newspapers and three magazines 'cause you ain't gonna be heard from for a long, long time.

I tried a thousand calories a day, some days I was through at eight o'clock in the morning. I tried Stillman, the water diet. Eighty ounces of water every day, you carry a bucket wherever you go. Two weeks on the water diet I wore Depends. I dreamt of June Allyson. And the Dr. Atkins diet. No carbohydrates, every morning when I wake up, I go on a stick. It is called the ketone stick. If the stick turns purple I am losing weight. My shoe turns yellow, I missed the stick.

My wife came up with the greatest diet ever in the history of the world. She gets up at ten in the morning, two cloves of garlic. Four in the afternoon, a quarter of a pound of Limburger cheese, and from a distance she looks thinner.

way that no one else understands. We're like cops and hookers in that way, we have our own understanding. Let's say I had a really bad set, I could call Joy [Behar] up and she'd totally understand what I'm talking about, in a way that nobody else could. I don't know so much what it's like now, but when I first started there were fewer of us, it was much cozier, it was much friendlier, I think. Now, there are so many comedians that it's different. I would walk into a comedy club, it was like Cheers. I knew everybody. I knew the bartenders, the waitresses, the other comedians. It was a very homey kind of feeling. Catch a Rising Star, the old one, the one on First Avenue, that was my main club, it was like home to me. So that didn't feel bad at all."

Carol Leifer is an all-for-one-and-one-for-all kind of comic. "When I came up, there was so much more of a feeling of camaraderie. It was the heyday of stand-up comedians in comedy clubs. All of us used to watch the other comedians a lot from the back and there were certain ones who were comedian's comedians, like Larry David, Gilbert Gottfried, and guys like that. Even if they were dying, the comedians were laughing, knowing how funny they were."

For some comedians, the audience is a piece of cake compared to performing in front of their peers. Howie Mandel says, "Oh, the worst thing you could possibly do is perform to a room full of comedians. The response that you get is, 'That is funny. That is very funny. That is hilarious,' or 'That will work,' which doesn't sound as good as 'Ha ha ha.'

"They don't laugh, but they appreciate and understand the mechanics. That's also just a by-product of really not sitting back and enjoying comedy as much as kind of analyzing it, and saying that'll work for me. Also, the element of surprise is lost. It's like a film critic trying to enjoy a film like just a Midwestern couple that goes out on a Saturday night. If you're breaking anything apart and analyzing it, it's not going to hit you the same way."

According to Red Buttons, you should go out and find a group of comics and perform. "It's the greatest audience. We love that. I've done Roasts all my life. You give me a professional audience, I'll take it any time of the week over any lay audience, because then you can do your best stuff, your hippest stuff. They'll get anything. They are the sharpest audience alive, the people in the business."

David Mishevitz is one of the new kids on the block, and living in the thick of the LA comedy club life. A life where often your audience consists of your fellow comedians. "A lot of the open-mike nights out here, it's just comedians and musicians. It's the same comics that go there every single week. One thing it does for some people, you write new material because you have no shot at getting the old bit over every single time. But in the back, unless a comic comes up and says something specific about something I said, like, 'Man, that was funny.' 'All right, cool man, thanks,' more than likely he saw one thing and then he went out to have a smoke and came back in at the end. It's interesting to try to corner someone and be like, 'What do you think I should ...?' and they're like, 'Oh, wait a minute. I don't know. I've got to go.'"

Shecky Greene also finds that comedians aren't the noisiest members of the audience, but he certainly respects them. "'That's funny' is exactly how they respond. It's typical. It's a respect that they're enjoying it. I'd like the guys, instead of laughing, to say, 'That's great, that's good, I wanna take that, we should have that, should be a debate, do that, you shouldn't do that with the ... you should do this.' It's a wonderful fraternity of comedians and I really love every one of my fellow comedians. I can't stand some of the jealousies they have. People who were making millions of dollars still had jealousy in this business."

Jeff Foxworthy agrees that comics aren't necessarily the ones you'll hear guffawing in the back. "From some-body who grew up appreciating humor, I thought when I first got into this that comics would just be in the back of the room laughing at each other—it's not the case at all. I remember one night, right when Jerry [Seinfeld] started getting big, doing concerts and things, I was opening for him at the Fox Theater in St. Louis. I went out and did my thirty minutes or whatever it was and then I pulled up a folding chair and sat on the side of the stage and just watched Jerry. I loved to watch him, he's a great comic. But I was sitting there and about thirty or forty minutes into his act this lady tapped me on the shoulder and she said, 'You don't think he's funny?' and I said, 'I think he's great!' She said, 'You have not laughed one time.' I'm like, 'Well, yeah, I have in my head.' I'm sitting there watching, going, 'Oh, man, that's such a great joke. This is great.' I guess on the outside I hadn't been laughing."

Rick Newman admits the comics are onto themselves in the laugh department. "When it's a show, an important show for the money, a comedian never wants the industry sitting in front, they want the general public in front. Because someone in the industry will be extremely appreciative and understand how good that comedian is, but won't be able to sit there and have the same reaction as an audience member, who will just laugh. You turn to your colleague and you go, 'That's funny.' Some comedians just make you laugh out loud. There are some comedians who do that, but industry people and comedians are a little more reserved with their reaction."

At some point in time, some brave soul got it into his head to stand up in front of a group of people and make them laugh. Now, I'm sure all of the know-it-alls out there know precisely when and where the art of stand-up comedy started, but for the sake of just plain fun, let's hear what the experts have to say about the origins of their craft:

Rita Rudner says, "Well, gee I don't know that answer. I'm sorry, I wish I could impress you. I think it might have been Steve Allen, I think he might have started it, 'cause he's the oldest, but he's dead now so I can't make fun of him. Well, let's see, I know the Catskills, vaudeville—vaudeville was before the Catskills, right? Burlesque, I know it started with visual. It must have started with visual and then somebody just started to talk in the middle of dropping his pants and then somebody came along and said, 'I think I'll keep my pants on.' Does anyone know? Oh dear. I never thought about it. I know it happened before cable, but that's all I'm sure of."

Don't worry, Rita. Nobody scored very high marks on this one, although Richard Belzer did earn extra credit with his Bodkin theory (see sidebar).

Red Buttons admits, "I have no idea, but I have a feeling that it's always been there. I think some caveman described hunting that day in a very, very funny way or wrote it on a cave wall in a funny way, so people grunted or did whatever they did in those days. I think it's been with us forever."

Jerry Stiller adds, "I would have no way of knowing that except that I studied about the Greek theater and I understood that the first actor had a mask. When he spoke with that mask he then became god-like and the theater became a pulpit. These Greek comedies and dramas affected people in a unique way. What they saw on stage changed their thinking. John Guare, a great American playwright, said, 'A play can change an audience. When they leave the theater, something within them will have changed.'

"I think the first time something happened that was funny was when the first actor, Thespis—from whence thespian comes from—came out with a mask and suddenly the mask fell off his face and he said, 'OOPS!' and the audience laughed. So he kept it in."

Well, Stiller isn't actually that far off the mark with the Greek angle. Even Aristotle took an educated guess. It seems the grand pooh-bah of philosophers surmised that comedy arose from the phallic processions that were a common feature in the Greek countryside. These guys would parade around with a phallus pole, shouting obscenities and being verbally abusive to anyone they passed. What? You don't find that funny? Tell that to the Friars Club the next time they invite you to one of their legendary Roasts. Anyway, once on stage, one of the actors wore a red phallus and he was considered the comic—maybe the guy with the biggest one became the

BELZER'S ODD BODKINS

While many of the comedians weighed in with their theories of the evolution of stand-up comedy, Richard Belzer went to the head of the class. Not that he necessarily knows the real scoop, but he gave the longest answer so he rates his own box here.

"A bodkin is a Jewish wedding performer, and this is where I think a lot of the genesis of Jewish humor, and in particular, aggressive stand-up comedy comes from. Bodkins were wedding performers in the little villages in Eastern Europe. They would do an hour or two hours, rhyming in Yiddish, like rap, but hysterical jokes. A lot of them were incredibly filthy: 'When the bride goes home with the groom she is gonna lift his beard and find his penis ... and you know she doesn't have breasts ... she has penises for breasts ... and the baker is fucking the mayor's daughter.' They would do the most vicious, hysterical material. They have them to this day. They fly them in to Brooklyn weddings from Israel; there are some famous bodkins.

"There's a whole tradition of them for at least a thousand years. They're the most vicious, scatological, filthy comedians, like

first headliner.

Howie Mandel conjectures, "I think it was purely an accident. Whether you were in class in school and somebody said something, the teacher said something, or something occurred to you, it was like a chemical reaction. You quipped back because in your mind that was the natural response to what was happening. And then there was this reaction, the class looked at you and you thought, 'Oh my God, that felt good.'

"I would imagine that same thing happened even at the beginning of time. Some guy did something because it was his natural reaction and then he got this kind of response and then he thought, 'This feels good. Everybody's looking at me, they're responding to me.' It's a sense of power. We all thrive in having this little sense of power. Maybe he tripped over a rock and everybody laughed so he got up and he tripped over it again, and

Buddy Hackett on acid. I mean, just amazing, but vicious. There were bodkin trials, where one bodkin accused another bodkin of stealing his material. Someday I'm gonna do a play about a bodkin trial because there are transcripts of these trials, where these guys would get up and do their material for the rabbi.

"A really heartbreaking story: In the eleventh century, there was a huge massacre of Jews in this one village, and it was just a horrific event, so depressing and sad that the Rabbi of the village said, 'There can be no more merrymaking. There can be no more singing. There can be no more joke telling. We have to be in mourning.' And the bodkins said, 'We don't qualify. We're not merrymakers.' They had a whole discussion about it and they let the bodkin perform. The bride would often run crying from the wedding party. Everybody would be hysterical. For a while there, I forget how many years, bodkins were the only form of entertainment in this area. So you can imagine the emotional investment the audiences had. They weren't allowed to sing or dance, but this guy gets up for two hours, stands on a table, and just eviscerates everybody in the village."

every time he did that he kept going for the laugh and that was nice. As much as an audience loves going to a comedy show, I don't think anybody enjoys it more than the comic having an amazing performance. There is no better feeling and I think that goes right across the board."

Dick Capri doesn't know how it happened either. "Maybe a caveman got up there and said, 'Hey, a funny thing happened to me ... this dinosaur ... I slipped in dinosaur shit ... it was so funny, I laughed. I was trying to make fire ... I worked so hard on the fire and the dinosaur came over and pissed on the fire.' And he told his friends, 'Hey that's funny.' 'What does funny mean? Are you sure it's funny?'"

Carrot Top thinks it was probably just out of instinct. "Some guy picked up a rock and did something with it, 'cause I think the first guy was a prop comic. I think there's just an instinctiveness to everybody to make people laugh, it was just naturally gonna happen."

Jeffrey Ross recalls, "I was in Cuba for the millennium. A buddy of mine was getting married down there and he asked me to come down and on New Year's Eve we are three or four hundred miles from Havana, we're in the jungle. This little fuckin' town, full of deprived, depressed, poor—when I say depressed, I mean economically—twenty-four hours a day, people who drink, dance, and fuck. Castro squashes them and they get right back up. We're at a New Year's party eating pig off a stick. I've been there about a week already, so I have a little bit of Spanish working and what I can piece together from high school Spanish. I was able to throw off a couple of bits, impressions. These are people I have nothing in common with who are in the jungle, they don't even know what Y2K means, they don't have computers, they don't have television, they never heard of Mickey Mouse, but here I am at twelve-thirty on New Year's Eve cracking them up.

"They never heard of a stand-up comic and I realized that I was naturally funny, that comedy is a basic human interaction. We weren't communicating much better than cavemen could talk to each other."

Susie Essman acknowledges, "Comedians are really storytellers and I think that that's the oldest form of entertainment. Some Neanderthal, someone I dated, would tell a story—it's an oral kind of art form."

Caroline Hirsch thinks, "It actually started in the Civil War. There were elder statesmen that tried to give a little slant to their speeches. That's how it evolved over the years. Then came vaudeville, with blackface. It has an interesting history. In vaudeville, the funnyman went on first."

Okay, enough already! I'm sort of sorry I opened this Pandora's box of trivial pursuit. Obviously, there's a gazillion schools of thought on just where this odd tradition of stand-up comedy arose. Whether it was baboons, or cavemen, or court jesters, or fast-talking politicians, I don't care anymore! The bottom line is that it's here to stay.

Before I totally bury this thread though, I do think

JEFFREY ROSS

Jeffrey Ross has received critical acclaim for his Friars Club Roast spots on Comedy Central. He has also appeared on several other Comedy Central programs such as *Pulp Comics, Lounge Lizards,* and *The Daily Show.* His other television credits include *Six Feet Under, Politically Incorrect, The Drew Carey Show, Late Show with David Letterman, The Tonight Show with Jay Leno,* and *Late Night with Conan O'Brien.* His film appearances include *The Adventures of Rocky & Bullwinkle.* Julia Louis Dreyfus' NBC sitcom *Watching Ellie* is among his television writing credits.

ENOUGH WITH THE BREAD ALREADY

Your smile blooms like a bright summer flower
Your hair flows down like a soft rain shower
Your eyes are like open seas, blue from coast to coast
So how come your ass looks like a truck?
Enough with the bread already

HEY, WAIT A MINUTE

Her long tan legs
Her soft sexy voice
Her dark bedroom eyes
Her large protruding Adam's apple
Hey, wait a minute

Rick Newman sums things up pretty well. "We have some interesting looking people who get up and say, 'Hello,' and it puts a smile on your face, really makes you laugh. I'm positive that before that, before there was language, there were people who were able to grunt and get a laugh out of three or four or five or however many people in their cave. I think the way that we appreciate a painting, we appreciate somebody who can make us laugh. It's such a wonderful gift—both to be able to do it and to be able to respond to it."

There is something about this art of stand-up comedy—but don't call it that around Bernie Brillstein, who says, "It's not an art. Bullshit, bullshit." Well, whatever the hell it is, there has to be something at your core to make you pursue it so vehemently. When I brought this up to Jeff Foxworthy, he told me, "I would hate to go to a psychiatrist and have it figured out because I'd be afraid I couldn't do it anymore. In the beginning it was probably wanting approval or attention, and now that need for attention has, I guess, been satiated but I still love doing this. There is probably something terribly, psychologically wrong with all of us. I remember I had been doing it for three or four years and one night, right in the middle of a set in Jacksonville, Florida, it dawned on me—what makes me think what I have to say is more important than any of the other three hundred people in this room? It was almost a panic attack. You gotta stop thinking like that. But I'm sure at an early age I found out that if I made people laugh they liked me."

You hang around these guys long enough and something is bound to rub off on you, which is not a bad thing, especially if you are thinking about being a stand-up comic. They're a lot of fun and they possess a refreshing honesty about their lives and their craft—so stick around and get to know them better.

48

MAYBE IF I JUST STAND HERE THEY'LL ALL LEAVE

...There's a first time for everything—even laughs

I'm sure the first time the Wright Brothers decided to take their plane to Kitty Hawk for a spin they had more than a few reservations about the whole idea. It's never easy getting up there without a net to catch you, but that first time can be the most nightmarish of them all. Granted, a stand-up comic's first time out isn't as life-threatening as Orville and Wilbur's may have been, but then again, they only had to stay up there for twelve seconds! Whether you're a hundred feet above the ground or on a raised platform, palms sweat and stomachs churn, and sometimes the only way out is to curl into a ball and pray you'll wake up in a nice comfy bed.

Eventually the class clown has to prove his mettle without using the teacher as a straight man, and the family cut-up needs to broaden her horizons beyond making fun of Uncle Murray's toupee. As any successful comedian will tell you, not every bird can fly out of the nest with ease and grace, but once you've done it the first time—provided you haven't splattered on the pavement—there is no going back to a regular job.

"I was working as a waitress and in order to make that bearable I used to just do impressions of all the customers and the Chinese kitchen staff," says Susie Essman, describing the genesis of her stand-up. "So all my friends that I waited on tables with, I had them laughing all the time because we had to do something. They all said, 'You know, you've got to do this,' and somebody found out about this place on Carmine Street called Mostly Magic. They had a Tuesday night open mike and we just went and signed in and I did it. I wrote three minutes of material, which I probably did in a minute and a half, and all my friends were there, which was like, what was I thinking, inviting all my friends? And actually, that night, Paul Herzich and Bert Levitt, the people who eventually opened up Comedy U, were there and they said, 'We thought you were great, we're opening up this comedy club. Do you want to come work there?' I was like, 'Whaaaa, what?'

"About two months later they called me up and said, 'We opened the club, we'd like you to come in and work.' And I did. Otherwise I don't know if I ever would have become a comedian, because I was too scared and I couldn't have done that whole thing, that waiting on line, taking a number thing. But they brought me into their club and they gave me tons of stage time and I developed there. Then I went to the Comic Strip and Catch a Rising Star and those other clubs. So I wasn't planning on being a comedian but then about three months into it I was like, 'This is the exact thing that I should be doing with my life.'"

But what about the laughs? If a comedian doesn't get them, then what's the point, and how do they have the moxie to try it again? According to Essman, "I did get laughs that first night. I did and then—this happens to a lot of comics I find—the first night they kill and then they die thereafter. It's just something about the magic of that first night. I've heard this before from other people. I did really well that first night. Then I started not doing so well and doing well and not doing so well. I mean, even though I had a lot to learn, I did have a natural ability to be onstage and make people laugh.

photo by Richard Lewin

SUSIE ESSMAN has been making people laugh all her life by voicing what everyone else is thinking, but afraid to say. Her television appearances include *King of Queens*, Larry David's *Curb Your Enthusiasm*, *The Tonight Show*, *Politically Incorrect* and *Law & Order*, among others. She has also performed at Friars Club Roasts, some of which have aired on Comedy Central. Her film credits include *Volcano, Teenage Mutant Ninja Turtles II, Punchline*, and *The Siege*. Susie regularly appears in all of the major comedy clubs presenting her bold, original humor.

"The first night, I remember sitting on the floor of my living room, rocking myself back and forth. I threw up, I had diarrhea. I was terrified. And I was like that maybe the first eight, nine, ten times I performed, and finally I said to myself, 'Wait a minute, if you are going to do this, you can't go through this every night.' And then it kind of just went away."

Apparently such ailments are an occupational hazard, as Howie Mandel can attest. "I didn't used to be able to eat before a show because I would be sick. I'd be nauseous, and then as I got more and more popular I'd be doing shows every day and I was dying of starvation because I wasn't eating. It was terrifying, but terrifying in the same way as a thrill ride. The bigger the roller coaster and the better the roller coaster and the closer you feel you are coming to death, the better that ride is. You come off and you're twisted upside down, you feel like you almost fell out, you're thrown ten stories into the air, and you're nauseous and you go, 'I thought I was gonna die. Wow, I've never been on anything like that before—let's go on it again!'

"To me, that was what performing was like. It was the most terrifying thing. So many times, behind the curtain, I'd be shaking and try to hold myself. If I stood still I probably would have passed out. I'd hyperventilate and I hadn't eaten, and I just felt sick. But then I went onstage and I heard the laughter and everybody was looking at me and then I said, 'good night,' and they liked me. They enjoyed what I did!"

Like Essman, Mandel fared well his first time out of the comedy gate, in spite of his physical state. This naturally funny guy, visiting LA with his friends, found himself onstage at Mitzi Shore's The Comedy Store on an open-mike night, "I got up on a dare, not to pursue comedy. I got up because it would be a fun thing to do on a vacation. I did what entertained my friends and entertained me, and I thought I was funny and I was really happy with it. I would have been happy with a great story to tell about my vacation. Did I know that the room would also be in line with me? Or at least Mitzi Shore would be in line with me? She said, 'That's very good, come back tomorrow night.' Or that a producer would be there and say, 'Oh, that's perfect for my show, *Make Me Laugh*, come back tomorrow night.' I chalk that up to luck—that my sensibility touched the nerve of somebody else's."

Most comedians will tell you that this inherent need to perform was a part of their psyche from before

MITZI SHORE has been overseeing the operation of The Comedy Store comedy club in Los Angeles for almost thirty years. Under her ever-watchful eye for talent she has cultivated the careers of some of the top comedians of the last three decades. David Letterman, Tom Dreeson, Elayne Boosler, Jay Leno, Steve Landesberg, Howie Mandel, and Richard Pryor are among the talented individuals that honed their comedy craft under Mitzi's aegis.

they can even remember. "My mother told me that when I was two years old, anybody who walked in the house, I jumped on the table and started to sing songs. My first time in front of an audience was on the stoop on the Lower East Side of Manhattan, where I'd be singing songs when I was three years old," remembers Red Buttons. "I wanted to show off. That's what we're all doing in this business, we're showing off."

Lily Tomlin desired the spotlight early on as well, taking ballet and tap at the Department of Parks and Recreation of Detroit. "I used to put shows on as a kid," says Tomlin. "As soon as we got a television set, I was always making up some kind of a show to do and trying to cast other kids from my apartment building in it. I thought anything, anything that could hold an audience's attention was entertainment. I would imitate people I'd seen on television like Bea Lily or Imogene Coca or Lucy or anyone else, or Jean Carroll, who was the very first stand-up woman I ever saw.

"I did a little bit of everything they did. Rather than a stand-up, I was probably the world's first performance artist. Because I would imitate my father, I would cut a rope in two and restore it, I'd do magic tricks. I'd put on my mother's slip like an evening dress and throw pearls around my neck like Bea Lily. I would tell Jean Carroll's jokes and maybe do that mock striptease that Imogene Coca had done on *Your Show of Shows*."

It was all in preparation for that special stand-up moment. "I was always doing monologues and character pieces, didn't really draw the line. To me, that was stand-up too, if I was up there by myself in front of an audience and if that's what I chose to do. That was just my style," says Tomlin of her burgeoning comedy persona.

"I'd heard about the Improv as a place you could work out and the first time I went to the Improv I pulled a whole big deal. It was from the days of the Improv in New York when the window looked right out on the street. I used to have a lot of antique clothing from thrift shops, I had evening dresses and fur wraps. They were really ratty in the daylight but at night they looked fabulous. In fact, the ankle-strap shoes from that time were the first pair of shoes Ernestine wore. I'm sure I was doing monologues and little takes and spins and whatever it was, but it was certainly unconventional.

"I lived on 5th Street between 2nd and 3rd Avenues and I'd get done up in these outfits. I had this blue velvet halter dress with an old white fox stole, ankle straps and all that stuff. So I'd take the subway up to the theater district and I told Budd Friedman, the owner of the Improv, that I had to go on at a certain time, I had to go on within a certain window like nine o'clock or nine-thirty. Then I'd get off at the theater district where the limos stand around waiting for people in the theater. If you gave one of them a ten they'd drive you someplace while they were waiting for people to come out of the theater. So I'd give a guy, like, ten bucks because I wanted him to wait for me. So I pulled up to the Improv in the limo, and I got out in front of the window in all this garb, and I swung in. I went on fairly quickly and did like, ten or fifteen minutes or something, then I swept out and got in the limo and drove away. And that was my first time at the Improv."

With all that brouhaha going on who has time to be nervous? "I'm sure I was," admits Tomlin, "but you're in a state of denial. You sort of suspend your own disbelief that you can do it. I'm sure I was nervous but somehow I made it through."

Rita Rudner holds firmly to the adage that there is safety in numbers, even when it comes to doing stand-up. "The first time, I did a double act because I was too scared to go on by myself. I was on Broadway in *Annie*, and we went to Catch a Rising Star late at night, and my friend Richard and I decided we would do songs and in between songs, tell jokes, because we didn't know what a joke was and we knew how to sing. We brought an accompanist with us and we got on at two in the morning and there were three people in the audience. Richard hated it, but I liked doing it so I came back the next week and I tried an act myself."

Sounds like she hit the ball out of the park her first time going solo there. "No, no, uh-uh." Oh, sorry. "If it works the first time, you're doing someone else's act. I had no idea what I was doing but I enjoyed the process of finding out, and I liked being up there. People kind of laughed between what I thought was funny."

What possesses someone like Rudner to change direction in her career, from the predictable schedule of Broadway to sleepless nights on the comedy circuit? "I don't know. I was in therapy, but I didn't ask and I don't know. I know I love doing it. I'd been dancing for quite a long time and I realized that stand-up comedy was where there weren't a lot of women and dancing and singing and acting there were thousands of women. So I decided to try it and I guess I had some kind of dormant aptitude or talent for it. I certainly had a dormant interest. I started to think about stand-up a hundred percent of the time."

"I didn't start out as a comedian," says Jerry Stiller. "The first connection I remember was being on the stage in the third or fourth grade, in Brooklyn. Mrs. Cantor, the teacher in this public school in East New York, needed somebody to sing in the assembly and they asked me to sing *Waterboy*, which was a spiritual they used to sing in those days. All the classes were there, we sat and I sang, 'Waterbo-o-oy, where are you hidin'? If you don't come, gonna tell on your mammy.'"

In case the full impact of his rendition isn't apparent on paper, Jerry really did break into song as he told the story, and nearly brought me to tears. Okay, maybe not, but Paul Robeson certainly would have met his match.

"And the lil' Jewish kid was singing this and I'll tell you, at the end of it they applauded and they went crazy. And then I sang, 'Wagon wheels, wagon wheels, keep on rolling wagon wheels.' I didn't know what was going on except at that point, when I heard the applause, I knew then that I wanted to be an actor.

"The next thing that happened, which got me to that next place, I was doing Adolf Hitler in a high school play called, *Hitler Goes to Heaven.* In that one I played a comic character, Hitler being comic. They sold war stamps, and the play was so well received that we did it twice, and all I knew was that these laughs were pouring in on me. I guess I started out as an actor and then I thought, 'Well, maybe I could be a stand-up comedian,' you see? So there was an amateur show at a settlement house on East Broadway and I put my name down and I went out, and I guess I must have performed for about ten minutes. I was just doing stupid things, trying to do impressions, talking to the audience and nobody listened. I had no material. I was so naïve. Like, Milton Berle would just string one joke after another, I thought they would listen to me. I didn't even have jokes. They told me I stunk. I can't even repeat the lack of response. At the end of it all, my mother just walked down the stairs. She was humiliated."

As you will discover along the way, if perseverance is not in your vocabulary, then stand-up comedy will *not* be on your résumé. It is, however, on Stiller's. Apparently mama's opinion didn't enter into his drive to pursue the craft. "I did a show called *Girl Crazy*, a Syracuse University show that played downtown Syracuse, and it went over very well. In that show I did these three impressions: Peter Lorre, Maurice Chevalier, and Jimmy Durante. After the show closed, there was a nightclub way out of town called the Club Candee, and the guy who ran it would audition acts. He said, 'Listen, come on down, if you can bring in a college crowd, we'll put you on.' I remember auditioning for him and he was eating a bowl of spaghetti while I was doing my act. He never even looked up. He said, 'Okay, you got the job, twenty-five bucks. You get a piece of every person who comes in here.'

"I went on and did that act, and I killed them. It was incredible what went on. He said, 'Okay, you wanna come down here next Sunday night and work with the regular audience?' I came down the following Sunday and I followed an act called Jerry and Turk and all I know is—I died. I said, 'What the hell is this? A week and a half ago they were screaming.' But I didn't give up."

Even Stiller admits that perhaps he should have, at least on that particular act, "It was just a bunch of one-liners out of Robert Orbin's joke book. 'I just flew in from LA and boy are my arms tired'—stuff like that. I really thought that would be funny. I wore a funny hat and I waved my arms and then I did my three impressions. By the time I got to the impressions nobody gave a damn.

"It went through my head that I needed a partner, so I kept looking for someone. I always felt that couples were funny. I did *The Colgate Comedy Hour* as an extra, and in the show were Jack Carson and Jack Gilford. In between the dress rehearsal and the show that night at the Center Theatre, I went to a cafeteria and sitting at a table was Jack Gilford. I looked at him and I said, 'Oh, Mr. Gilford, Mr. Gilford, can I speak to you?' He said, 'Sure, sure come over here. Aren't you in the show?' I said, 'Yes, yes, I'm one of those, you know, an extra.' He says, 'Sit down, sit down. What'll you have? Have a sandwich.' And I said to him, 'Can I ask you a question? I wanna be a stand-up comedian.' He says, 'Tell you what, get someone you can bounce off of, preferably a girl. A good looking girl.' He says, 'It'll be a lot of fun.' I said, 'Really?' He said, 'Yeah.' Then he picked up my check."

Although Stiller didn't take Gilford's advice imme-diately, he did eventually find that female partner. As luck would have it, he didn't even have to look that far, she happened to be sleeping in his own bed. He and Anne Meara met while both were struggling actors in New York but it wasn't until after they were married that they joined their funny forces to become one of the most popular comedy teams in show business—Stiller and Meara. "Some years later Anne Meara and I started working on an act. I was brought up listening to radio and listening to people like Burns and Allen, Fred Allen and Portland Hoffa, Mary Livingston and Jack Benny. I always felt that these people had their cake and could eat it too. In other words, they were married to the person they were working with and that brought them together and they would never lose each other in any way. It was like a permanence, instead of waiting for the phone to ring you would always have an act."

Stiller isn't the only one who proved that imitation is not just the sincerest form of flattery, it's a good way to make a living ... or, at least, try to. "The very first time I performed was when I was at school. I did impressions," says Dick Capri. "I did impressions because there was another kid that did them. I never knew how to do them, but I heard how he did them. So you hear a guy doing Peter Lorre, 'Oh, that's how you do it? You talk through your nose. Oh, I didn't know that.' So I was an impressionist, but I could only do an impression of another impressionist. I would steal impressions, I could never originate one. A great impressionist will hear someone speak and they'll have a good ear and they can do an impression of him. I would have to do an impression of the impressionist doing an impression of him. I made a living out of doing impressions of impressionists.

"Doing impressions, you're entertaining the people, so it's not as hard as if you're just going out and doing comedy. Comedy is tough. Somebody says, 'Hey, this guy sounds like so and so,' 'Oh, yeah, fine,' that's all you have to do. Then I would put a joke with the impression and then I would get laughs. That's how I got by for many years. In those days I was doing Groucho Marx, Edward G. Robinson, Ed Sullivan. If you did an impression of someone who was very hot at the time, they just loved it. Everybody loved to see an Ed Sullivan impression.

"I came to New York and I found an agent who booked amateurs. Instead of comedy clubs, they had amateur shows in these little clubs. If you won you got five bucks, if you came in second you got three bucks, if you came in third you got two bucks. The first time, that was quite a moment. I came from Reading, Pennsylvania. I called my mom, I said, 'I got to New York, I'm here a week, and I'm already on television.' It just happened like that. I was too young and dumb to be nervous.

"When I started, we had to try to get a job in order

to show how bad we were. You know how tough it is to get your first job? They're gonna pay you to be bad. It's very difficult. Now, you go out, 'Okay, I'm gonna be a comedian.' Okay, take a number and they'll listen to you. No one wanted to listen to me. I had to get a job to prove how bad I was. That's why it took me so long to get to where I am.

"I was doing impressions and then I started doing some little sight bits. In those days, everybody was doing impressions and the guy that was managing me said, 'Kid, get rid of the impressions.' Everybody said, 'Be yourself, if you want to make it in show business, be yourself.' I had no idea what that meant. I don't know how to be myself. I'd never done jokes. Slowly, I put more jokes in my act and dropped the impressions, and eventually I dropped all the impressions and became a comedian. Then I got happier. When I was an impressionist I was very unhappy because I wasn't myself, I was always someone else. I had no personality."

Speaking of personality, Richard Belzer's got that by the truckload, "My whole life I had been told, 'You should be in show business.' I was thrown out of every school I ever went to for being disruptive and funny, you know, class clown. My classmates were shooting milk through their noses. I was making everyone laugh, and I got thrown out of the room, usually. In 1971, I answered an ad in the *Village Voice* for *Groove Tube,* which was a kind of underground video show—satire of television and film. I answered an open audition call, almost on a dare. Some friends and my then wife said, 'You're so funny, why don't you go down there?' The line was around the block. I'd never done anything in show business but I had always done impressions and characters. I just exploded at this audition and I got hired on the spot. Played ten roles on the show, then we did the movie, then I got the courage to do stand-up. I'm one of the few people that started as an actor and went to stand-up rather than the other way around."

Why Belzer would prefer stand-up over acting, only a therapist can figure out. "I was always terrified of being

RICHARD BELZER is a comedian, actor, and author. On NBC's *Law & Order: SVU,* he recreated his role of Detective John Munch from NBC's *Homicide: Life On The Street.* Richard's film appearances include *Groove Tube, Night Shift,* and *Scarface.* He honed his stand-up comedy skills as the emcee of New York's popular comedy club Catch a Rising Star, moving on to numerous appearances on *The Tonight Show* and *Late Show with David Letterman.* He has written two books: *How To Be a Stand-Up Comic* and *UFOs, JFK, and Elvis: And Other Conspiracies You Don't Have to Be Crazy to Believe.*

in front of a live audience. I thought of being an actor, where you had scripted material and you could rehearse, and the idea of going up there with your naked face hanging out and just jokes was terrifying. It was for months after I started, too. I did spoofs of musicals for my friends and I did impressions and I did characters. I just put together a hodgepodge of what I thought would be a set. I was terrified. I had to have two martinis before I went on and walk around the block and almost go to the bathroom in my pants. For months and months I was utterly terrified, but once I was on stage it was usually okay.

"The very first time was amazingly good. The second time I went on I bombed horribly. For some reason that first time was magic. I was hooked. And the next time was awful. I didn't start doing stand-up until I was twenty-seven years old, and I realized, you know what, this is what I have to do, I'm going to use the word, my 'calling,' my destiny. It's true in my case. I had been a newspaper reporter, a school teacher, a dock worker, a truck driver, a census taker, a jewelry salesman, a free-lance writer. I did everything and I wound up in show business. I loved being a newspaper reporter. If I wasn't a comedian, I'd be a journalist today, I think. I certainly enjoyed teaching ... but the jewelry salesman thing! I mean, I was pretty good at whatever I chose to do, it's just that I was never really satisfied. I wanted to do something creative. I wrote poetry and plays and articles, but I'm really meant to be a performer. I think I was terrified to do it until finally that was the only thing left."

Belzer honed his stand-up craft at Catch a Rising Star. "Belzer became my main emcee for seven years and really perfected his art with the ability to be able to be up there and he didn't have an act," says Catch owner Rick Newman. "He would work the audience the whole night long and that gave him his sharpness, being able to do that night after night, getting up and being spontaneous. And he learned, which was very interesting. Belzer has that acerbic dark side to him and he's so quick and so funny and he had to perfect his art so that he would win the audience over first. Then he could turn against the audience and make fun of them. That's a very important part of what a comedian has to do. You have to win the audience over before you're able to pick on them."

"Being an emcee is the greatest training in the world," says Belzer, "because you come up on stage— 'Good evening ladies and gentlemen, welcome to the show, anybody from out of town?' You know, that cliché stuff that everybody now knows was new then. To me, that was the most fun, to pick up a woman's purse and improvise off the contents, or to ask somebody what they do and then talk to them for five, ten minutes sometimes and getting things out of people in the audience that people were amazed I was able to do. It was just fun too, because it forced me to be spontaneous. They gave me the raw material of their life and I would guesstimate one way or another.

"Monday night was audition night, and people would line up outside the club, get a number. Comedians got five minutes, singers got one or two songs. In those days it was comic, singer, comic, singer, comic, singer, and I loved those days. I loved them then and I love them in retrospect because that is what show business is all about. People lining up and trying to make it, realize their dreams. Among the people who auditioned for me were Jerry Seinfeld, Larry David, and Bill Maher, so there were genuine discoveries. It was fun to try and find someone."

Anthony Clark was one of those someones who paid his dues working the comedy club circuit. "I remember every night trying to get up at Catch a Rising Star. I mean, you're trying to get stage time from Jerry Seinfeld and Rodney Dangerfield, Richard Belzer, Richard Jeni, just unbelievable comics. One of my fondest memories is just sitting at the bar one night and looking at the kids waiting to go up, I called it my freshman class at the time. It was like me, Chris Rock, Jon Stewart, and Adam Sandler, so I think all of us did pretty well. I'm pretty proud of everybody. But truly we were just sitting there looking at each other like, 'Are we ever gonna get up?' It was very frustrating."

It stands to reason that Clark's first sitcom, *Boston Common*, revolved around life at a Boston college, since his stand-up roots followed a similar course. "I think I always wanted to be an actor. I kind of fell into stand-up because I went to Emerson College and Boston in the mid '80s and late '80s was just booming with comedy. I think there were seven clubs there at one point, open seven nights a week. I mean, anybody that got laid off from a factory would start doing stand-up. You couldn't keep people out of the clubs. Emerson had a huge reputation for comedy because its alumni include Jay Leno, Steven Wright, Denis Leary, Spalding Gray, Norman Lear ... Boston at the time was putting out everybody."

With all of that comedy around him in Boston, iron- ically enough, Clark's first time alone on stage was eleven hundred miles south of Bean Town. "I was in Atlanta doing summer stock theater and David Cross, who had his own show on HBO, *Mr. Show*, went on at the Punch Line and suggested that I write five minutes while I was down there and give it a try. That was my first time on stage. It was in between my sophomore and junior year in college.

"The Punch Line is a legendary comedy spot and I sat around all summer trying to get on stage. Finally, at the end of the summer, I think I had prepared so much by not getting on stage that when I finally did it was unbelievable. It was a great response and I was addicted. I've never taken any kind of hard drugs but I can imagine what that would be like if the euphoria is the same as getting up on stage; having a packed house of two hundred people just go crazy for you the first time you've ever done it. I went right out of the side door into the parking lot and I felt like I was going to projectile vomit. All of my friends were like, 'Dude, it wasn't bad,' but I was physically ill afterwards. That wore off in a few hours and I was addicted to it. There was no coming back.

"I had done a whole lot of acting in high school and college but it was a completely different thing because there was no one to hide behind, there was no one to blame it on. It's not like being in a band, where you can hide behind an instrument or you've got five other guys up there with you. It's just you and a microphone and a microphone stand and the crowds don't give it up until somebody rings the bell. I've been told all my life that I was humorous and all that, but not until the point when I actually got up there did I realize I seemed to have a calling for this. And it felt good because I really am not that good at many other things. If I hadn't been an actor I'd probably work in a drive through at KFC right now."

Like Jerry Stiller, who took Jack Gilford's advice, or Anthony Clark, who had David Cross's encouragement, Carol Leifer found her nerve via someone in the know: "I went to SUNY Binghamton in upstate New York, with Paul Reiser, and he was the one who really turned me on to the whole stand up thing. He would play tapes of himself going on at Catch a Rising Star and little places. I mean, this was before comedy clubs, so it was like, 'Who is this guy? Vic Damone? Going on at nightclubs during the summer.' He told me all about how at Catch a Rising Star, anybody could go on an audition night, so I tried it and I was hooked. I always say to Paul, 'If I hadn't met you in college, I don't know if I would have found that route to it.' Starting standgg-up and going to those audition nights, having him around to do it with, really made it a lot easier than doing it on my own.

"The first night that I went on was like out of a dream. I remember I was number five that night and David Spade was the emcee and I went on and I had put this little five minutes together. I did so great the first night. It was amazing. But in looking back now I see it was because it was audition night so the audience, if you're halfway decent, they'll really root for you. I had a great time slot. So much of stand-up has to do with where you go on in the night, who you follow and all of that. When I walked off, Rick Newman, the club owner, shook my hand and it was like, 'Oh my God. I feel like I'm ready to go on the *Tonight Show.*'

"It was the second time that I went on that I totally bombed. It was late, the audience wasn't into it. I remember a guy heckling me. I had no idea what to do and I did too much of an aggressive comeback to him. Now, having done stand-up for as long as I have, I know that when somebody heckles you, it's a very intricate kind of dance, knowing when you go for the jugular and when you don't. So, second time I went on, same material—died. I was horrible and I realized that there are so many elements that go into being a performer that you can't judge it night by night like that. It was like, 'Okay, now I get it. It's not all like the first night.'

"I had done little stand-uppy things in college so it wasn't that strange to perform. And growing up being kind of a ham, it wasn't nerve-racking or crazy for me at all. It felt like something I was going to do once, go back to school, and forget about, so I wasn't as fearful as maybe somebody going into it who's leaving a thriving career. A lot of the people I came up with, like Dennis Wolfberg, who has since passed away, and Joy Behar, they were adults and had careers that they were leaving to pursue stand-up. I always had a lot of respect for them because they were really putting something on the line, as opposed to someone coming out of college and, instead of going to Europe for a year, trying stand-up comedy.

"I have always liked the immediate access of stand-up. I feel bad for actors who are trying to break in, it seems much more of a maze as opposed to stand-up, where you go to a club, you find out when they have an open-mike night, you sign up, and that night you're a comedian. There's very little red tape. I got so much great feedback from the established comedians at the time—'Hey, you got something, you should do this, you should hang out.' Once you pass the audition at a club, the big invitation is, 'You can hang out now.' It seems funny looking back—'Hey, you can hang out now'—that's the biggest validation you can get. But to become a regular at these night clubs and have the affirmation of established comedians makes you feel like you're doing something right."

"I started in my late thirties, basically, the way Phyllis Diller did," says Joy Behar. "I can't imagine how you would start in college because comedy, getting up in front of all those people, is one of the hardest things that you can do. I don't know if you know this, but the number-one fear, according to the *Book of Lists,* is the fear of public speaking. The number-six fear is the fear of dying. In other words, people are more afraid to talk in public than to die. So, I think that I was too scared, too insecure as a young person to try it.

"I won a contest at Queens College, a speech contest, so I was always good at public speaking, but I was also very scared and I just couldn't take the vomiting. I was naturally good, but you know what? Even before that, when I was in junior high school, I went to a dramatic workshop and I took acting lessons. They offered three things: dance, acting, and speech—and I always excelled in the speech class. That was where I was really meant to be. It took me almost forty years to figure out that I could do it professionally. I was a teacher before that, and I also was good at speaking to people as a teacher. So it really was the thing for me, and having been very funny and crazy as a child. It just wasn't meant to be until I got older. Emotionally, I was not prepared to take the rejection and the difficulties of stand-up, so I didn't do it for that reason.

"I grew up, came of age during the '60s and '70s,

and that was a time when the only people who were really funny were Cheech and Chong, and that was really not my style. George Carlin was doing stand-up and Phyllis Diller was coming out at that time, and Elayne Boosler, and a few other people, but very few comedians were really hitting at that time. In the '80s, when I was older and more mature, I hit a comedy boom and started working immediately, practically immediately, so my emotional obstacles disappeared and the times were right for me to make some kind of impression in the business.

"It's one thing to say, and I hear it often, 'I'm really funny at parties.' It's quite another to do comedy in front of people when you are required to be funny. As a professional, being funny is no longer optional. If you're witty or you can put a lampshade on your head, great. But now take that same skill and put it in front of people at a club and you will see how the bodies drop."

Though Behar really began her upward climb in the '80s, she'd already had a shot at a career change during her years as a high school English teacher. "I auditioned for *Saturday Night Live* in 1975. I liked the show and a friend of mine and I had written this bit about an Italian woman who gives the neighborhood news. I called up the talent coordinator, his name was John Head, which is a double-whammy right there, and I got him on the phone. I was in Queens—Forest Hills—and I called him up and said, 'Listen, I have this bit that I think would be really funny in the show,' so he said, 'Really?' I couldn't even believe I even had him on the phone. So he said, 'Say it to me,' so I read him a couple of the bits and he said, 'It's funny, come and see me.' So I went in and he was trying to develop talent, so he worked with me a little bit and then I auditioned for Lorne Michaels. I performed the bit at the Improv, at ten o'clock at night with the *Saturday Night Live* producers there and a full house. John Head had set it up, so I got the best spot.

"I have to tell you, I killed. I had diarrhea, I was nauseous, I was incoherent before—but I killed that night, and I scared myself. I never got on *Saturday Night Live* for various reasons, I think that at the time people there would have liked to have bought the material to do themselves. That period of my life was weird because I kept praying that I wouldn't get on. Friday night they would call me and tell me whether I was going to make it or not and I'd be lying in bed at my house in Queens with my husband thinking, 'Please God, don't tell me that I'm going to do it.' I was terrified to do it. I had nothing under my belt. I just had this bit that they liked. I didn't get on, so then it became, 'Okay, now let's see how you're going to do this.'

"I was going to acting school. I was at HB studios studying acting and I was just determined to stay on track. Then, in 1979, I had a near-death experience. It was an ectopic pregnancy and I really was in very serious danger of dropping dead. When I came out of that, I kind of had a different resolve about the world. I thought, 'You know what? I really almost died, so how bad can it be to die on stage? It changed my head around. It became like, 'Hey, so what? Big deal. What are they gonna do to me? What can they do to me?' So I started doing stand-up.

"The second time I got up was a couple of months after the first one for *Saturday Night Live*. Now, John Head was not there with an audience. The audience was like maybe three drunks from New Jersey and a couple of other people. It died like a dog. The same thing that had killed, now died. Now, since there was nobody around to tell me anything, I assumed it was my problem. I didn't realize that the circumstances have a lot to do with how well you are going to do. I used to say to Silva Friedman, the owner of the Improv, 'Can't you give me an early spot, like at ten? I do really well at ten.' She said, 'Well, everyone does.' So I then realized, you have to be talented, you have to be funny, but you also have to have the right circumstances. I'm still nauseous. I still don't need any Ex-Lax. All I have to do is give myself an appointment for a set. None of us suffers from constipation, let's put it that way.

"A lot of young people will ask me how do you do it? I didn't know how to do it. I had no idea how to go about it. The first thing that I did was a character who

RED BUTTONS

Of Milton Berle:

He's a beautiful man. We're talking about a man who went to an orgy and stole the grapes. A man who believed you should close Radio City, but keep the Rockettes open.

I WAS THERE

I'm always there ...

In Detroit at the annual we hate Japan parade ... I was there.

In Miami at a Cuban Yankee go home rally ... I was there.

In Geneva at a Henny Youngman ban the bomb concert ... I was there.

In Harlem at a Lenox Avenue block party to celebrate the Australian Yachting Cup victory ... I was there.

In Bensonhurst, at a waiter's union hemorrhoid scratching contest ... I was there.

In Chicago at an old age home for retired Mafia hit men who take turns knocking off the night nurse ... I was there.

At a Lourdes pilgrimage of Spanish herpes sufferers who caught it while dipping to Julio Iglesias ... I was there.

was actually giving news information, she would say, 'Only a hail of bullets marred the festivities as wedding bells rang for Carmela and Angelo Cartucci at Our Lady of the Most Precious Blood Church.' So it was a bit that I wrote and I could almost read it—I was a character. It was not *my* persona. I had to figure out how to get beyond the character and bring myself into my stand-up. I didn't even conceive of that. I couldn't even figure that one out.

Some of the biggest people in the history of the world never got a dinner. I looked it up, some of the biggies since the beginning of time:

Adam, who said to George Burns, "Dad, can I have my allowance?" ... never got a dinner.

Moses, who yelled when the Red Sea divided, "Surf's up!" ... never got a dinner.

George Washington's dentist, who said to George, "The teeth look good, knock wood" ... never got a dinner.

Quasimoto, who said to his mother, "Get off my back" ... never got a dinner.

Sunny Von Bulow, who said to her husband Claus on their honeymoon, "Stop needling me" ... never got a dinner.

The Invisible Man's wife, who said to Invisible, "I don't care if the neighbors say it looks silly, don't stop" ... never got a dinner.

Tom Thumb, who gave Mother Goose the finger ... never got a dinner.

Toulouse Lautrec who said to a tall hooker, "I don't have to stand for this" ... never got a dinner.

Aladdin who said to his wife, "I know it's not a lamp, keep rubbing" ... never got a dinner.

"This is my feeling about starting, I think the beginning of stand-up is the hardest time, because fifty percent of it is confidence—minimum of fifty percent, maybe more. If you have the confidence then you get behind what you're saying and you sell it to the audience. I always admire the young new comedians that I watch who are completely in denial. Especially the boys, they're in much more denial than the women. The guys get off the stage, having died, and you say, 'How'd you do?' 'Oh, I had fun.' 'I'm glad you did, because nobody else seemed to.' They have no concept that they bombed. A lot of these people go on to be big stars and know how to do it, and I think that that's one thing that I wished that I had had more of, denial.

"Denial is what gets them back up there. Or they'll rationalize, 'It was just a bad house,' or they're very, very driven. A lot of people are just driven, they're compensating for a bad childhood or something. A lot of people have gotten much, much better just because they had to keep doing it. I never had that ability so I had to be broke and have a near-death experience to get to it, and a divorce. I had to have no money, no husband, and no fallopian tubes and that's what pushed me to do it. There were so many obstacles for me to overcome. When you have no money, your ego takes a backseat. You can say, 'Okay, I bombed,' and then they pay you like twenty dollars or fifty bucks and you say, 'Hey, this is not a bad gig.' So I'll get up again and try it again."

"The very first time that I got paid to do a comedy act," shares Freddie Roman, "I had been a master of ceremonies up in the Catskill mountains. I had been a social director with other people, but then I was able to book myself at another hotel as the comedy star of the evening for twenty dollars or fifteen dollars, whatever the hell it was. It was at Jabultovsky's, in Somerville, New York. I remember vividly, I had a pink dinner jacket, black tuxedo pants. I was the cat's meow. It was 1957, so I was twenty years old, and I did a medley of stuff that I stole from everywhere I could steal. I had to do thirty minutes, and up to that time I had never done more than ten. I did impressions, bad impressions. I did jokes that were going around in those days: 'The lady walks up to the hotel owner and says, I've been in this hotel for two weeks, the food is poison, plain poison—and such small portions.' That was one of the standard jokes in those days. Yet the audience accepted it.

"I went back to work there four weeks later. They were happy with me—I was cheap, they were happy. What possessed me to even have the balls to get on stage and tell people that I'm a comedian at that point? You were young and carefree and you wanted it badly and you did it. And that's pretty much what it was. I had more balls than anything else in the beginning. You must."

"All my life I was forced into the position of entertaining in a funny manner, that shows that I was born to do it. But I fought it. I wanted to be the traditional nice lady, get married and have these children, and be a housewife. In 1955 that was what you did," says Phyllis Diller, who was thirty-seven years old when she reassessed her life. She had become that housewife and mother, raising five children. She was also a career woman, working as a publicist for a San Francisco radio station, a newspaper writer, and a columnist. "It wasn't exactly stand-up from the very beginning. That was simply what I'd been doing as an amateur in the neighborhood—on call. Anybody who wanted a little entertainment, they'd call me. Sometimes they'd even assign me—they'd want something about motherhood or something, and I would write a show and go and do it. I was really getting some good experience right on my own block.

"This is the beginning of television, you realize, and my husband is watching TV and he sees, for the first time in his life, comics on the air. People like Art Carney, Milton Berle, Nanette Fabray, Imogene Coca—he's watching all these people being funny on television and now he's looking at me real funny. He starts nagging me, 'You've got to become a comic.' For two years we argued about this, because, I pointed out, we had these children, which he wanted to ignore so I could be a comic.

"You know, he was right. I finally said, 'Okay,' and from that day on my drive was, how do I become a comic? By the time I started this, my kids were six to sixteen and I was sitting at my desk at the radio station wondering how I was going to start. So I called the Red Cross and said, 'I have a show, where do you want it?' They said at the Presidio, the military base. So I went there and they pushed the piano into a room with four hospital beds. I took my son, who played the banjo. I played the piano, sang, and told jokes and did what I'd been doing all the time for the neighbors and the PTA—

and these guys were bored to death. One of them threw up, another one re-enlisted, and two of them died!"

Regardless of her memory of the event, Diller was asked back to perform yet again. This time she solicited the help of her friends from the radio station and performed in the psych ward. "There were thirty-five nuts shuffling around in white pajamas!"

Diller's first professional stint, however, was at the San Francisco nightclub, the Purple Onion. "At first, I couldn't get used to the lights, oh my God, the blinding lights, that would just make you crazy. The next thing, I couldn't get used to the sound of my voice on a mike, and then, there's people out there! I was a housewife! I had a limited vocabulary, words like 'pablum,' 'diaper,' 'oatmeal.' I had a big chasm to jump. It took years because I didn't understand showbiz, I didn't understand anything about it, but little by little by little I learned."

"I got into it the old-fashioned way," says Stewie Stone. "I grew up very, very poor and my father was a hoofer in vaudeville, a tap dancer. He always talked about show business and I had a feel for show business. I remember as a kid the greatest moment of my life was my parents taking me to downtown Brooklyn to see *The Jolson Story*—it wasn't Lou Gehrig, *The Pride of the Yankees*, it was *The Jolson Story*. The only thing my father could give me was five dollars a week, I said, 'What's that gonna do?' He said, 'Well, you're gonna take drum lessons, 'cause I think you got rhythm and if you're a smart kid you'll practice and you'll be able to go to the mountains in the summer and play drums in the band. That'll get you a summer vacation and then, if you're really my son and you're smart, you can put yourself through college playing drums, 'cause we can't afford to send you to college. Whatever job you have, you can always work weekends playing the drums and this will augment your life.'

"It sounded silly, but from the drums I went to Brooklyn College and then I was in all the wedding and Bar Mitzvah bands. I said, 'I don't want to do this any more. I'm a drummer, where am I going?' In those days, if you did something extra they paid you five dollars extra.

If you sang, you got five dollars extra. I couldn't sing so I would emcee the candle-lighting ceremony or whatever. A friend of mine said, 'I have a great idea, we'll work up at the Concord, we'll work Monday through Thursday and we'll come home weekends and play weddings and Bar Mitzvahs.' So I played drums at the Concord and if it rained we did a show in the morning in the Night Owl Lounge, which was the bar, and I started to get up and do jokes. I put five jokes together 'cause I wanted to impress the girls—you're funny, you impress the girls. I went into show business to get girls.

"When I was there the social director said, 'You're such a funny kid, you should stay on the staff and learn.' So I went on to the social staff at the Concord. I was making thirty-five dollars a week on the social staff and going home weekends and playing drums. Then I would come in to the city and go to agents, strip joints. If you drove to Connecticut you got fifty dollars. If you drove the stripper up you got five dollars for gas but if you fooled around with the stripper they didn't give you the five for gas. So if the stripper said, 'You wanna fool around?' 'No, I want the five for gas.' Then my friend passed away and I became the social director at the Concord and I was still going away and working these strip joints in Syracuse and Boston. That's where I met Norm Crosby and all the guys.

"I gave up drums, I figured I'm either gonna sink or swim. I was always funny on the stoop with the guys, like I talked about my friend taking out a girl, 'Oh, she was so ugly ...' 'Oh, what a girl you picked up, she could pick up her socks without bending over,' and all the guys would laugh. I thought I was funny, so I went to the amateur nights at these joints in Brooklyn and I would try and translate what I did on the stoop—died like a dog. So then I would play drums and tell jokes and it was funnier, I played the tom-toms, little corny things. I had to keep going, this was it. I had nowhere else to go.

"We didn't have the luxury of being bad, 'cause in those days there were no comedy clubs. You got a bad report in a strip joint you didn't work for six months. A friend of mine saw me doing a bathing beauty contest at the Concord, he said, 'You're funny, you wanna work Playboy?' so I started working the Playboy Club. I was doing fifteen weeks a year at the Playboy Club as a comedian. I put twenty minutes together, I was doing pretty good at the Playboy Club, and my lucky break came. I worked the Holiday House in Pittsburgh with Frankie Avalon. He said, 'You're funny. I'm gonna take you to Bachelor's Three in Fort Lauderdale, I'll give you five hundred dollars.' So I went. Joe Namath owned it, it was a hip joint. I was a big hit. The guy said, 'I want you to work with Frankie Valli and the Four Seasons.' I said, 'I never heard of them.' This is twenty-nine years ago—he's my closest friend now. I performed with Frankie for ten years straight after that. I went on to work with Englebert Humperdinck, Steve and Eydie, Paul Anka, every major star that worked. So that's how it happened."

David Brenner carries his comic chops in his genes as well. "I probably have one of the strangest stories in the business. I was a late-in-life child. My father was a vaudeville comedian, song and dance man, so that's the genetic thing right there. I grew up in a house in which my father, any chance he had to see old films, or on television, any of the old timers, he would say, 'Oh, you've gotta watch this guy.' The Marx Brothers. The Ritz Brothers. Jack Benny, of course, was his favorite. George Burns and Milton Berle and all the old timers. He was just a guy who loved to laugh. He was funnier than all those people put together. I never met anyone so funny in my life. So, I grew up in a house in which humor was important. But I never thought I would go into comedy. It was one of the last things on my mind to become a comedian.

"I was doing documentary films. I was writing, producing, and directing documentaries. I was the head of the Documentary Department of Westinghouse and Metromedia Broadcasting. A very serious trade, very serious career. After years of bumping my head against the wall and thinking, in my youthful naïveté, that I was going to change the world if I give them the answers—I just decided I was going to quit documentaries. I didn't know what I wanted to do, and I had enough money to squeak by for almost a year and I thought, I've been working since I'm eight-and-a-half years old, and I took the time off, the year, and I thought, well, I've gotta do something, you know? I've had a work ethic since I was a kid. I had always gone to comedy clubs and everyone always told me, 'Oh, you oughta be a comedian.' So, I went there and I figured, 'Oh, I'll goof, I'll do stand-up comedy for a while.'

"The first time I went up on stage I destroyed the audience and the next thirty nights, I bombed. I couldn't figure out why did I do so great the first night and why I bombed or just got chuckles. I don't get it, I'm doing the same thing I did opening night. Then I realized that was the problem. I was doing an impression of myself, because the first night I just got up there and winged it. It's been my style ever since. The routine I told when I first got up was my experience, the first time I skydived, I just told what happened. But, you know, when I was a kid hanging out on the street corner, which I did every night, or at the poolroom, or both, I didn't plan what I was going to say when I met my friends. I didn't think, 'Well, I'm going to talk about my sister falling down the steps. I'm going to talk about my dad's car breaking down.' I just got up on the corner and whatever we were talking about I was making fun of, that's what I had to do. I did it the first night and I didn't do it the subsequent thirty nights. I wasn't ad-libbing, I wasn't winging it."

Obviously, that thirty-first time on stage was the charm, as Brenner worked his way straight to Carson's couch within that first year. "You've got to remember, I wasn't going to be a comedian. I only did *The Tonight Show* to validate the year I took off in my life to do stand-up. I thought I was going to become a screenwriter or a movie director because that's what I did for television. I thought I was going to go out to Hollywood. I didn't really want to go to California, but I thought, I'm going to have to end up in Hollywood and make movies. That's what I was really leaning towards in this transition, this interruption. I went out there on the Carson show with the attitude that I was going to do that, and then the next day I was going to seriously contemplate what to do with my life and stop doing comedy. But by the end of the next day I had ten thousand dollars-worth of job offers and I knew I'd hit the mother lode. So, in other words, I started it as a lark, and it was one of the longest larks in history." To hell with practicing to get to Carnegie Hall, get your ass on *The Tonight Show,* everybody.

The trend in the '90s was to become a stand-up comic so you could get your own sitcom within a month or two. Apparently David Alan Grier wasn't aware of this, seeing as he was a somewhat established thespian before he decided to bite the bullet and go the comedy route. "I met Robert Townsend when we did *A Soldier's Story* and we shared a trailer, and he would go on and on about how he wanted to do these movies. He had a friend, Keenan Ivory Wayans, and he would talk about how they were gonna do this production company and stuff. I met Keenan when I went out to LA for pilot season. They were all comics and I would hang out with them and go to comedy clubs and it was just by osmosis that it started. I started like, 'Oh, I can do that,' and out of boredom, when I wasn't working, I started going on stage.

"It started as a dare. Robert and Damon [Wayans] and those guys were like, 'Go on stage, have you gone on stage yet?' Finally, I was just harassed into it. I wrote these five little minutes of comedy and that's how it all started. It was fun. Five minutes is such a long time to be on stage. That's where I started and it was a release, I never really thought I was going to be touring or anything. I would just do it for my sanity and because that's what I wanted to try.

"The first place I performed was the Laugh Factory, it was like the black hole of Calcutta. Nobody went in this club. It was this teeny, tiny club on Sunset and I figured, well, no one will ever see me here, so that's where I went on the first time. I had already been on Broadway and done some films. The funny thing was, the first time I performed at the Laugh Factory, I stood in line with everybody else and I got a spot and I went on, and you

RYAN STILES appears on the popular ABC sitcom *The Drew Carey Show,* playing the role of Lewis, the luckless janitor. He began his career as a stand-up comedian at seventeen, working in strip joints in his native Canada. Ryan discovered a different side of stand-up when he became a member of Canada's highly acclaimed Second City comedy ensemble, an improvisational troupe. From there he appeared on Britain's popular improvisation show *Whose Line Is It Anyway?* Along with his sitcom work, he also currently appears on the American version of *Whose Line Is It Anyway?* Ryan has also starred in the films *Hot Shots!, Hot Shots! Part Deux,* and the Academy Award nominated short *Rainbow War.*

can only perform like once a month. Well, within three weeks, three commercials I did and this movie came out and one of the guys in line was like, 'Oh, my God. I can't believe it. One spot on the Laugh Factory and you're, like, huge.' I never had the heart to tell him no, I already actually had a career. It was pretty funny."

Did Grier get the laughs he expected? "No, you never do. Not in the places you expect. You go, 'Oh, this will be funny'—no. I wrote this one little bit that was like, whatever, let me just do this, and people *really* laughed at that. The audience always tells you what they think is funny—it's kind of a strange thing."

"I quit high school to do stand-up. It went over well with my parents," laughs Ryan Stiles. "I was the class clown and I hung around with guys who were kind of the same way. I had three older brothers and they were all really funny and my dad was funny. The humor was always there as I was growing up. While other kids were listening to The Monkees and all that kind of stuff, I used to listen to Bill Cosby. I always loved that way of life I guess.

"My dad was a commercial fisherman and in the daytime I was working in the fishing industry, so I would get up at four in the morning, cut fish open and take their guts out all day long, then at night I'd go do stand-up stinking like fish. And then of course I was still high from the stand-up so I'd sit around and drink till two in the morning, then get up at four and go work with fish. I definitely don't ever want to do that again. This isn't really hard work. I think any actor who complains about the hours he has to work, how hard it is and stuff, should really have to go out and do what normal people do.

"When I started doing it there weren't a lot of people, it was during one of those lulls in comedy which we're heading into again, I think. At that time, the main guy was probably David Brenner. It was around that era, so in, like, '78–'79, I was up in Vancouver and this comedy club was opening and there had never been one there before. Around that time, every city was opening up comedy clubs and they had an ad in the paper. I took a bunch of friends down with me and luckily at that time nobody was really very good. I found it hard to write new stuff; that was my thing. I kind of did a combination of my own stuff and then I stole some George Carlin stuff. I think everybody stole."

While most kids at that time were worrying about who to ask to the prom, Stiles was busy honing his craft as a professional in paying venues, "I was up in British Columbia, in Vancouver, at the time, in a lot of strip clubs. I was under age, I had a fake ID, and introduced the dancers and stuff. You get a little cocky. I remember one night, at that time there was a big gig for me at the Queen Elizabeth Theater, it was just a huge theater. I opened for Sheena Easton. Then an hour later I'm emceeing the strip contest. It was from one level to the other. I think it's a lot different now, I think comics aim for that really good ten minutes to get themselves a series. I think back then, you wanted to get forty minutes together so you could headline. We usually went on with two other comics: One would open, one would emcee, and one would headline. I was just trying to get a lot of material together at that point, but you work for twenty dollars and you had to pay your own gas and you had to get the money off the bartender at the end of the night.

"I was a teen working at a strip joint. I was in heaven—it was great. Of course, I met my wife when I was pretty young so I've been with the same woman, because any woman who is going to stay with you when you're making fifteen dollars a gig, she'd be with you when you start making a little bit of money. I find a lot of guys just drop their wives when they make a lot of money but I'd rather be with somebody who was with me when I made nothing."

Stiles found an even more fascinating side of comedy in improvisation. "Howie Mandel was actually the first guy I ever did improv with. He suggested we do improv and I had no idea what it was and he kind of led us through it. If I'd only done stand-up I wouldn't have had the opportunity to work with the people that I've worked with. I worked with Catherine O'Hara, Robin Williams, and John Candy when I was doing Second City in Toronto—I mean, these people I never would have had a chance to work with if I was still doing stand-up. To me, it was a blessing that I didn't have to go home and write material and work out new stuff. In improv you just go in and make it up and forget about it. I prefer it that way. I love it that way."

George Wallace says, "I wanted to be a comedian since I was six years old. I tell people, we're in the business because of Red Skelton, Redd Foxx, Red Buttons, and Pinky Lee—all people of color. I would watch television—Milton Berle, Johnny Carson—at the time when I was a kid. Moms Mabley, Jackie Leonard, everybody was on with Merv Griffin in those days. I would watch these guys tell jokes and I would go to school the next day and tell the same jokes and people would laugh, and I just thought, 'Man, making people happy is the greatest thing in the world.' When you make people happy, people want to be around you. When you walk into a room, if you're not a cause for a smile, then something is wrong.

photo by Brian Dougherty

JEFF FOXWORTHY

Jeff Foxworthy exploded onto the stand-up comedy scene with his best-selling *You Might Be A Redneck If ...* humor books and triple platinum CD's. 2002 marks the release of his *The Blue Collar Comedy Tour* feature film, based on his highly successful tour. His popular ABC sitcom, *The Jeff Foxworthy Show*, turned his southern-style humor into a national sensation as well as earned him a People's Choice Award. Jeff received the American Comedy Award for "Best Stand-Up Comic" in 1990. A regular on shows such as *The Tonight Show* and *Late Show with David Letterman*, Jeff also has an HBO special and two Showtime specials to his credit. He is the author of eleven best-selling books.

EVERY SINGLE HAIR ON HER BODY

I have learned from my wife, looking good takes a little time. I know when we're preparing to go out for the evening the four words that I dread hearing the most, it's my wife's voice coming out of that bathroom—"I hate my hair!" "Well, I'll just call them, tell 'em we ain't coming tonight." Never, ever do you hear men say, "I hate my hair!" 'Cause as long as it's still there, we like it and we're not gonna say anything ugly about it that might make it get up and leave.

And if men do worry about hair, we only worry about the hair on our head. Women worry about every single hair on their body. Before we went on vacation last summer my wife said to me, "I have got to go get ready for bikini season." Which to me means buying new sunglasses. You see, in thirteen years I have learned, you can move your eyes, just don't turn your head. Wives can hear those neck muscles creaking. And there's nothing more embarrassing than watching a girl walk across the front of the pool in her bathing suit and you end up face to face with your own wife—"Hi. Listen, I was just thinking we ought to ask her to baby-sit for us tonight, shouldn't we? You and I could go out and have a nice lobster dinner and maybe I could buy you some new jewelry, you like jewelry don't you? I'll buy you a lot of jewelry."

Now what my wife meant when she said she needed to get ready for bikini season was that she was about to go have a procedure done to her that is called a bikini wax. To hear her describe this horror, apparently she pays somebody—pays somebody—to pour lava hot, scalding wax on her inner thighs and then the two of them chat for a little while until the wax has dried and then the woman grabs the wax and yanks the hair out. If you ever hear of somebody doing this to me, rest assured there was a gun to my head because you yank the hair out of my inner thigh, I will tell you where my grandmother hides her money.

That's the most horrible thing I've ever heard of. We should implement that as a penalty in our judicial system—"You've been found guilty of breaking and entering, for the next twelve months you are required to get a bikini wax every two weeks." "No, your honor have mercy on me." "And if I catch you back in here, you're gonna have to have a butt wax too." I'm sorry, I don't know where that came from. You guys are gonna be in bed tonight, asleep, I'm gonna be staring at the ceiling—"Butt wax?" Sounds just like something you buy in the drugstore, doesn't it? But not an impulse purchase, no—"Excuse me, what aisle is the butt wax on, please?" "You want the scented or the unscented butt wax?" I need the unscented there's a lot of dogs in our neighborhood.

You know, that's just the beginning of it, then you have the leg hair. Guys, have you ever had your woman take your razor, shave her legs with it, then she'll put it back on the counter, you pick up that same razor and shave your face? You can get the bleeding to stop. It takes a team of trained professionals, but you can get the bleeding to stop. Lord, I don't know what a woman's leg hair is made out of but you get enough of it together you can clean a rusty grill with it. Nothing on this planet feels as good as a freshly shaven woman's leg, and few things are as deadly as one that hasn't met a razor in a while. It actually has a grain to it. You know, you rub it one way, its not too bad, the other way, severe tire damage. And married men know this. That's because every married man here tonight's had this little conversation where he's lying in bed with his wife, "Hey, baby, you wanna fool around?" "OK, but I haven't shaved my legs in five days.' ... "That's ok, we'll just wait." Well, it's like having sex with a cactus. Not that I've ever had sex with a cactus.

Somebody should be happy that you're there and that's the kind of life I try to live."

Wallace had several friends trying to make the comedy grade, a grade he wanted to make as well, but with a little more forethought than most. "They were hungry, didn't have a place to work, didn't know where they were going. I said, 'The hell with that.' I wanted to make some money and work. That's why I came to New York, when I left college, to make a lot of money quickly. It was always in advertising sales—hoping I'd make the money and get myself a financial cushion and then start show business on my own. It's what I wanted to do, make money telling jokes.

"Twenty-five years ago I was twenty-four and vice president of an advertising agency in New York City making fifty-plus-thousand a year. They said, 'You're gonna quit this job and go tell jokes?' 'It doesn't matter to me, I don't worry about it. I'm gonna do all right.' I went out to Los Angeles and next thing you know, I was writing the Redd Foxx show. I did that for a year and he was doing my jokes. But that's still not doing it right, I want to do my own jokes. So I've been working since I started.

"I had to do all the clubs in Los Angeles. I would go up on stage after Robin Williams was killing people. But when you have the attitude like, 'I don't care. I want to get on that stage'—I didn't even have the sense to know that I was following somebody who killed, Rodney Dangerfield or Richard Pryor, it didn't bother me."

Wallace immediately jumped from small comedy clubs to *The Tonight Show* to his first paying gig, opening for Natalie Cole before 17,000 people. Wasn't he petrified? "No, I'm stupid. That's what I wanted to do, put me out there. I did a good job."

Like most successful comedians, Jeff Foxworthy seems to have type C blood (the comic kind), but he too got there via the suit. "As I look back at my life I think, 'God, what else would I have done?' When I was a kid, I would save my allowance and buy comedy records— Cosby and Flip Wilson and Newhart. Then, as I got older, it was Carlin and Pryor. I would memorize them. I would go to school and do them, get in trouble for making people laugh in class.

"I always had a fascination with stand-up. As a child, I can remember sneaking, peeking around the corner to watch the comedians on Johnny Carson, and I didn't care about watching the singers or the actors, I wanted to see the comedians. But I think probably, like most people, I didn't know that this was something you could do. I guess I thought God put about five comics on the earth and that was it. So I got out of high school and went to college and went to work at IBM. Worked there for five-and-a-half years, wore a suit and tie everyday. I look back at that and I'm like the face from the poster of *Home Alone*, I'm like, 'Oh, my God.'

"I was the funny guy at work. I was the guy that made people laugh in the break room, the guy who would do impersonations of the boss and get caught doing them. A bunch of guys I worked with went down to the comedy club every week and they kept telling me, 'Fox you gotta go down there and do this. You're funnier than these people on amateur night.' I had never been to a comedy club so I went with them one week and I watched. They used to have, probably still do have, the amateur night before the regular show. I watched and I thought, 'Alright, I'll do this.' And I went home and wrote a few jokes about my family and called the club to find out what I had to do to get on the next week and they said, 'Well we're not doing amateur night, it's the first week of the Great Southeastern Laugh-Off'—one of these big laugh-offs that they did all summer. They said, 'Why don't you wait till the end of the summer?' Well, at that point, having seen it, I wanted to do it. So I got all my co-workers at IBM to call the club and go, 'Is Jeff Foxworthy gonna be on? 'Cause if so, we'd like to bring twenty people.' Well, after about seven or eight calls they were like, 'Yeah, he's gonna be on,' and three guys showed up from work.

"I won the contest the first night on stage," says Foxworthy, who only remembers one bit that he did that night. "I said, 'Why is it that fathers, when they cut their toenails, don't do like everybody else and throw them in the trash can? Why do fathers leave them in the ashtray in the den so the whole family can come by and observe and admire them? Father toenails are not like anybody else's, father toenails, you need, like, bolt cutters to cut them off with.' That's the only thing I remember doing that night, but they laughed.

"I look back and go, 'God, that shouldn't have happened,' because the others were working comics. I felt a mixture of emotions in that it was petrifying to be up there—I mean, it's one thing to do it for the guys you know in front of the water cooler and another thing to stand in front of three hundred strangers and do it. I was terrified. I don't think I could even look them in the face. But at the same time, and it just sounds hokey, but a minute into it I was like, 'This is what I want to do.' Then I went up and did a few amateur nights and I thought, 'I'm quittin' my job,' and I quit a month later.

"I watched some of those other people who would just go up week after week and not get laughs. Thank God they laughed at me the first time. I'm serious, I don't think I would have done it again. Obviously, the positive end of it made it worth facing the fear. I know some guys who continue to feel that way. I quit being scared pretty quickly but there's been occasions since then—I can remember standing behind the curtain at *The Tonight Show* while they were on commercial break and thinking, 'Oh God, I don't know if I can do this.' But for the most part I think I'm lucky because the guy I am on stage is pretty close to the guy I am—so it's not like I have to get in a mindset or something."

The evolution of a prop comic may not be as riveting as, say, the Scopes monkey trials, but Carrot Top doesn't monkey around without his stuff. "I was always full of jokes. My dad would come home, he worked at the NASA Space Center, and these old government guys sat around all night and just told jokes. I would take these jokes to school and people would always say, 'Hey, what's your joke of the day?' and I'd have a joke for them. When I got into college they had a talent show and my roommates were like, 'Dude, check out this talent show,' and I said, 'Yeah, we should go to that,' and they were like, 'Go to it? I thought you were gonna be in it.' I said, 'I don't have an act, I just have jokes,' and they said, 'Who cares dude? It's a talent show.' So I went up there and I just told jokes. It went over great. So I went to the local comedy club, the Comedy Corner in West Palm, and that's where Foxworthy and everybody else was going to play and stuff, and I went to a talent show there and they said, 'What the hell are you doing? You can't just tell jokes.' I said, "Well, why not? I did it at the other talent show.' They said, 'This is the real deal, you have to have your own act.'

"I went back to the drawing board. The props really came about by accident. It was twelve years ago. I was in my dorm and I had this sign, it said Neighborhood Crime Watch, this was the new thing in all the neighborhoods. So I came on stage and I said, 'Sorry I'm late, I was in the neighborhood,' and I hold the sign up and I say, 'How good is crime watch if they're not watching their sign? It took me ten minutes to unbolt this sign, it takes two seconds to go through somebody's window.' So I was already off to a big start. So then I went to another road sign that I had, and I had a really good opening with these little visual aids. Being in West Palm, down in South Florida, I had a hat with an old lady's head on a spring and it would bounce back and forth and I said, 'This is for old people to wear when they drive so you can see their head.' I was killing in the first three minutes because it was all stuff that they had seen. It was local, it was topical. The club owner came up to me and said, 'Now you got it. That's great. The whole prop thing, this is really cool.'" So I suppose we have that club owner to thank for Carrot Top today.

Gilbert Gottfried began his career before comedy became all the rage. "I wasn't funny as a kid, but I'm not funny as an adult either. Back then, the idea of saying you were gonna be a comedian was like saying you were gonna be a terrorist. Because that was crazy talk, but after awhile, especially after the comedy boom, it was like one of these things where it seemed like a career option. I was a teenager, I don't know, like either fifteen or sixteen. I went on stage, I think at the Bitter End, when they used to have—I think they used to call it hootenanny night—'cause comedy hadn't started yet.

"You basically showed up early, waited around for a few hours there and you signed your name and most of the people there were folk singers. I went on and I did some imitations, mainly Humphrey Bogart, Peter Lorre, Boris Karloff, stuff like that. I always think, was I funny or was I too stupid to know that I wasn't at that point? I remember people always asked me, 'So what are you hoping is gonna happen? Did somebody discover you yet? Did they give you a TV show yet?' 'No.' This went on for years, going into clubs like that, and eventually the Improv and Catch a Rising Star. The big success was getting on stage at all. Usually, you waited the whole night, then went home.

"I remember at one point, some club, not a real club, the basement of a church, was having a comedy night. I think they offered seven dollars, which at that point, was like hitting the big time. I worked hard for that seven dollars. All the other comedy clubs paid nothing. They had a strike at one point, the comics were asking for money, and that's when they got so-called cab fare, it was like five dollars or something. I supported it. I didn't perform at the places, but I always had a mixed feeling, I had an old codger feeling about it, like, 'These damn kids. When we started out in comedy, we got no money and we didn't get a free ginger ale!'

"When I started getting time on stage, sometimes they'd put me on at three o'clock in the morning, when there were three people there and they were drunk. I'd just start doing anything that popped into my head and then I started getting good. I started to get strong at getting up at four o'clock in the morning and just going nuts and doing anything that came to me. After awhile, they didn't want to put me into the prime spot 'cause they figured, 'Hey, we got someone who works so well here.' It may have been the time frame because after awhile I got very popular among the people in the club. The comics and people like that would come in to watch me when I had bits that worked. I would get bored doing them and see what just popped into my head. One time, someone at the Improv said to me that the reason he didn't put me on stage was, 'I never know what you're gonna do next.' And he said, 'It's always funny. It's always hysterical, but I never know what you're gonna do, so that's why I don't put you on.' And I thought, 'So much for the name *improvisation.*'"

David Mishevitz has been at the stand-up thing for over three years now. During these interviews he was in the process of hanging up the suit-and-tie gig he had as a media buyer with BBDO West, a prominent advertising agency. How he could leave a company whose Eastern division holds the Pepsi account is beyond me, but it's his life I guess. "I just put in my two weeks. I have enough saved up to cover my expenses for however long I need to right now. I just kind of cross my fingers between now and then about doing some voice-over stuff, which I've been lucky with, and put all my focus on stand-up and some writing things that I have going on."

It's fascinating that at this moment Mishevitz is embarking on a journey that doesn't always end at Destination Fame. Yet his roots are similar to many comedy greats. "I wasn't the class clown but I remember staying up real late and watching *A&E's Evening at The Improv* and *Two Drink Minimum with Jake Johannsen.*" What got him up on stage the first time, you ask? "Probably a couple of Budweisers. The first time was at a place called Hitchcock's in Chicago, which is now The Monkey Bar. I did it a few times and the coolest thing about it was there were two guys, Bill Gorgo and Jimmy Wiggins, comics from the Chicago area. They used to sit with four or five of us before the open-mike portion started and not only talk about bits we were doing, but talk about the room, about how to handle yourself in different situations and stuff like that. I found that and the writing process much more interesting.

"I had a little piece of paper that I wrote down key words on and I had it taped to the outside of a book, just there, so I didn't have the whole joke. I got maybe a couple of laughs, maybe some people's attention here and there. I got through everything I wanted to get through, and I stood up there for the time, so that was all right. Initially, I had never done anything like it, just speeches. Communications majors gave speeches all the time. But I dug it right then. I got a couple of laughs. Nobody said, 'Oh, my God, get out of here.' After I'd done it maybe six times, I'd just go and watch a lot of comics at a place called The Elevator. I don't know why I didn't try to get up again there. I was always changing jobs, there was always something like that." Well, now he's got a lifetime to prove himself—or not.

"I'm an Italian, and Italians were not allowed to be comedians," says Pat Cooper. "If you said something at the table you were a buffoon. You were not allowed. 'How dare you? What gives you the right to think that you are funny? Who do you think you are to disrespect your mother, your father at the table? Dip the bread in the sauce and shut up.' Now, a Jewish kid says something at the table—another Milton Berle! That's the difference and boy, I admire the Jewish culture. I followed the greatest Jewish comics on the planet. There were no better comics than the Jewish comics when I grew up. I'm talking *on the planet*. They were dynamite and great. Alan King, in my opinion, was one of the great monologists. Shecky Greene and Jack Carter and Jan Murray and George Burns and Jack Benny, I grew up in that era and I learned and I watched and the idea is, you don't give up.

"Hey, I bombed when I started out. I was doing 'take my wife, please.' I was doing everybody's jokes. I was bombing but something within me kept driving me. I'd go to the Paramount, the Strand Theater, and watch the comics and I would turn around and say, 'That's for me.' Everywhere I'd go, in the schools, I would be funny. People laughed at what I'd say. I would talk about the lamp maybe, they would scream. Before you know it, somebody comes over and says, 'Hey, you know what you oughta do,' and you do it, boom. You have twenty, thirty minutes together. I've done a lot of things where I've failed, but failure is success if you stay with it, if you say, 'Hey, I know what I've got, and ain't no one gonna tell me.' I've got things. Ain't no one gonna do Italian stories. They'd say, 'You can't do it.' Meanwhile I got on Jackie Gleason doing it. 'Whoa,' they said, 'Oh my God, he did it.' All of a sudden all the Italians who were afraid to say they were Italians, 'I'm Italian.' Jackie Vernon, who I loved, nobody knew he was Italian. Now everybody will say, 'I'm Italian.' Even Jews will say, 'I'm Italian.' Which is okay, but I learned from the best and the best without a shadow of a doubt were the Jewish comics, and I have not seen their equal yet.

"My first moment was treachery. Treachery. It was in the Fox Theater, many years ago, an amateur show. My sister was singing *Ave Maria*. The emcee said they were short an act and my sister said, 'My brother makes noises with his mouth.' They said, 'What do you mean he makes noises?' 'Well, he does impressions of bandleaders, like Tommy Dorsey.' So I went on there and the prize was twenty dollars and second prize was a watch. My sister sang *Ave Maria*, you coulda heard a pin drop. I went on after that and did Charlie Barnett's theme song, Tommy Dorsey stole the show off her, and I got the twenty dollars. My family didn't talk to me for months, for months! They said, 'You stupid, how could you do such a thing to your sister?' I said, 'Well, she called me up.' What did I know?

"From there I met Joey Adams who took me on the tour of amateur shows, and I got more confidence. Then I got married and my family said, 'Get a job. Go to work. You're stupid. You can't be funny. They didn't know. They didn't understand. Nobody was in show business in my family. Nobody was in show business in my ex-wife's family. 'You're an idiot. Go to work. Here's what you do: Monday, Tuesday, Wednesday, Thursday, Friday you get paid, Saturday, you go buy steak, Sunday you eat macaroni and then you die Monday.' That was it. So you could not step out of that mode if you were an Italian. I was called a rebel. They said, 'You're a disgrace to your mother and your father.'

"I'll give you an idea, I'm crying one day outside my apartment, the neighbor says, 'Patsy, what's the matter, you're crying?' I said, 'My mother, she wants to put my head in the oven.' She says, 'Well, that means she loves you.' I say, 'Let her put your head in the fucking oven, then she'll love you.' Now, to me, that's humor. They thought, how could you say that about your mother? I said, 'I don't know what to say, that's humor.' That's when I said to myself, 'That's a funny line, man. I can throw lines off.' See, I'm a gambler, I play Russian roulette with comedy.

"I'm fourteen years old and I walk into the confessional booth and I tell the guy, I'm not telling you nothing, you dirty rat, and I'm doing Cagney. The priest told my father and my father beat the shit out of me. That was funny, but it was sacrilegious in my day. Today it's hilarious. So I was ahead of myself. I'm doing impressions, now priests go, 'Pat you're wonderful.'

"Years ago, before television, you had to go on the Pantages Circuit, you had to go on the Loews Circuit. There were like three or four different circuits of theaters. When you were on the Loews circuit you had to try to get to the next level, to work the Palace. When I worked the Copacabana, television was still in its infancy. Then people started watching television and anyone could have headlined the Copacabana, and they did."

Jeffrey Ross wears the stand-up comedy mantle as comfortably as Columbo's well-worn trench coat, but this line of work was never his intent. "Interestingly enough, I never wanted to do it and I've always fought doing it. I took a class taught by a comedian, Lee Frank, in New York, in '89. I was going through a crappy time in my life; living with my grandfather who was ill in New Jersey, and I didn't have much of a social life. I was a writer. I was writing training films and industrial films and I took this class to make my writing tighter. I didn't really think about it as a stand-up. I did it as a communicator, just to make my writing a little more accessible. I was writing very dry scripts.

"My grandfather was the funniest guy I ever knew and probably my biggest comedic influence. I thought comics were strictly tuxedos in the Catskills, and it was something that I would never ever be. I was the son of a caterer in New Jersey and I had never even been to a comedy club, if you can believe that. When I took the class I didn't even realize it was for stand-up. I thought it was a different type of writing class. In essence, it was one of those happy accidents, 'cause I got up in a class and I really enjoyed it. There were nice people and cute girls and the teacher was cool. It was a three-hour break every Tuesday from my miserable existence, which was taking a bus from New Jersey to New York and working all day in a little office with my partner, and getting nowhere. It was a hobby and I really loved it. I excelled right away.

"I did all the open mikes. The last class was an open mike at the Eagle Tavern on 14th Street. I was so excited about doing that, by the time we got to the last class, that I went the night before to the Ye Old Triple Inn on 54th Street and did that open-mike night, just to get the butterflies out. That was my first time in front of an audience. I drank, if I recall, one or two shots—I don't usually drink—just to completely numb me, and I got laughs. I went up and told stories about the kosher catering business and some kind of lame jokes about my name, Lipschultz. Horrible stuff. I remember something to the effect of, 'Everyone wanted a Louisville Slugger in my little league team, I got a Hebrew National salami.' Cornball Jewish jokes.

"It sort of worked. I think I was funnier than the material. I was funnier when I got heckled and lost my place than when I actually told the jokes. I remember getting interrupted by some guy in the front row. I remember freezing, not knowing what to say. I lost my place in the script I planned. It's only now, years later, that I realize I can just wing it. But I do remember getting a few big laughs, and if you have a few good jokes, like Miltie says, they all remember the home runs. Maybe I hit a couple of singles and got a couple of laughs. That was such an incredible feeling and I walked off stage and there were these two cute girls there and they talked to me. They said I was funny and I thought, 'Wow! This is great.' It was like being in a band, but I didn't have to play anything or drag any equipment around.

"That's when I realized I could seriously do comedy as a hobby. I'd only been up that one time and I had a failing business and a dying grandfather and it just wasn't in the cards, it was strictly a goof. I did the open mike at the Eagle Tavern and I started recording myself and I quickly became sort of a regular on the open-mike circuit in New Jersey and New York. My family was not supportive, but they quickly became supportive when they came to see me. I wasn't funny for years. It's just years of, you know, you drag your cousins and your aunt to see you, then you bomb, it's just horrible.

"I was a beginner, I had no acting experience. I had done some DJ-ing in college. I had no professional writing or performing or acting or even public speaking. I had a New Jersey accent that I wasn't sure people could even understand if I left that area. I just kept doing it as a hobby and I went out to the Hamptons and I had a quarter share in a house, and there was a comedy club there that I talked my way into. I said, 'Put me on and I'll bring six, eight friends,' and they did, and I remember I got some laughs and the owner gave me fifty bucks. I couldn't believe it. That was sort of a gift, because I wasn't supposed to get paid. It was a short time later, at Catch a Rising Star, that Louis Faranda handed me my twenty bucks from the bartender. That was really the first time I got paid."

"I remember watching *The Tonight Show* with Rich Little and Phyllis Diller and Joan Rivers and thinking, 'That would be really cool. Too bad I don't know who gets to do that, but it isn't me,'" says Jim Gaffigan, who eventually figured out that it certainly could be him. "I was a class clown. I come from kind of a funny family, like, I'm considered third funniest in my family." So how come I'm not interviewing his brothers Mitch and Joe who, he tells me, fill the top two Gaffigan family funny slots? "Because I think some of it comes down to gumption or chutzpah. Stand-up is, in a way ... I mean I love it, but in a way it's kind of a thankless endeavor, there's not a lot of money in it. It really is something you kind of do for yourself and in a way it's kind of like sky diving, you know?" When you consider all those comics who say they spend their moments just before going onstage throwing up and whatnot, he just might be onto something.

"People would always say, 'You should do stand-up,'" says Gaffigan, "I actually took an improv class because I had a fear of public speaking. Somebody that I was in the improv class with was gonna do this stand-up kind of seminar thing and he dared me to do it so I did. He ended up bailing, but I fell in love with it. I did it at Rose's Turn [in Manhattan], which is where, I think, Woody Allen did stand-up first too. It's a cabaret bar, but they had this showcase. The weird thing about stand-up is, in a way, there are no rules. When you're writing a film script there are tons of rules, but that still doesn't mean you have a good script. And sometimes the people who go against those rules are the most talented.

"I definitely had a big problem with stage fright. I remember just trying to act like I had at parties and in small groups, and joke around. But it was definitely terrifying. It was definitely, like, 'this could be really humiliating.' The first couple of times it went well and then it got really humiliating."

Some comedians are just naturally funny and some know funny people. Norm Crosby had both going for him. "I was the funny kid around my neighborhood, the funny kid at school. I got to know a lot of the comedians that came into Boston. I got to know Pat Henry and Dick Capri and people like that—for years. I wasn't even in the business, I was working in a shoe company, doing their advertising. I was a commercial artist, I wrote copy, I laid out the ads, everything. I was an agency unto myself and I used to dabble and play around with comedy and on the weekends I would seriously think about booking dates. So my friends brought me to their agents in Boston, 'Here book him somewhere.' A guy gave me a date, it was New Year's Eve. It was my first show.

"They put the show on so it would coincide with midnight. I was the emcee, the comics were always the emcee, and I was the one to say, 'Hey, happy New Year!' I had, as was the custom in New England, two strippers, two belly dancers on my show—that's what they feature— a girl singer, and me. Well, I put the singer on and she was okay. Then I put on one of the belly dancers … and then put on the second belly dancer and I'm looking at my watch … then I asked the singer if she'd come back to do a couple more songs. I left myself about eight minutes.

"I was scared to death, petrified. I wondered why I dared to do it, and finally I got up and I was trying to do my jokes and at that point they were really blowing their horns, turning those ratchet things, blowing their whistles, and screaming and carrying on. The bosses were in the back watching, so I put the strippers on and I stretched. When a stripper was finished, I walked out and said, 'Wasn't she great? Come on, hey, come on back here, they loved you.' She had nothing on! 'Come on back.' I stretched it so that all I had to do was a couple of jokes—one joke or two jokes, I don't even remember if they laughed. I said, 'Okay, folks here we go, ten, nine …' and it was time '… Happy New Year!' I went back to the agent, I said, 'Please, I know.' He said, 'No, they loved you. The guy thought you were wonderful. You kept it right down, you did it on time.' I got away with it.

"I got twenty-five dollars for the job and I thought that was fantastic. That's when I started to do club dates, because I realized it was too tough to do the nightclubs. You see, the [comedy] clubs were really crummy places and the audiences were crummy people. They weren't sophisticated, intelligent, and I was trying to do clever stuff. Then I had an opportunity to go into New York. That's when they started to do the local civic things, the club dates where I was hired to perform at private affairs in nicer venues. I became a big hero in a small town, a big fish in a small pond. I was doing the Governor's Birthday Ball and the Chief of Police's Banquet and the Mayor's Charity Day, and I was working a little bit better type of club. I was starting to feel better about myself, that I really knew what I was doing."

Bernie Brillstein remembers hooking Crosby up with his first Copacabana gig, "The owner, supposed

BERNIE BRILLSTEIN is a producer and successful personal manager as well as a highly sought-after creative consultant. Brillstein helped launch the careers of such prominent comedians and artists as John Belushi, Jim Henson, Dan Aykroyd, Gilda Radner, and Dana Carvey. As a founding partner in Brillstein-Grey Entertainment, he has been responsible for such groundbreaking series as *The Sopranos* and *The West Wing*. His autobiography *Where Did I Go Right? You're No One in Hollywood Unless Someone Wants You Dead* was a New York Times best-seller.

owner, was Jules Podell who was an amazing character. Little guy, about 5′6″, shoulders like this … talking like this," [talking in a gruff tone], "I said, 'Norm, no matter what you do, if you're a great hit the first show, don't go up to Mr. Podell. Stay away from him. Don't go near him, 'cause he's crazy.' Norm kills at the first show. He's so high, he's taking bows, you know, comedians love to take bows, and he sees Podell and he starts walking over to him, like, to take another bow, and then he remembers what I said and he stops and turns away. Podell knocks on the table with his pinky ring and gets one of the maitre d's and he says, 'Get Norm.' He brings Norm back in front of him and he's sitting at a table with a cognac and he says, 'Crosby, what am I, a fucking monkey? You come over and stare at me? What am I, a fucking monkey?' Norm says, 'No, sir, I just … ' 'Don't stare at me.' "

Many comedians start young, but Samm Levine started as a fetus. Alright, maybe that's a stretch, but it's just a little stretch. "The first real performance that I was asked to do, by professional people, I think I was still thirteen. There was a showcase at Carolines Comedy Club. There were eighteen-year-olds there and there were also nine-year-old kids there. There was one comic whose act was so clearly written by a post-menopausal woman in her mid 50s, but he had the nerve to get up there time and time again and tell the jokes. 'I was born during the Great Depression, my mother's ... ' nine-year-olds do not write jokes like that. I know a lot of nine-year-olds, I was one. I didn't know what the Great Depression was.

"When I was younger, I definitely used to tell my jokes in the style of Richard Jeni and hell, sometimes I'd just tell his jokes. What the hell, why not? Who was listening? A bunch of sixth graders. But the life was definitely for me. As far as I can remember that's the point when I said, 'That's it. That's clearly what I'm gonna be doing for the next twenty, thirty years. It was the first time I was asked by a real club to do comedy for real people. I was so happy. It was one of the best days of my life, truly it was, because I really didn't know what to expect. Up to that point I'd played Bar Mitzvahs and what are they gonna do, not laugh at this twelve-year-old kid who's a friend of the Bar Mitzvah girl or boy? So up to then I had really friendly crowds, this one, I had to prove myself." More power to Samm for thinking beyond his years.

By contrast, here's someone who has underwear older than Samm ... heeeere's Shecky Greene! "I had a brother two years older than I am, we used to do all the dialects. I don't think there's any dialect that I can't do. I sang very well when I was a kid and that got me in front of an audience. In school, I was always a class clown. I started the drama class. I really didn't think I wanted to go into show business but I was around a girl who was a dancer and I wanted to show her something, I wanted to show her I could do that. The first show that I ever got paid for was in Chicago, for a group of Jewish people. I went out and I told some stories and I sang, and instead of singing a Jewish song I sang *When Irish Eyes are Smiling*, which was brilliant. After the show was over, I said to the guy who gave me ten dollars, 'Did you like it?' He said, 'The chicken was better.' I was gonna call my book, 'The Chicken Was Better.' It really wasn't that petrifying because those particular things that I did, it was something that I was doing all the time—tell a few jokes, sing a few songs. You're only petrified when you know you've got to do it again. This time was gonna be the only time and then out.

"You gotta go through a lot. I don't think today I would have gone through what I went through. I mean, I was younger and it was fun for me. Every job, I was quitting—I'd work a job, then I was quitting. I was gonna go back to school. So I always knew that I could quit, but then I went back to school one day and I didn't know what I wanted, so I said, 'Well, this place in Milwaukee wanted me, another place wanted me, so I just stayed in show business. But I never really had that drive, that Mr. Show Business and Broadway and movies. I never had that. I was offered movies, I never did them. I really hid out, like in Vegas. Vegas was like a retreat for me.

"I hosted the Griffin and the Carson shows a lot and that early television, I didn't enjoy it, never enjoyed it, I used to get panic attacks. Thank God for Zoloft. I had a fear. I had a legitimate fear of being on the stage, so when I would work on the stage I'd entertain the audience, get a standing ovation. The minute I got off that stage I would have a panic attack, go into a depression. So that made me drink, made me gamble. I did a lot of things that were self-destructive, because I couldn't handle it.

"When you start to make a lot of money, and I mean it started off with ten dollars then it went to fifty dollars, then it went to a hundred and fifty dollars, then it went to two hundred dollars, then it went to a hundred thousand, then it went to a hundred and twenty-five—yeah, I stayed in it. I brought a doctor out on the stage with me because I didn't want to lose that kind of money. People always said, 'What'd your partner do? He never talked.' There's things I've done, my career shoulda been over a hundred times but I've been very lucky."

"From the time I was fourteen I wanted to be in show business," says Kevin Meaney. "I was a big fan of Steve Martin. I loved Steve Martin, that was my kind of style. People would come up to me in high school and say, 'That guy, you ever see that guy Steve Martin? He's doing your act.' I'd go, 'I don't even have an act. I'm a high school kid. I don't have an act and now this guy is doing my act?' I understood that he didn't steal my act, but I was kind of like him in a loud and crazy way, just, you know, different from the other guys getting laughs. I would do comedy in a different way. So I knew I had something. I did a few plays. I did Neil Simon's *Come Blow Your Horn,* the first play he ever wrote, and I played Buddy, the younger brother. I remember getting such big laughs off the lines that Neil Simon wrote and thinking, 'I love to get this laugh from the audience, but I want my own act, so I have to come up with something as good.' I knew the laughs I could get if I had the right material. I knew that much, that the material was very important."

Like most comedians their first time out, Meaney was in for a rude awakening. "I wrote a bit with my brother Jack, the Home Lobotomy Kit. Remember the *Saturday Night Live* "Bass-o-matic" bit with Dan Aykroyd, where he put the fish in the blender and they blended it up a bit? It was sort of based on that type of a sales guy selling the Home Lobotomy Kit. 'Introducing a new foolproof end to migraine headaches, daily stress and strain, it's new and it's easy, it's Popiel's Home Lobotomy Kit. Simply shave your loved one's head using your electric razor ... ' I had memorized the whole thing and I got up on stage, this was out in San Diego— 'Introducing a new foolproof end to migraine headaches, daily stress and strain ... ' You ever forget where you are in the middle of something? All of a sudden I had nothing to say!" In the biz that's called "going up" and it's never pretty, especially if it's your first time on stage.

"Comedians had really pulled the wool over my eyes, because I had been to Catch a Rising Star right after high school and I had been to the Improv and I had been to the Comic Strip and I'd see the comedians get up on stage. I remember David Sayh and David Brenner and Bob Shaw. I remember heckling Bob Shaw and going up to him years later, 'You remember that heckle that I did to you?' thinking that he would remember because it was so brilliant, you know. They fooled me so much that they would just get up on stage and talk about what happened to them that day and I thought that's what you did. I mean, I didn't know any comedians, I didn't know somebody to ask, 'Well, how do you do this?'" Where's Paul Reiser when you need him?

"They just seemed to get up there and talk about what happened to them that day or the day before, or with their girlfriend. It just seemed so natural for them to get up and talk. So I thought, 'Well, I could get up and talk, too.'" Along with the cursed Home Lobotomy Kit, Meaney chatted it up that first time out. "I didn't really even have anything written out. I just kind of got up there and talked and I failed miserably. I wasn't comfortable on stage, it was stressful, I had people looking at me and I thought, 'What do I do now?'

"I don't think anybody can be prepared. Even if I was prepared and I went in there and did great, I don't think it would have mattered, because it's not really what you're doing on stage, it's who you're becoming on stage, and it takes a long time to become somebody. You're not going to have a career in a night. So I knew that I might fail for a year, I had that insight. It would be that long, maybe longer, before I could start making money. That was an objective. I don't come from a family that can support me just because I want to do stand-up comedy, so I had to go out and try to make money doing it.

"Nobody said, 'You can't do that—why don't you go into the fire department?' I mean, I worked at B. Altmans & Co. and when I left that, my mother said, 'How could you leave that job? People work there their whole lives. You're a manager there. You manage the Charleston Gardens Restaurant. You'll always have that job. They give you benefits and everything. Now you're leaving that, to do what?'

"I had no guidance counselor—I think now they would probably say, 'This is a funny kid, maybe he should go into television or something.' Or, 'Maybe he has a career in comedy, maybe'—but nobody ever said that until I got to college. A professor of mine said,

'You've got something really special. You've got the ability to make people laugh. I've never seen anything like this before in my life,' and he was the guy who finally said to me, 'You can do what you want to do, just go out there and get it.' Nobody before had ever said that.

"Everybody said, 'You're really funny, you're very, very funny, you should do this—you should go to these open-mike nights and stuff.' I never did it in New York, because I never wanted to subject my family and friends to that, and have them say, 'Maybe you shouldn't do this. He tried it, it wasn't good.' That's why I moved out to California where I didn't know anybody. I said, 'If I can do this, I have to do it in front of people who don't know me, where nobody knows who I am. I don't have a relative, I don't have a friend in the world out here.' So I ended up in San Francisco. I got on the open-mike nights there and learned how to do it in front of nobody who knew me. I was being judged raw. So then eventually somebody says, 'Yeah, that's pretty funny, what he did there.'"

So, now you've heard the experts, and they're saying that getting up on stage the first few times boils down to making sure that: your stomach is empty; you've voided your bowels; your self esteem has been stored as far away from your tear ducts as possible; and that somewhere nearby is an open bar and possibly a stripper. On the upside, if you have the stamina—both physical and psychological—to endure the trauma of accepting the fact that one can indeed be the loneliest number you will ever know, then you just might pull off this stand-up thing after all. If all else fails, just toss your brain into Popiel's Home Lobotomy Kit and press purée.

CHAPTER 3

GOTTA GET A GIMMICK

...In case my jokes fail, my voice will still be heard

George Burns held a cigar between his fingers ... Jack Benny clutched a violin ... Groucho Marx painted on a moustache while Chico wore a little hat and Harpo kept mute ... Sophie Tucker was the last of the Red Hot Mamas ... Señor Wences put a wig on his hand ... Martin sang while Lewis mugged ... Berle wore dresses ... Foster Brooks and Joe E. Lewis drank ... George Jessel excelled in eulogies.... They all had a gimmick, something that made them unique, memorable, and funny. They are also proof that once you find your niche you can go places reserved for the immortal, funny few. Hell, even Gypsy Rose Lee had a famous gimmick that left her alone and naked on a stage—not so different from the experience of a stand-up comic.

There's more to being a stand-up comic than standing up and being funny. You need that comic edge to be remembered. As any ad exec will tell you, it's product recognition that's going to bring people back to sample more of your merchandise.

If you don't believe ad execs, then how about Norm Crosby, who insists, "If you don't have an identity, if you don't have something that's yours, unique to you, then you become one of the mass e pluribus unum and there's no way for the audience to remember you. Most of the guys from my era—my peers—looked alike, dressed alike, same haircut, same tuxedo, basically, same material. So

NORM CROSBY, aka the "master of the malaprop," has appeared on television's top variety shows including *The Ed Sullivan Show* and as a regular on *The Dean Martin Show.* He has brought his unique comedy to casino showrooms, nightclubs, and the banquet circuit. As corporate spokesman for all Anheuser-Busch products Norm appeared in several of their beer commercials. Because of a hearing affliction, Norm has a special interest in the problems of the hearing impaired and was the first National Chairman for the Council for Better Hearing. He received a star on Hollywood's Walk of Fame in 1982.

how would you go home and say to somebody, 'I just heard a funny guy, 'bout average height, had a tuxedo, funny.' 'What did he do?' 'Oh, he talked about his house and his wife and his car.' How in the world would you know who that is? But if you said, 'He insulted everybody.' 'Oh, that's Don Rickles.' If you said, 'Oh, he talked funny and screwed up the words,' 'Oh, that's Norm Crosby.' Or, 'He was droll, monotone.' 'Oh, that's Jackie Vernon.'

"At the Improv, Budd Friedman will put on fifteen comics in one night. Each kid—ten minutes—they come out, they're dressed alike. They wear jeans and sweaters, and they think they're being different and they don't realize what they've done, they've traded the tuxedo for another uniform. It's a uniform. They all wear the same thing. If one did it, it would be unique. You would say, 'Wow, that's different.' But they all wear the same sneakers, the same jeans, and the same sweater, they become a whole category of acts. You can almost put them in a bag and pick out one and it's the same exact thing as the next other one. It's important that you don't let that happen. See? You have to have a hook. You have to have something that you hook them with—that they remember.

Long before they know your name, they have to remember you for something and if you have that, you got it made."

Crosby is best known for his malaprops, a gimmick that didn't come to him overnight. It was when he was invited to perform at the Latin Quarter in New York that he realized he needed to find his own hook. "What I was doing at the time was taking stuff from Ed Sullivan. I would take a joke, a line, a premise, something, from each of the guys. The guys that I was taking from were all the New York comics. They were all on television—the Jack Carters, the Shecky Greenes, the Buddy Hacketts, the Jan Murrays. I said, 'My God, how can I go into New York and do that stuff? Everybody will know it's theirs.' I wanted to do something different. I was thinking about material and every subject had been covered. Every possible theme. Every motif. Every possible topic had been done to death. I thought, 'I can't come up with anything new—my house, my wife ... '

"So I started to think about something that I could do that would be my own, and that's how I came up with the word manipulation—it became my trademark. I knew people who actually spoke that way. One of the reasons I had so much success is that people can identify with it and everybody knows somebody who talks that way. I used to get tons of mail: 'My Aunt Heddy used to say, it's as obvious as the speck on your nose.' People would write me and give me these things.

"I worked at a club in Springfield, Massachusetts, and the boss became my friend. We used to play golf and hang out, and he loved the girls in the show, the girl singers, the girl dancers. He'd book 'em and he had eyes for everybody. So he came to my dressing room one day, there was a little girl dancer on the show who was cute. Some of the acts would stay there, in Springfield—it was ninety miles outside of Boston—and some acts would commute to Boston, because it's not that far. So he said to me, 'Find out if the girl is staying over or if she communicates.' I knew he didn't mean that—and it just planted a seed. I started to think, 'What a great way to go, not only worry about the material, but how to present the material. I don't think there's anybody in the business who's presenting the material differently. I thought about it and I started to do it and, unfortunately, the people I was working to at the time didn't know the difference.

"I worked these clubs and I'd say, "When the Eucalyptans vanquished the Trojans they pushed them out of Troja down the Aguanemenon Valley into the Connecticut Turnpike and they stabbed Brutus in the ventricle with a rusty shim and he got rigamotion of his lobitary duct and he clapsed on the steps of the Acrocolis and they wrote down that he died from clapse.' I swear to God, they would sit there and look at me and say, 'Yeah, okay.' Then the boss would call me in the kitchen and say, 'What are you doing? Geography? Don't you know any jokes?' So it wasn't easy.

"But I persevered. I kept playing with it and doing it and then I discovered that the better the places that I worked, the more intelligent the audience, the funnier it was, because they knew the difference. So, finally, I got to do my first Ed Sullivan and my first Johnny Carson, and Johnny stood up at the desk and said, 'It's a joy to hear somebody do something different in comedy. God bless you, Norm. That's so funny, that stuff.'"

"The best thing a critic ever said about me was, 'He's the only comedian I've ever seen where the audience leaves wondering if *he* liked *them*," laughs Richard Belzer. "In some way, covertly or overtly, I hope to inform people about politics or human behavior or show business. Some things are just purely silly and funny, but I'd like think there's a thread running through what I do, that there's a bit of knowledge encased within the humor. I feel I was compelled to do that intuitively and it wasn't ever by design. Once I started working I realized that I wanted to talk *about* something rather than *around* something.

"My main influences were people like Groucho Marx and Lenny Bruce and Richard Pryor, people who weren't necessarily nice, but had some intrinsic charm. There's just something about—I don't want to say being nasty—but being brutally honest that I found appealing. I didn't know how I was gonna be at first, I just went up because I felt compelled to go on stage. But then I realized that politics and improvisation, dealing with an audience, were my gifts. I was an emcee at Catch a Rising Star for many years, and you start out the night by saying, 'Where you from?' and bringing up to twenty-five, thirty acts a night—you run out of material. So I got to talk to audiences a lot, which I found to be great fun. It forces you to be funny on your feet. I mean, I like to ad lib and improvise, so that's always been a part of my persona—unpredictability.

"I think the audience, at the risk of being immodest, is won over by the wit and the intelligence and just the forcefulness of what I'm doing. I kind of mug them into liking me. There are many really explosively funny nights where I decimate someone who just keeps coming back for more, and it is funny, but I don't think it would be funny in the telling. I mean, there was one time—Alec Baldwin loves this story—where this woman just wouldn't shut up and I said, 'I'm gonna take you up on this piano and just fuck you into unconsciousness if you don't shut up,' and for some reason that just got a huge laugh. Because of the dynamic, it just built up to a moment where I had just had it. The more grotesquely sexual, the bigger the laughs.

"A lot of times it is just about what the person does for a living—okay, you get up, you go to work, what's the first thing you do? You just take them through their day and just find laughs in their ordinary everyday life that they never looked at before. I just really press them, 'What's the first thing you do when you get to the office? There's just a lot of texture to that, for me anyway."

While Belzer is the master of working the audience, it doesn't work for all comedians. Phyllis Diller has a different tack. "Oh, it took me years to find out how to get on ... how to say hello. Because, you know, some of the lines are so corny. 'Anybody here from Cleveland?' Ugh. 'Are you having a good time?' Ugh. If you let any one of those people start talking you might as well go back to the hotel. And anytime they say, 'Are you having a good time?' they're asking for it. They are never gonna make it. You should come out and you should be in charge from

PHYLLIS DILLER

Phyllis Diller has headlined in venues all around the world as a professional comic. A "late bloomer," she started her career at the age of thirty-seven when she was a working housewife and mother of five, employed at radio station KSFO in San Francisco. She starred in three television series and has made guest appearances on hundreds of top-rated shows. Her film career includes such movies as *Splendor in the Grass, Boy, Did I Get A Wrong Number, Did You Hear the One About the Traveling Saleslady?* and *The Sunshine Boys.* She appeared on Broadway as Dolly Levi in *Hello Dolly.* Phyllis has written four best-selling books: *Phyllis Diller's Housekeeping Hints, Phyllis Diller's Marriage Manual, The Complete Mother,* and *The Joys of Aging and How to Avoid Them.*

Fang thinks formal sex education means watching porno films in a tux.

President George W. Bush has an ancestral home in Kennebunkport—a town named for a really bad wine sold only in shoe stores.

I was on a flight where the food was so bad, the stewardess demonstrated the air sick bag.

What do you get when you cross a Jew and a WASP? A pushy pilgrim.

Fang fights with everybody. He had a big fight with the gas company and he had a big fight with the oil company. We heat our house with liniment.

Doctors say you can enjoy sex way past eighty, but not as a participant.

Fang dragged our mangy mutt into a restaurant and the manager said, "Can't you see that sign?" Fang said, "So who's smoking?"

My purse caught on fire. My VISA card overheated.

I told Fang he could watch half of "Laverne & Shirley." So he watched Shirley.

One big drawback to bigamy, even if you get divorced, you're still married. In Arkansas, if you get a divorce, are you still cousins?

They've started building the President Clinton Library. They're welding RV's together.

When I told my daughter the Christmas story, she said, "Madonna played Bethlehem?"

Math deficiency affects ten out of every six people.

This morning I picked up some unfinished furniture. I bought a tree.

Barbara Bush was afraid they'd hire Roseanne to play her. She needn't worry. They've hired Leslie Nielsen.

What a lousy hotel. They stole towels from us. The bridal suite was in the basement.

A cop stopped me. He said, "Lady, you were going sixty miles an hour." I said, "You idiot, I've only been out ten minutes."

An officer asked Fang for identification. Fang said, "You're a cop."

My car is a lemon. The windshield wipers are on the inside. The only time they could do you any good is if you've lost your rear window and you're backing through a blizzard.

I'm a lousy driver. I have to pull off the road to blow the horn.

My mother talks to herself, then complains she hears voices. She listens to her records everyday. She doesn't play them, just holds them up to her ear.

Fang is two tacos short of a plate. His ducks don't fly in a "V."

My mother-in-law, Moby Dick—when her stomach growls, you'd better pick up a chair and a whip.

the first moment. There are people in the audience who want to be a part of the act, you have to ignore them. Otherwise they will still be having that conversation throughout."

Diller gets that first laugh out of the way without uttering a sound. All she has to do is take center stage in one of her wacky outfits. "I learned early that I had to make some reference to either what I'm wearing or my hair, something about me. That was the way to say hello. Oh, I've had some great outfits. I had one dress that looked like metal, and I said, 'There's a tinsmith inside still working on it,' stuff like that. Or, 'It's left over from Camelot.' That's the way to get on—for me.

"Nobody new is doing a look. They all just come out in what they would wear, the girls in pants. But pants weren't in when I started, so my look developed. I don't like to wear pants—I'm not comfortable. And my theory is, if you're uncomfortable, you're not chic. My look evolved. I wanted to tell them that I was flat chested, but I had really big boobs. I've had a reduction. So I went to the shapeless outfits, so I could tell them I'm flat and skinny. There are still thousands of people who think I'm really skinny, actually they think I'm tall and skinny. I'm short and dumpy. But I do this with clothing.

"I was losing hair badly because I was bleaching it myself and I went to a salon in New York and they said, 'Lean over and take the shower brush and brush it over [your head] every chance you get.' They felt that circulation, I suppose, would help. I was too busy. I was at a peak, in New York, doing maybe seventeen little interviews a day and I would go out on stage without remembering to comb it back. It caught on. I realized, hell, this is working. You'll go with anything. First it was just my own hair and then I did the wigs and now it's grown to a fright wig."

Don't think Diller is insulted if you tell her you're laughing at her in her getups, or at her deprecating humor about her fictional husband Fang or her terrible sex life. "That's what I want to happen during the whole show. It's like priming a pump. You see, everything in a comic's life, to be funny, it's got to be all wrong. Everything's got to be bad." As for that material, "My kids used to be little kids, I'd talk about that. Now I've got grandchildren, so I've kept it up. I don't do a lot of talking. It's just a few words and laughs. Laughs are all you're aware of."

Gilbert Gottfried also weighs in on the audience participation angle. "What I've noticed about the comics who say, 'Where are you from?' is that in a way, they're like fortune tellers or clairvoyants who go up to a group of people and say, 'Someone here has the letter R in their name. Is there someone with the letter R? Now, let me see if I'm right about this, are you having trouble with your job? Someone has trouble with their job.' And eventually, what I find with these people who do 'Where you from?' is that they'll have a joke about taxi cabs and they'll go, 'Hey, anyone in this audience a cab driver.' 'No?' 'Well, what do you do for a living.' 'I'm going to school.' 'Oh, you go to school. You ever take a cab to school?' 'No, no, it's two blocks away.' 'You ever have any friends who worked as cab drivers?' And eventually by pushing and shoving, they get the audience to say something about a cab. 'That's interesting, 'cause cab drivers ... ' and then the audience goes, 'Wow, he just thought about that on the spot!' "

So it's safe to assume Gottfried won't be asking people where they're from. As a matter of fact, I'm not exactly sure what he does up there—and neither is he. "Yeah, I'd like to know. I'd like to know what I'm doing in the business. It's very sad. I might quit after this interview. You helped the American public." Nah, I don't deserve that much praise. Gottfried is still working hard, using his unique style. "I've got all the material to choose from that I've built up over the years. I mean, I don't have it in my mind that I'll do this one after this one. It'll be a mixture of some bits that are prepared and whatever hits me—usually a chair hits me or a bottle. As far as writing it down, I've always been bad at that, it's always like something comes to me on stage—if you remember it afterwards—but no, I've never really written stuff down."

Gottfried admits that his stage persona might be off-beat, but there are many who clearly enjoy whatever bon mots pop into his zany head. "People would tell me that I was just fucking around on stage and think, 'What are you doing? You should just do your act.' The interesting thing about 'just do your act' is that your act, as far as they are concerned, is something you've done before. So if you did something about elevators and then the next time you did something about onion rolls, they'd go after the onion roll thing, 'How come you didn't do your elevator routine? That's your bit. What are you fucking around with that onion roll thing?' Then, next time you're on stage and you do something else, they go, 'Hey, how come you didn't do the onion roll?' So it's all about stuff they've heard before.

"One of the comedians around the circuit when I was starting out was Jerry Seinfeld, and just to entertain myself and the other comics in the back, as the audience was scratching their head, I'd start imitating Jerry Seinfeld on stage. That would make the comedians laugh but the audience was coming up and saying, 'Why are you fucking around? No one knows who the hell Jerry Seinfeld is.'" Gilbert is clearly a man ahead of his time. "I'm like Galileo—and basically as funny as Galileo." But don't ask him where he gets his material, be it his family or the lady at the deli. "You know, if I knew that I'd be going there more often for all my material. I have no idea, it's just something that comes into my head. One thing I always hate, when people say to me stuff like, 'Boy, if you came to my job you'd get so much material,' or 'Boy, if you sat with my family during … ' I'm thinking, 'no, I wouldn't.'

"I remember, when I was first struggling to get on at the clubs, people would give me important advice like, 'Why don't you go on the Johnny Carson Show?' And I'd think, 'Never thought of that one—I should do that.' My decision was to hang around a club all night … gee, *The Tonight Show*?"

Early advice isn't the only thing Gottfried is cynical about, since he apparently has a persona that everyone wants. "I can't tell you how many meetings and auditions I've had where I was their number one choice and the only person they wanted for it, and I wound up not getting it. Where I walk in and they go, 'You know, the whole reason we're making this movie is just for you. You are the only person we want for this,' and they go for someone else.

"One time, I was up for a part and they were saying, 'Oh, you're the only person we want for this part. Anything you wanna do with it is just great. We just can't wait to work with you.' It was just this done deal, and then my agent calls and says, 'Oh, they're going with someone else on it.' So I said, 'Oh, who are they going with?' And he says, 'Dustin Hoffman.' I was sort of sitting there wondering like, when in Hollywood anyone was ever going, 'Hmm, Hoffman, Gottfried? Gee, just can't decide.' It was actually Mumbles in *Dick Tracy*. I don't know when the names Dustin Hoffman and Gilbert Gottfried were ever mentioned in one sentence. I think the only time is when someone says, 'I've seen Gilbert Gottfried act and he's no Dustin Hoffman.'"

What Gottfried might lack in Hoffmanisms he gains in gimmick. "You don't know how your personality developed, but it just did. So, I never had an answer when people said, 'The way you are on stage, is that like an uncle you had?' I have no idea," says the manic comedian who is soft spoken when off stage. "I'm like Perry Como, I've often been compared to Perry Como. I am the Jewish Perry Como, I think. Which is what Hollywood's been looking for—they put the word out, 'We want a Jewish Perry Como.'" Now that's a gimmick!

"Taking a particular moment and making it into a funny moment," is George Wallace's modus operandi. "What happened with George Bush—simple things in life make you laugh—George Bush committed a faux pas last year at the Kennedy Center in Washington. George Dubya saw Stevie Wonder in the audience and he said, 'Hey, how ya doing Stevie?' waving at him—for what? See, I pick up on little things like that. That's what I like.

"A lady came up to me at the airport and said, 'Mr.

Wallace, you're mighty quiet today.' I'm thinking, well, hell, I'm standing here by myself! Little things like that. Little stupid things that people say and do. You read the newspaper and it says some man was in the hospital and he had an unexpected heart attack. As opposed to what? 'How about a round of golf today?' 'Okay, but you know what, we gotta get it in before eleven-thirty, because I'm expecting that heart attack to hit me around noon.' I take stupid things people say and put a twist on them. That's my job. To just put a twist on everything.

"My persona on stage is just to go up there and have fun. I'm in a living room and we're all family. Everybody's a family. We're just talking, we're in the kitchen, we're having a drink, we're eating together, 'How ya doin'?' When I'm on stage, people don't mind talking back to me, just like in the living room. And that's the atmosphere that I like to create when I walk on stage. It's not a show, I just happen to be up here with the mike, but it's everybody's show. That's the unique thing about a personality. You have to project that image that, 'Hey, I'm okay, you can talk to me, I'm your friend.' When we're saying hello to an audience, we're doing a lot of things instead of saying hello. We're finding the mood of the audience, we're finding out if it's tough, which direction to go, do I need to come fast with the jokes or do I need to just talk to the people? Do I need to just say, 'What are your problems?' Whatever. When we're saying, 'Hello, how are ya, what's going on?', we're sizing up the room.

"It's so easy to win an audience over when you walk out with a smile and just let them know you are a real person, you're not just delivering jokes. I know a lot of my friends can deliver jokes very well and they write great jokes, but I think the best thing to do is go up on stage with a personality. I know some comedians go on stage, they do their jokes, everybody leaves, and you might remember the jokes. But the personality should be the main thing. You wanna be liked.

"They always know you are in control because you got the mike. That keeps you in control. A lot of my act is audience participation, so they speak when they're spoken to. When I go out, I know what I wanna talk about. I know they can relate to what I'm talking about, otherwise I wouldn't be doing it. First of all, I know these people have paid to see me. When people come out to the club to see *you*, they're coming out to have some fun. That's the great thing about a comedian, it's not like a singer, a comedian, you gotta deliver, you're making people laugh.

"My best bits are that people can say some stupid things. I take their little clichés and turn them around. Stupid, simple phrases. You know, some guy says, 'Makes you feel like you been hit by a Mack truck.' Now, who do we know that can tell us how it feels to be hit by a Mack truck? I think a Ford Ranger'll do a real good job on your ass! Simple things that people say. You go to the doctor and the nurse says stupid shit, 'Are you here to see the doctor?' 'No, lady, I'm here to twist your boobs! Of course, I'm here to see the doctor.' Simple things like that. The pilot is always saying stupid things, 'If there's anything we can do to make your trip more comfortable, please don't hesitate to ask.' And I'm thinking, 'Well, what about that first class seat up there nobody's sitting in.'

"I watch TV, and I'm going, 'Stupid commercials.' Like Gatorade—I'm not drinking anything that I'm gonna sweat the same color that I just drank. When I watch TV I watch it differently than most people do. There's a commercial running right now, who the hell is gonna take a Viagra before they get in a race car and drive it two hundred miles an hour? It's simple things I look at in life. My job is to say what everyone is thinking."

"I just wanted to be who I was," says Rita Rudner. "That was my ambition because every person is unique and I didn't want to do comedy the way comedy was being done before. So I wanted to take who I was and bring that to the stage. I really paid attention and I decided not to do a comedy rhythm that existed, not to portray a comedy attitude that existed, and to see the world through my own eyes the way someone who was brought up the way I was would see it.

"So that's an area where I could be criticized or I could be complimented, either one. I have a very specific viewpoint. I was an only child, I had to go from there. I was overprotected; I was a ballerina; I was Jewish; so those were all my springboards."

"If you want to get abuse, be a prop comic." Care to guess who that might be? Carrot Top explains, "I don't know why prop comics are looked down upon so much because I think to be a prop comic is just another side of being a comic. Every joke that I do visually I could say as just a joke but what I do is, I have the visual aid. What I do combines stupidity and cleverness."

In spite of the cleverness, Carrot Top still feels like the odd man out. "Ever since the very beginning, right at clubs they're like, 'Carrot Top, oh, God, he's that guy with the props.' My show is kind of a rock show, there's pyrotechnics and lasers and lights and props and music. I have a whole stage set. It really is like a big rock show. I do a two hour show and probably an hour of it is props and an hour of it is storytelling and stand-up and a whole bunch of things you don't see unless you see that live show.

"I'm not competing with George Carlin or Dennis Miller or Janeane Garofalo or any stand-up comics, because I'm not doing anything close to what they do. Each prop is kind of an invention, as opposed to a play-on-words. Some are really clever and some are really stupid. That's what I like about Carlin, he will talk about farting for twenty minutes and then talk about abortion. I used to think that was so amazing, that you could talk about farting and then talk about abortion in the same twenty minutes, and I thought that was brilliant. It could add stupidity and cleverness in the same show. So I've always been a fan of kind of being clever and kind of being a little silly."

Speaking of silly, this is probably a good place to ask Carrot Top about his name. "When you're a redhead you're always given nicknames, so my real name is Scott Thompson and there's a Scott Thompson from *The Kids in the Hall*. So I thought, there's already a Scott

Thompson, I'm not going to be Scotty Thompson. Carrot Top really just came because people would say, 'Hey Carrot Top' and I thought, 'You know what?' As a marketing thing, too, it just worked and so I, really on a whim, just took it one night. The emcee said, 'What's your name?' and I said, 'Carrot Top.' He's like, 'What?' I said, 'Carrot Top' He's like, 'Carrot Top?' I said, 'Yeah, just do it,' and I went on stage and it worked. I say to my friends, it's like a blessing and a curse. It's been successful for me but at the same time it's, 'Aw shit, I'm gonna be known as Carrot Top the rest of my life.' That's okay, there's been Red Skelton and Ice Cube and Ice T and Queen Latifa—there are other names that are probably a little wackier than mine.

"I make fun of myself. I'm a big fan of self-deprecation. I think it's like a one-man show that is kind of funny. I don't necessarily think it's strictly stand-up comedy like a Bill Maher would do, it's kind of a mixture. I don't tap dance or sing, but there's a lot of a throwback to vaudeville days."

Speaking of vaudeville, if there is one comedian who couldn't be any farther from it, both in years and style, it's Samm Levine, now twenty. "When I started, my style could not be more old school, could not be more Sid Caesar. You know, set up, punch line, rim shot. Could not have been more one-liners." Then again, maybe vaudeville will never really die. Check out this real material from a thirteen-year-old stand-up: "So people are always pickin' on me 'cause I'm so short and everything, and you know, I just decided to stand up for myself and just say, 'Hey, you know what? I am short and there's absolutely nothing I can do about it, so you just get over it Mom, okay, I've had enough.' There you go, that's a one-liner—bang, bang—and that would probably have been ninety percent of my humor. At the time, I couldn't think of any better way to do it. I had trouble coming up with really huge routines. Like Rich Jeni will do twenty minutes on one subject, he'll do twenty minutes on feathered hats. God bless him, he's brilliant. I couldn't think that way yet.

115

"It's definitely evolved. Now, I can spend a little bit longer, I can spend three or four minutes on one joke if I want, looking at it from different angles. The humor is not so wholesome as 'So get over it, Mom.' The dirtiest thing I ever opened with—I was seventeen years old and on a bet—respectable club—I walk out onto the stage—I deliberately tell the emcees never say how old I am, to introduce me like I'm another comic—and I walk out on stage, 'Hey everybody, how ya doin'? I'm Samm Levine and I gotta tell ya, pussy tastes bad at any age, that's all I'm sayin'.' The look on the crowd's face was all I wanted. After that, they were mine, they couldn't believe it. When I was seventeen, I looked fourteen, and to see a fourteen-year-old kid open up with something like that, I felt like, I only wish the rest of my act were that blue."

What is the rest of that act, anyway? "I would say it's a little bit of everything, and it's the right combination when it all clicks together. I am firmly a nature and nurture kind of guy, and I think that the nature of your upbringing has a lot to do with it. I always used to make the joke, 'People would ask me, 'How'd you get so funny? Are your parents funny?' and I would say, 'Oh, no, we have cable. That's how I got so funny, I watch a lot of TV.' You know, of course, I'm kidding. It has a lot to do with my parents, just 'cause my father was always trying to tell jokes and I love him to pieces, but God bless the fact that he's a dentist and didn't attempt to go into stand-up or anything remotely pertaining to the arts. I can't tell you how much I've wanted to do a bit about the awful material that my parents give me.

"I get up there these days, I just try to connect with the audience. I try to bring them into my world. I try to get them to look at my parents the same way I do and then they can visualize their own parents doing the same thing. I try to use my appearance and, patting myself on the back as I'm saying this, use my wit and play them off each other, 'cause you usually don't see fifteen-year-old looking kids on stage. Looks are very important in this town, a kid telling jokes about politics, you don't see that and I think that's funny. The last time I went up, after a joke that did so-so, I brought out a joke I never had any intention of using. It's a joke that I told when I started doing stand-up, but I think it's still just as good today as it was back then—'So what's the deal with this Watergate thing ... alright ... I mean, if Kissinger and Nixon can't get their act together, what hope is there for, say, Ali McGraw and Steve McQueen? ... really.' The crowd loved it and I was surprised because a lot of that crowd was younger guys. They were guys and girls in their mid to late twenties, but thankfully, I guess I picked a topic that was memorable enough that everybody knew it, but not obscure enough that I was gonna alienate everyone.

"One trick I first saw in the Catskills, at Kutshers Country Club, by Paula Poundstone, who could not have been more on top of knowing what everybody in that crowd would connect with. She would sit on the edge of the stage and talk to the people in the crowd. She'd talk twenty minutes to one woman from Hohokus, 'cause she thought it was a funny name of a town. I always had that in the back of my mind, just talk to them, talk to the crowd, find out the general feeling. Where is everybody from, how long you been here, what are the schools up here like, does anybody go to college, what's the average job here, is everybody in the computer industry, is every-body somehow affiliated with coffee? Find out stuff like that and go with the humor you have on that. Even if it's never worked for me in LA or New York, never, even if I've bombed with it every time, I just have a feeling. I think that I always wanted to do that but was always too scared 'cause I was always worried somebody would say, 'Yeah, I'm in insurance,' and I would have nothing. I'd go, 'Oh, okay.' I better not die on stage."

Who the heck is Lily Tomlin when she's up on that stage? "I don't know. I just do character monologues or quirky bits. I don't know what to call it. I always wanted it to have some relevance, to be content-full. By content-full I don't mean necessarily have an agenda or some specific political or social message, it was more out of my soul, in a way. Whatever pleased me. It might be a com-

LILY TOMLIN has starred in motion pictures, television, animation, theater and video. From her early days working in nightclubs and comedy clubs such as the Improv in New York to her groundbreaking appearances on *Laugh-In* she has been creating memorably quirky characters that have endeared her to audiences around the globe. Just mention the names Ernestine and Edith Ann and Lily Tomlin immediately springs to mind. She has received several Emmy Awards and has guest starred on numerous television shows, including *Murphy Brown* and *The West Wing*. She earned a Tony Award and critical acclaim for her one-woman Broadway Show *The Search for Signs of Intelligent Life in the Universe*. In films she has starred in *Nashville*, *9 to 5*, *The Incredible Shrinking Woman*, *All of Me*, *The Beverly Hillbillies*, and *Tea with Mussolini*, to name a few.

mentary on some social issue, but it would be more artful.

"One of my earliest monologues was Lucille W., who's addicted to eating rubber objects. It was really meant to be a commentary on what was acceptable as an addiction in the culture. A pretty obvious thing, especially for someone who was in her twenties. It's Lucille doing a kind of an AA confession about being addicted to eating rubber objects.

"I would collect old movie magazines from the '40s and '50s. Once, I read an article where one of the physical trainers at the studios said, 'The most perfect body I ever saw was on Lana Turner and she had it once for two weeks in 1942.' Those kinds of things have fascinated me. One of my other earliest monologues was the world's oldest living beauty expert, Madam Lupé, and that was because I was fascinated by the double standard in the culture, women always having to be so young and attractive to be desirable, and how ephemeral that youth and beauty is. Madame Lupé's face was all deteriorated because she was the world's oldest living beauty expert, and then she would rejuvenate her face with exercise and emolients, and then she would sneeze and it would all fall down."

Tomlin's material is filled with characters gleaned from her astute observational abilities. "If I was in a restaurant and I saw an interesting couple I would do everything to try to hear what they were talking about. People just fascinated me beyond anything else and it all extends from growing up in an old apartment house. I was madly in love with the people who lived in that building because they were all so different. It was an evolving neighborhood that had been fairly upwardly mobile, middle class professionals. By the time my mother and dad moved in, who were like poor white southerners—blue collar—some of the older people left in the building were on pensions and they couldn't really leave.

"My apartment building was like the center of the universe for me. Some neighbors were very political, some were absolutely apolitical, some were educated, some were totally uneducated, and I was at home in every apartment. I lived to go visit people and get inside their apartments. I saw them in so many circumstances—vulnerable, angry, pathetic, beautiful.

"We used to have a line when we'd do shows in the theater, we'd say, 'There's a thousand people out there tonight who wouldn't be caught dead in the same room together,' because it would be such a diverse audience. I did a concert once, in Concord, California, and people would send me notes backstage, each as sincerely involved with my career or my material or as big a fan as the other person. They would be horrified if they knew they were comprising the same audience.

"I used to just love to go out the stage door in a theater run, especially when I was doing *The Search for Intelligent Life in the Universe* on Broadway because the audience was so diverse—a well-dressed yuppie couple would be there and three or four middle-aged women from Nebraska or someplace, in print dresses

119

with pocketbooks, and two or three punked out kids with mohawks, and it would just be wonderful. I was thrilled by it. I guess I would like to see the world as that commonality, whereas usually people think everybody's different from them."

Tomlin has certainly proven herself in crossing over to pleasing a diverse audience, but that style wasn't honed overnight. "Even after I was on *Laugh In* and Ernestine and Edith were so popular, I went to play Marvelous Marv's in Denver. Literally, they'd come because I was on *Laugh-In* and they loved Ernestine and stuff like that and I would just do maybe a little bit of Ernestine, a couple of minutes. I'd also be doing other stuff, long monologues that were real moody and more like short stories or little playlets although I thought they were hilarious. I'd do great business because I was so well known from those early television days but I played almost literally to silence. Show after show after show. Jan Sterling, the actress, was in town, in Denver, once and she came to one of the late shows with her cast— she was doing a play there.

"Marvelous Marv's used to give me an apartment in the building, it was housed in some high rise, and you'd get an apartment upstairs over the club. After the show, which was pretty silent, everybody went up to my apartment and Jan Sterling gave me a big long talk. She said, 'It's not that people don't like it, it's different to them, they don't understand, exactly, they haven't had the experience of this kind of thing, particularly in a club. You just cannot stop doing what you're doing.' So I'd get bolstered by that. I'd think, 'Oh God, these people just don't get it, or I'm not funny,' and then someone would come along and give me a big pep talk and I'd feel great. I'd be revved up and could go out and do ten or twelve shows before I hit a downward spiral. But I think every time you go out you just think it's an aberration, 'Next time I go out it's gonna be great.'

"I always wanted everything to be wonderful. Joan Rivers had one of her first TV shows out of New York, one of those early shows in the daytime. In the wintertime it was really hard to get an audience, they'd literally pull people off the street. I was brought on one time as a young stand-up who was just starting out. I did the world's oldest living beauty expert that day in the studio, and the audience just howled.

"I go to the elevator to leave, and there is literally a bag woman getting on the elevator—no teeth, ulcerated legs, just really in bad shape, and she looks at me and says, 'Oh lady, you were funny today. You gave me such a good laugh and I needed one.' It sounds corny, but that was really leveling for me. When she said that to me it was, figuratively, like an intake of breath. So that's how I want everything to be. I want the experience to be like that. I don't always achieve that but something that makes you laugh and moves you almost simultaneously so that you can't believe that you've had that experience. I thought that was what was wonderful to do. I thought that's what was worthwhile delivering to an audience."

For Jim Gaffigan comedy takes on many styles. "I started off doing self-deprecating jokes, then I was a little bit social satirist mixed in there with impressions. In searching for your persona, you might go through different stages. There are different types of comics: There are clowns like Robin Williams or Carrot Top—there's just a playful silliness to them. Then there are social satirists like Lewis Black or Bill Maher, who comment on society. There's the jokesman who just lives or dies by the joke, like Dave Attell. Then there are great storytellers like [Dave] Chappelle and Louis C.K. I think storytelling is the hardest. Then there are joke tellers who are observationalists also. There are preachers like Keith Robinson, just trying to convert someone to some point of view. Then there are simple observationalists. I would say I'm kind of a combination of clown and observationalist, which is not that rare.

"I'm definitely a product of environment. In New York City there's a certain level of impatience with the audience. There's a certain level of immediacy and it kind of hinders the storytelling or the really truly profoundly offbeat. Some of that is environment, it's the showcase environment of only doing ten or fifteen-minute sets or only doing five minutes at an open mike or whatever, whereas in places like San Francisco or on the road in Minneapolis, you can be more of a character.

"I think that developing a stand-up act takes awhile, because you're dealing with finding your personality on stage. That's easier said than done because it takes awhile to feel comfortable. Then there's the question of what's universal." Ah, the universal appeal—you've either got it or you don't. That ability to make sure your audience actually relates to the jokes you tell. Which often means nix the one about your buddy Rocco and his new girl-friend, 'cause nobody but you and Rocco will be laugh-ing. "They'll tell a joke and it might be kind of funny among their friends, but there isn't that intimacy so it might come across as racist, or sexist, or just inappropri-ate because there isn't that level of intimacy. That person might not be racist or sexist but there's a certain level of intimacy that you need with the audience."

Gaffigan often uses the self-deprecating gimmick in his act—something that audiences, more and more fre-quently, are relating to. "I have some nice credits but the reality is I'm not widely known, so I'll go up there and I'll address what the audience is thinking. I'll be like, 'Yes, hi, how are you? I've never heard of me either.' It stops them from going to the negative place, which is, 'Who the hell is this guy?' Some comedians will go up there and disarm the audience in different ways, but they'll set the tone. Dave Attell usually goes on stage and says something highly irreverent. Pat Cooper's kind of that way. It shocks right at the beginning so that people are like, 'Alright, he's gonna be irreverent.'"

"I think I'm a throwback to another time in come-dy," says Kevin Meaney. "I'm more traditional, in a way, where I don't talk about sex or my personal feelings about lovemaking and dating and marriage. I mean, mar-riage, I'll talk about the institution and how my wife drives me crazy, but I couldn't bare my soul like Richard Lewis, talking about his first time, when he got the crabs … I couldn't, I couldn't. Keep that to yourself, why

KEVIN MEANEY's comedy includes physical humor, impersonations, and music. He was a special guest star on *Saturday Night Live,* making several critically acclaimed appearances. Kevin went on to star in the CBS sitcom *Uncle Buck,* based on the character John Candy created on film. He's had his own specials on HBO and Comedy Central and appeared in HBO's *Comic Relief.* Kevin's numerous stand-up appearances include *The Tonight Show, Late Night with David Letterman, Good Morning America, Live with Regis & Kathie Lee,* and many others. Kevin opened for Jerry Seinfeld during his Broadway concert at the Broadhurst Theatre. He earned an Emmy award in 1985 for his performance in the PBS series, *Comedy Night* and made his film debut in Penny Marshall's *Big.*

would you tell anybody that? That's probably one of the reasons why I don't talk about the time I made love to an Amazon woman. I just can't—'and she wrapped her legs around me'—although I found it funny, I would be embarrassed. I wasn't raised that way, you don't talk about anything like that. You don't talk about sex or anything, nothing like that.

"I like being physical on stage. I love sweating and getting the audience all riled up. That's the way I like to present what I do. I'm very loud and joyful. People must think, 'What's wrong with him? This is bizarre behavior!' But it's just a release. I love doing that. I try to make a little cartoon and you visualize my mother, you visualize me as a small boy, you visualize my mother screaming at me, so there's little windows, little pictures that the audience can draw in their own heads of this disciplinarian correcting me. I like to talk about family. I like to talk about growing up. I like to talk about my new family and my wife. I'll delve into some politics here and there, but basically everybody does. I'm not that unique in my topics, I just present the material a different way.

"I know some musicians, they'll play the piano and then they'll do stand-up but they won't do the piano and the stand-up at the same time. If I played the piano, I'd be up there on the piano and I'd be singing. I'd be doing everything with that piano, that would be my act. If I played the saxophone, I'd probably have a closing bit with the sax. I don't know why you wouldn't incorporate it. I dance a little bit, I'll throw a little dance in there. I sing, I can do that. I can do some impressions, so whatever talent I have, I use it on that stage."

Anyone who has ever seen Meaney's musical renditions knows he is a master of multi-media zaniness. "The *We are the World* song came from the hype that was given to the song before it was released. I was all wrapped up in that hype, as everybody was, and I listened to it and I said, 'I gotta do something on that bit.' I recorded it off the radio and I did something that night at a college I was working at." Meaney's "something" involved a takeoff on all the artists who sing on that recording, inclusive of their various hair styles and sunglasses. His imitations ran the gamut from Michael Jackson and Bob Dylan to Cyndi Lauper and Tina Turner. "You figure the bit would last maybe a year, two years at the most ... I can't get rid of it. I can't. The people want to see it. It's a great closer. It just evolved from that first night I did it, but I felt what the audience felt when I played it the first time and I didn't even know what I was gonna do. The audience just got so wrapped up in the song. It's a beautiful song."

Meaney also sings with Sinatra—well, in a Natalie Cole/Nat King Cole sort of way. They croon *The Coffee Song* together. "I said, 'Let me find a song that I can sing with Frank Sinatra, like on his *Duets* album.' I've been actually working on a couple more of these type songs, it doesn't necessarily have to be a duet. I really like to use multi-media, to have fun with that.

"People like to see the personal aspects of my life," says Meaney, who admits he's come a long way in developing his stage persona. "It was a gradual thing. You eventually get a little bit better and you say, 'I got beyond the Home Lobotomy Kit.' Once I started personalizing my act, that's when I started to get recognized with people in clubs and television, movies, and radio—once I started making it very personal. You come up with your own style, you have to be unique and you have to be yourself onstage. You can't copy somebody else."

Rick Newman witnessed a variety of gimmicks running Catch a Rising Star. "One of the great stories: Larry David, who started out as a stand-up comedian, used to come in and get up on stage. We'd have a packed house. He'd get up to the microphone and, starting at his left, gaze at the audience, moving slowly, scrutinizing them before he said a word. All the way to the right, doing a one-eighty of the audience, and then just shake his head and walk offstage without saying one word. Or, he'd just say, 'Never mind.' It was always funny. Total confusion with the audience, 'What the fuck was that all about?' But Larry didn't care. All I had to do was have someone else ready to go up. I always knew, 'Okay, Larry may not do his act here.' There were times when our next comedian was not there or was late. I learned to have either the emcee ready to jump back up on stage or another comedian just standing there waiting to see if Larry was gonna do his set or not. But that's Larry. When he did a set he was a funny fucking comedian.

"Belzer had a line that he would always say: 'Props, the enemy of wit.' But, the fact of the matter is, there are a few people who can pull off prop comedy to a degree. Andy Kaufman was certainly one of them. Sometimes it works and sometimes it doesn't. One of Andy's routines that used to drive me out of my fucking mind and that I hated because it would never work, he would put a sleeping bag on the stage. Then he would crawl into the sleeping bag with a book, take a flashlight, and then zip the sleeping bag up so you couldn't even see him. He took the microphone with him with the flashlight and the book and he would start to read from the book. Sometimes he'd stay up there for ten minutes." The prop bit that Kaufman is probably best known for is taking the theme song to *Mighty Mouse* and playing it on a phonograph on stage while mouthing the words. According to Newman, "Mighty Mouse was very funny and very visual. Mighty Mouse always worked. I never saw Mighty Mouse not work, but then he does this sleeping bag thing and ... wha?

"I feel that you have to give the artist a fair amount of liberty to do his art as long as he is capable of delivering most of the time. Again, the nature of what a comedy club is, some things aren't going to work. An audience that goes to a comedy club nowadays stays no matter what. They know that they are going to be there for one show from beginning to end. But in the beginning of the comedy club scene, around the early and mid '70s, it was just one continuous show. So I would start my show sometimes at eight-thirty or nine o'clock, and in those days it would go until three in the morning. Either the audience didn't leave and I wound up putting on thirty acts in the course of an evening, or they weren't educated enough to understand that someone else was going to come on after this act. So, I did have some problems sometimes.

"There were times when there was a routine that they might do that I would say, 'You can't do that tonight. I'm not saying you can't do it tomorrow night and I haven't stopped you before, but you can't do that tonight. You gotta go with the strong stuff.'"

Shecky Greene elaborates on some theories of what makes a comic successful. "I never used to watch too many comics in nightclubs. I didn't realize until I started watching them that I was a personality myself. First, there was Shecky Greene—Shecky Greene's *talent* was all secondary to who I was. I had to get to like the audience, to get the audience to like me. I think that's very important for most performers, to get to that audience—and they have to know you first, unless you've got such a reputation they know what you're gonna do. Dean [Martin] had that charisma. There was a persona about Dean that when he was working with Jerry [Lewis], you always

looked at Dean—there was something that you just gravi-
tated to. There are a lot of performers like that, a lot of
successful people, like Johnny Carson. I mean, Carson
may have called himself a comic, but he wasn't a great
comic. You wanted to see Johnny Carson 'cause there
was something nice about him. I think that's basically
what it was with me. When I wanted to get out of the
business it was because I found I was losing that. The
fear overcame me. I would worry about the fear instead
of presenting myself. It got in the way, it really did. I'm
semi-retired now and that's what a comic says when he
can't get a job. I'm semi-retired but really, I just like to
do a few shows.

"I had the ability for improvisation and I didn't
even realize it. I would go in and talk about my family.
I would go into whatever happened to me that day. I
would get up on the stage and talk about when I was
arrested in Vegas for being drunk—I made humor out of
all of that. I found out that I could take anything, any
subject, and make humor out of it. Bush making his
speech, every other word was a standing ovation and I
said to the audience, 'I'm taking Bush's speech 'cause he
got so many standing ovations and it's gonna be my
nightclub act now.'

"Even when I was making a hundred thousand, I
would never know that first thing that I was gonna do,
because that wasn't me. As I got to the big rooms in
Vegas, it was a bad thing not to be prepared with that
first thing. I'd walk out after a while and I'd say, 'It's very
hard to entertain people and make people laugh who
have been gambling.' I had to come up with something
verbatim that I did every night, and that wasn't me. A
lot of jobs I wouldn't take—big, big jobs—because I
didn't feel that they were the right audiences for me.
One thing I was good at, like Sid Caesar, was to just fall
into a character. I would walk out and hide myself in
different characters.

"I used to make up songs on the spot and people
would say to me, 'When did you write that?' I have the
ability, as I'm doing one thing my mind focuses on the

next. That ability for improvisation, I never even knew it was a talent. I would do it in lounges, all over, until finally these guys began to write, 'He makes up songs, he does this ... ' so it took me about forty years to find out what I really did for a living.

"If you do enough things, even an audience that's a little hostile, you can get to them. There are certain things that you know you're capable of doing. There's a joke that you know. There's a line that you know. If it's universal, it'll hit somebody.

"Because of the name Shecky Greene, they always call me a New York comedian, a Borscht Belt comedian. In *Time* magazine—'Borscht Belt comedian'; *Newsweek*— 'Borscht Belt.' Well, I played in the Borscht Belt, but I didn't start out up in the Catskills. The greatest entertainers in the world started in the Catskills, but there was the connotation—'Borscht Belt' was a reference to any Jewish comic. As I got older, it got progressively worse. Actually, I used to work in Duluth for Norwegians and Swedes, I used to work places that Jews never even knew existed. I worked in Hawaii. I think we had one Jew there—me ... that was me."

More of Greene's innovations were the personal problems he brought to the stage—and we're not talking about the School for the Dramatic Arts. Shecky's shtick was still comedy, after all. "It was like going to a psychiatrist, except I had five hundred to a thousand people listening. Saved a lot of money that way but it really was a wonderful catharsis for me. I think I'm the first one in show business, really, to talk about my Jewishness. I talked about the anti-Semitism in the Navy, that a guy saw my Jewish star and said, 'I won't ask ya what that is.' I said, 'I'm the Sheriff of the ship.' So, like that, I made humor out of things.

"My illness I made humor out of, my drunkenness I made humor of it. I could hardly wait to get on stage to talk about it. Thinking about a new routine that had nothing to do with that would be difficult but, using my own problems, wasn't difficult, 'cause it happened. Anything that happened to me, I used. I even talked one time about my first sex encounter, first time that I got a sexual disease, while I was in the Navy. They all told me in Panama, 'Don't go to that girl,' and I did and I shouldn't have gone and she had a mustache and it was just the worst thing in the world. To take a very serious subject and make it funny, that's the joy, that's the real joy. Matter of fact, I can hardly wait until tomorrow to see if something happens to me, 'cause I need new material. I may go out and get hit by a car and then I'll have something to talk about—not for long, but I'll have something to talk about."

Susie Essman literally gets down and dirty with audiences, but it's all in the name of fun. "Everybody's got their own style ... well, hopefully. There are a lot of people who don't have their own style but I think that's one of the most important things. There are certain people who go into a character. With me, it's not a contrived thing, it's who I am, an aspect of me that's heightened because it's on stage and it's performing. I would say ninety percent of the time I'm in the zone and I'm just in it. I don't remember the set afterwards. I'm just there, I'm just in it, clearly working the audience, spontaneous. I know I can be a little shocking but that's not my intent. I don't go for shock value. I just kinda like to talk about things most people think about, but won't talk about. I like to give people permission to talk about that stuff."

Most of Essman's time on stage is spent working the room, mingling with the audience. "I have to be so focused and listening so carefully and so connected to the audience. I think that that's really the cornerstone of what I do as a performer—strongly connect to an audience so that I'm actually speaking to them and listening to them and it's not just like I'm using them to get to a punch line. They feel this experience we're having together, and that's what I like to create. That's what I think is special about live performing.

"I'm surprised how uptight people are sometimes. If I'm working a country club that's an older crowd, for example, I can talk about sex all I want but I can't say the "f" word. For some reason that word unnerves them. I can say everything else. I can imply everything else. It's a generation thing, it's their generation. Whereas my generation is much more comfortable with the word. But we say "fuck" like it's nothing. It's meaningless. If I said, 'Ah, the fucking dog,' you wouldn't even think twice about hearing me say that, but my parents' generation— I wouldn't say that or the "c" word.

"A lot of times I'll go to these jobs and they'll tell me, 'You have to work clean,' and yet the dirtier I am, the more they're loving the show. There will always be one uptight woman who complains in the back or whatever. There's always gonna be somebody, you can't please everybody, you just have to go with the odds.

"There are times when I just go blank on stage and I can't remember anything, that's when I'm not in my flow. You can't be in the zone, in the flow all the time, but you can fake it. I've always tried to be in the moment and honest, so I'll talk about it and say, 'I can't remember a goddamn thing.' Or I'll look at my notes. I'll just say to them, 'My mind's a sieve, I can't remember a thing.' That's part of my style too, being very much in the moment and being honest with the audience and respecting them in that way. But sometimes it's just one of those nights. I had one not long ago, where I just went on stage and it was like there was nothing happening and I couldn't remember my material. It's a horrible feeling.

"Stand-up comedy is different from other kinds of comedy. I consider myself an entertainer—I'm not a performance artist. I'm not any of those other kinds of things. I consider it my job to make people laugh. Now, there's a lot of leeway in that area. Ideally, you want to make people laugh in the way that *you* want make them laugh. What I realized, very early on, is that it's not that hard to make people laugh if you are a funny person. But then you start to want to make people laugh in a particular kind of way. It becomes more about control on stage and technique. I'm not a message comedian. I'll go off on rants about things that are bothering me, but mostly I just want to make people laugh. I can't tell you how often people come up to me after a show and say, 'I needed that. You added six years onto my life. It's the first time I've laughed in so long. I feel so much better.' I really consider it a healing art form, I really do, and that's always been my goal. It's just to make people laugh without going low. (Well, it depends on what's low. To me, talking dirty is not low. Doing fart jokes is low. I don't like scatological. Sex is fine.)

"Here's what I like to do when I'm performing in a comedy club or at a private party: I like it to be a live experience. I like it to be an experience that we are all in together and we don't know what's going to happen. It shouldn't be like watching comedy on television. I want everybody to feel that we are all in this experience together, it is never going to happen again. That's when you go into the zone. That's when it's so incredible. Is it risky to go into the audience? At this point it's not, because I know what I'm doing. It's exhausting, is what it is. It's incredibly draining to work the way I work."

You can count on one hand how many stand-up comedians have earned Academy Awards, right? Whoopi and Robin. But Red Buttons is also a member of that talented elite.

"I think my acting and my personality play a big part in my stand-up. I have a kind of intimacy with the audience, too. I guess that comes from my long career, and also from the mixture in my career. I'm just not a stand-up comedian, I'm an actor, too. Not too many stand-up comedians can boast to that. I've had kind of a catholic career, and I don't mean in the ecclesiastical sense.

"The early years, you're scrounging around trying to find a style and see what your rhythm is, and it's just work, work, work, work, work. It's repetition. This is also a business where tenacity plays a tremendous role. Your style is your delivery, and your delivery is divorced from what you're saying. You can say anything, one thing has nothing to do with the other. When you first start, you're groping, you're searching, 'What am I?' Even if you're not saying it to yourself, it's there. Your personality is in limbo, especially in comedy, which is the toughest game of all, and it takes a little living to find out about yourself and the world, and be able to disseminate that information to an audience.

"The romance of being in stand-up is that there's always a little bit of a surprise, something that works better in one place than in another. You can go to a nightclub, let's say on 52nd Street in the old days, and kill 'em, kill 'em in this place. But then you can go right across the street to some other place and die. It has to do with the clientele. I think the audience reads you, it's a boxing match. It's like you're shadow boxing, you're in a gym, you're throwing out a couple of jabs, you're ducking, you're playing around, but after a while the experience takes over and you're able to tell where your audience is, intellectually.

"You never perfect anything in our business. Charlie Chaplin once said, 'We're all amateurs. We don't live long enough to become professionals,' and that's Chaplin, so believe me, that's the gospel! I don't believe anybody's ever perfected anything in our business. After awhile, you start to work into your rhythm. You know what plays for you, how to deliver, what to think about, what your approach should be. When you're first starting out and you're looking for a style, you take on a little bit of who you admire. Like, I loved Joe E. Lewis in a nightclub … Jimmy Durante. Little by little, you're a little piece of this, a little piece of that, and you make it your own and you change it so it's not recognizable. Then you find out what's working for you and you play into that.

"You take things, you pick and choose, like I do in my 'Never Got a Dinner' routine or 'I Was There' or 'The Things That I've Done.' I also did monologues in my act when I first started, a lot of acting things like, 'The Blind Fighter,' 'The Autograph Book,' 'The German Submarine Commander.' I didn't start out doing one-line jokes, but as time went on, I became more sure of myself and wanted to do some social commentary, so I started doing the jokes."

Don't ask Joy Behar what her persona is. "I don't know. You'd have to tell me. All I am is myself on stage.

I don't think that there is a big discrepancy between the way I am on stage and the way I am in real life." While Joy is chatting with the audience much as she would at a party, she doesn't necessarily let others get a word in. "I used to talk more *with* them, now I just have things I want to say *to* them. I have much more material and I don't have to schmooze them as much. I think comedians learn to do that when their material is dying. I discovered that when my material wasn't working, I'd say, 'Where are you from?' Suddenly a door opened, and they'd say something like, 'I'm from Jersey.' 'Oh, really? What exit?' These are the standard lines. The audience laughs, just because you come back with something, and if you have a real patsy in the audience, then you have a great set and you get paid. So that's how schmoozing starts, through necessity.

"I must have had confidence that I didn't even know I had. Kaye Ballard once asked me, 'Do you know how funny you are?' and I said, 'Not really.' She said, 'Well, you better know it,' and that was very good advice, because if you don't know it yourself, the business will beat you up. I think that the people who are good at schmoozing audiences have the talent, they just don't know it. It's not something you can develop—if you can't do it when the gun is to your head, you'll never be able to do it. Never. The way that I used to get myself to perform, because I was so anxious, is that I'd call up the Improv or wherever and I'd book myself some spots and then I had to show up. I've never missed a job on purpose, and I would never say I'm gonna be there at nine o'clock and then not show up. So the diarrhea would begin and then the vomiting, but I would be there anyway."

Today, Behar is comfortable with her audiences, so she keeps them fully abreast of where she's at. "There are a couple of rules that I have, and one of them is to tell the truth at all times. If I'm bloated or retaining water that day, I'll tell them. If I'm annoyed with something, I keep the spin going but I think it's important to say where I'm at."

What is David Alan Grier's gimmick? "It's just me. It's a heightened version because I'm performing, but all of the stuff is based on truth. Did it actually, actually happen just as I said it? Maybe not. Someone said that their father took a Learning Annex class with Spalding Gray on how to do a one-man show. Rule number one was to exaggerate, which is what comedy is. You take your life and you exaggerate. You don't honestly say exactly what happened verbatim, but it's source material.

"Being an actor, I would just write these long bits, like monologue kind of character things, and I never was myself. I never just sat there and talked about myself. It was, 'Imagine, if you will, dwarfs on Mars!' and then I would be off and running on, like, these five or ten-minute pieces. So finding my own voice, just like talking about my life and all that, took a lot of time. But I finally got around to it, and that's when my performances started working much better."

In spite of having worked on his craft for several decades, David Brenner finds his voice in the here and now. "I work from current events. If you want to know what my act is, go back about four, six weeks, pick up every copy of *USA Today,* the *New York Times*, and the *Chicago Tribune,* and the *Washington Post*. Read everything in the papers and then put a punch line at the end of it and that's my act.

"When I started, a lot of TV and nightclub people would come to see me at the Improv or Pips and they'd say, 'I don't get it. He's not telling jokes.' And friends of mine would say, 'Listen to the audience, they're screaming.' And the guy would say, 'Yeah, but I don't get it, it's not a joke.' I'm not talking about mothers-in-law. Some reporter, I think it was in the *New York Times*, wrote a review of me that said, 'He does observational material,' and that's what coined it. Since then, thousands of guys do what I do. I no longer do it that way because—especially to the younger people—I look like I'm doing someone else, when actually, I'm the one who started it and they're doing me!

"Richard Lewis had a great line, it sounds insulting

and maybe it is, but he said to me, 'You know what? You have a monopoly on the mundane.'" Brenner's observational bits tend to leave everyone saying, "My God, he just hit the nail on the head," lines which, over time, became standard for many comics. "Well, that's how I used to work. One night, I had the TV on to keep me company and Ray Romano's show came on. The plot had something to do with Ray buying his wife a diamond ring and then she couldn't find it, and someone said, 'Did you ever notice that when you can't find something, you always say it's gonna be in the last place you look?' They did—verbatim—all my lines about that.

"Now I do current events and I'm edgier and much more topical. So, instead of doing a joke about sitting on a newspaper on a subway and a guy saying, 'Are you reading that paper?' which really happened to me; instead of that (to which I replied, 'Yeah,' stood up, turned the page and sat down again), instead of that kind of line, I'm talking about Afghanistan, I'm talking about security in the airports, I'm talking about whatever is in the paper today. I go through the papers, cut things out, put 'em on cards, get up on the stage, flip the cards, and hope something funny comes out. If it doesn't trigger right away, then I go to the next card."

Because Brenner doesn't have a prepared act, per se, the jokes he makes on stage are often as new to him as they are to the audience in front of him. "It's like a subconscious thing, so that's why sometimes I crack up when I say something because it's as if somebody else said it."

Do you know this guy? He says that you do. "I think I'm the guy that everybody knows." Well, just in case, it's Jeff Foxworthy. "People are never nervous about coming up to me. People come up to me in the grocery store and it's never, 'Excuse me, Mr. Foxworthy,' it's, 'Hey, Jeff! Lemme tell you what my mother did last weekend.' I think I'm like a guy everybody works with or something. I remember early on, back when I first started doing stand-up, Steven Wright had just done *The Tonight Show* a couple of times and I thought, 'Boy, that's a neat style.

Should I be like that? Or should I be off-the-wall or should I be sarcastic?'

"Rob Bartlett is a comic from New York, a terrific comic, and I was lucky enough to work with him early on. Rob said to me, 'You know what? You just go up and do it every night of your life and your persona will develop and you won't even know it.' I guess it does, because now, if I listen to myself doing stand-up, I find sometimes that I accentuate words in a different place than you would normally do, and my voice kinda goes up and down and I'm like, 'Oh I guess that's my style. I didn't even know I had a style but I guess that's it.'

"Every time I do an interview people say, 'Do you just hate the redneck stuff?' Well, no. I was really stubborn early on when I first started getting out of the south. I would come up and work at Catch a Rising Star or Carolines or something, and the advice I always got in New York was, 'You know, Jeff, you need to take some voice lessons and lose that stupid accent.' I've always loved the south and at least a quarter of the country talks like this. Why do I have to lose my accent? So I was stubborn about it, and I always wore blue jeans and boots and it was good natured but I always heard, 'Oh Jeff, you're nothing but an 'ol redneck from Georgia.'

"One particular week, I was working at a comedy club right outside Detroit and they were kidding me after the show about being a redneck, and this club was attached to a bowling alley that had valet parking. I'm like, 'Okay guys, I know what I am but if you think you don't have rednecks, look out the window, people are valet parking at the bowling alley.' I remember walking back to the hotel that night thinking it was just going to be a bit, it was just a premise. Initially I said, 'A lot of people think everybody from the south is a redneck but I've been all over the country and there's rednecks everywhere, here's how you can tell.' I'm amazed by the longevity of this thing. I mean, I did my first redneck book in '89 ... I started to do calendars, the page-a-day calendars, and they are like the second highest selling calendars behind Far Side and Dilbert. Every year I think,

'God almighty there can't be three-hundred-and-sixty-five more of these.' But there are, I just keep a yellow pad on my desk and I stop and write a few down everyday, and at the end of the year I start adding them up and there are five hundred new ones.

"Part of the appeal is that they're one-liners in an age when nobody does one-liners. Nothing else I do is one-liners. But all people have to remember is a sentence and they get a laugh. It didn't dawn on me until a couple of years ago, it was like, 'Well, God, they're easy to remember, they're easy to tell, you can tell them and get a laugh.' For most people who aren't comics, that's the biggest problem—the jokes are too long. I can remember early on in stand-up, watching Leno one night. When he was in the clubs, Leno was just awesome. He would get into that last ten minutes and it was just rapid fire. I can remember him holding court at the waffle house after a show and just talking about the structure of jokes, saying, 'If you have a joke that goes dut dut dut dut dut dud boom! You gotta find a way to make it go bat a batta ba boom batta ba boom batta ba boom!' And learn to cut that fat and just get to the point. That's probably the biggest mistake people make when trying to tell a joke: they give you too much information.

"When you're first starting out, the fear is that if you try something new and it doesn't work, will you be able to salvage your set or is it all going down the toilet? I've reached the point now that I know, hey, if I try something new and it doesn't go over, I can save it, I can ride the ship and take it on into the harbor. I think there's something in the mentality of everybody who does comedy, that we kind of get off on that fear. You know, knowing how to fix it if it breaks.

"It dawned on me not long ago, I've been doing this eighteen years. And I was thinking, 'God, I remember when I was hoping I could do it for five. Please God, just let me do this for five years before I have to go back to work again.' I think we probably all have that fear, especially when you find something you love to do. I don't think many people really think when they begin a creative career that they're gonna be a star. I think they're just doing it 'cause they get off on doing it, whether it's singing or acting or stand-up, but I don't think they really think, 'Oh, I'm gonna be a huge star at this.'"

"I've always thought, I don't have a kind of character per se, like Roseanne did, or Judy Tenuta, or Emo Phillips, or people like that," says Carol Leifer. "I've always done kind of observational humor, personal, just talking about what makes me laugh. That's how I write my material, I just sit down and think about things that I find funny. I've always been complimented by comedians, mostly male, who have said, 'So much of your material, it's not female-based, it could be done by a man or a woman. So that's pretty much how I describe it.

"I've always felt that being a woman comedian has been an incredible advantage, especially back in the '80s when I was doing stand-up full time. Certainly women comedians were in shorter supply so it felt like we were in more demand for things. I got many more gigs, even if it was sexist, because someone was putting together a show, 'We want a guy, we want a black guy, we want a white guy, we want a woman, a singer,' so I always felt it was definitely an advantage. Maybe for women who are starting out now it's tougher, but then it was definitely a plus.

"My act is pretty clean. There's not many jokes in it that I couldn't do on TV. If anything they're a little racy, but I really don't subscribe to being dirty in my act, and that's something that I really learned from guys like Jay Leno and Jerry Seinfeld. It's easy to make a joke work if you add the word fuck in it or curse a lot, but if you sense that a group is a little older or more uptight, there are certain jokes that you kind of shy away from. So much of the stuff is dictated by attitude, your attitude on stage. I forgot who it was, I think maybe Richard Belzer, who said, 'When you do stand-up, you're kinda like the pilot of the plane. People in the audience sense if you're not confident, and then they lose confidence."

What's David Mishevitz got to say about his budding persona? "I don't have a gimmick. I do some social satire stuff and a lot of funny family character stuff, and I try to relate it in some way to the bigger picture or down to the smaller picture. I'm not the guy who just goes up and does, like, fifteen minutes about my family: here's my sitcom, here's my life. I just talk about little particular things that sort of happen to everybody."

Of course, Mishevitz is one of thousands of funny guys trying to earn a living doing comedy. He knows his personal style has got to stand out among the many. "I see a lot of people doing premises like road rage or things that piss them off. Most guys will be the victim, get angry, but in my act, I have this road rage where somebody cuts me off but *I* cheer for *them*. Try and take the other way out. I find the humor in taking the downbeat path.

"Folks come up to me and say, 'That's really cool,' especially when I don't have a really good set. I'll have one person come up and say, 'Hey, I really dug that.' Alright, then I try to figure out why. Why wasn't there more of *him* around? For a few months, I just tried working the audience, commenting on what they were doing and what they were wearing, and who they were with. I asked them what their jobs were, blah, blah, blah, and I started noticing that there were a lot of similarities in every show. So now I try to just go up and observe everybody. I give them some back story that they didn't think about to try to let them know that I recognize them in some way. Then I try to take them along wherever I want to go. In some respects, it's more fun. There've been a couple times where I hit a useless dead end, but I just keep beating it and beating it and even making fun of the situation. I kept trying to show them that there's still somebody in front of them who realizes what's going on."

"I only get laughs when I talk about myself," says Dick Capri. "When I talk about my problems, when I talk about my marriage, my discord, my bad eyes, my lack of hair. I have to talk about me. I cannot get a laugh talking about political stuff. I'll talk about my ex-wife, so I write down ex-wife jokes—she did this, she did that. I put them together into a story.

"The easiest thing for me to do is tell jokes. Doing a monologue, a whole routine with a point of view, that's

DICK CAPRI

Dick Capri has brought his stand-up comedy act to every major entertainment venue on two continents, including night-clubs, resorts, arenas, and theaters. He has worked with such singing sensations as Frank Sinatra, Liza Minnelli, Tom Jones, and Engelbert Humper-dinck. Dick starred on Broadway in the hit show, *Catskills On Broadway*, which played to sold-out audiences during its entire run. He has also made appearances on Comedy Central, including the highly rated *New York Friars Club Roast of Drew Carey*.

Ladies and Gentlemen, if you have never seen my kind of nonsense I'd like to tell you the type of comedy that I do. First of all, I don't use any four-letter words, and I don't do any obscene material, and I do not do the type of material that's accepted by many of the young people of today. I also do not have a booking in the immediate future, ladies and gentlemen.

My mother always wanted me to marry an Italian and when I did get married, I married a girl who was part American Indian, she had some Indian blood in her. When I called my mother I had to lie, 'cause if I tell my mother I'm not gonna marry an Italian, my mother goes right to church and squeals on me to the statues. So I call my mother, I'm all excited, I say, "Ma, I'm getting married." She says, "Are you marrying an Italian?" I say, "Ma, she's half Italian and half Indian. She's an Italian Indian." I figured she'd go for that. My mother says, "What's an Italian Indian?" I told her she was a Sioux-cilian. And she'd heard of them.

They have tempers you wouldn't believe. Fortunately, when my wife was gonna get angry she'd put her makeup on differently.

Three white lines over here and a blue one over here. I met her on the street with her new husband and I had to be polite, so I figured I'd call her by her Indian name, I figured she'd like that. I said, "Hello, Big Bottom." She said, "Hello, Little Bird." I didn't like that. I forgot about it.

My grandfather loved espresso. He drank ten, twenty cups of espresso every day of his life and that's strong stuff with all that caffeine. In fact, when he died, at the funeral, he could still mingle with the crowd. And you talk about spousal abuse, my grandfather was a battered husband. He did all the cooking and one day he got upset and he said to my grandmother, "I'm not gonna cook for you anymore." She said, "You don't cook for me, you're not gonna see me for three days." So he didn't cook for her and he didn't see her for three days but after the fourth day, when the swelling went down, he could see her a little bit out of this eye over here.

It's a family story. I don't tell that story when my family is in the audience. They think I'm a singer. I'm the only Italian that can't sing. I once sang "Mona Lisa" and the price of the painting came down. We can't help it, we hear music we sing. Spanish people hear music, they dance. Jewish people hear music, they say, "It's so loud here. Hear how loud this is?" I like the complaining. I like people to know what they want. Like this table of Jewish women in a restaurant and the maitre d' comes over and says, "Is anything alright?"

My family is a very interesting family. Recently, I sent to a genealogy research company and they looked up my family tree. Now, a lot of these genealogy companies, you know what they do today they put your name in a computer and out comes sort of a semi-history of your family. But how do you know if they're telling you the truth? This happened to be a very reputable company. It says the Capri family goes back to biblical times. It says I had an ancestor who actually attended the Last Supper. But you can't see him in the picture because he wasn't sitting at the head table. He was at table four, and he won the centerpiece. I also had an uncle important in the Renaissance. It says he worked with Michelangelo. While Michelangelo was up there doing the ceiling, my uncle was doing the closets and the baseboards.

the toughest thing for me to do. But just to tell you a joke, 'Did you hear the one about ... ' That works best for me. I can tell a great joke. I enjoy telling jokes. There's no point of view, you don't have to set it up. When I'm talking about my life, I have to set it up, it needs a prologue, but if I'm just telling a joke about two guys walking into a bar, that's easy.

"It makes the audience feel better when they know you're a loser. They love to laugh at a loser. That's why Rodney Dangerfield is such a big hit. He's a loser, he doesn't threaten anybody."

Talking about himself wasn't easy that first time Capri tried to drop his usual parade of jokes. "I sat with a friend of mine who wrote some material and he said, 'Show them you got balls, go out and open with it.' So I opened with the new stuff and I went right into the shithouse. It was death. In order to save myself, I had to go into the impressions, ' ... and so ladies and gentleman, Ed Sullivan.' I had no point of view, I didn't know how to talk and be funny. I was a performance comedian. Trying to just be myself, be funny out of a situation, was very difficult. The audience was just staring, waiting. 'Where is the funny?'

"I learned the formula. They said, 'If you want to make it in show business, you have to be yourself.' I kept trying to learn to be funny. I learned to be funny. It was always there, but I didn't know how to show it, how to do it. I just went out there and kept doing it and doing it and doing it." Capri's new style meant opening up to the audience. "If you look at them individually, you will never walk out on stage. Look at them individually and you think, ohmigod, how am I going to make this putz laugh? Like, in Atlantic City, you see the line going into the theater and you say, 'How am I gonna make this guy laugh, with the white belt and the suspenders and the socks with sandals? How am I gonna make him laugh?' In a group they're fine. I love an audience—I love an audience but I hate them individually."

Ryan Stiles took some time finding his comedy self. "I went through the whole thing—as a lot of comics do— about who I want to be like. Should I be like Rodney or should I be like so and so ... ? I think you really start to get it together when you figure out that maybe you should do it like *you*. There's a reason you're up there in the first place. I thought I should be like George Carlin or like Cosby, either speaking slowly or really hyperactive—and then I just started doing myself. Then, the material came a lot easier 'cause I was writing for myself rather than someone I thought I should be. The material comes out easier when you're writing for yourself.

"Unless you're up there just telling jokes, I think it's observational. I was a typical comic who told jokes, one joke would maybe have a prop, then I'd do a song thing. I'd kind of mix it up. I was never very political, I just did whatever struck me as funny."

Ask Stiles for a favorite moment and you'll get this: "I think probably when I did *The Tonight Show*. That's the only time when I stood backstage and my fingers got tingly and I was short of breath and I felt like I was gonna vomit." That was a *good* moment, he claims. But he was getting to a point about persona and style. "It actually happened on a night when Leno was guest hosting for Carson. At that time everyone aimed to be on *The Tonight Show*. Then, when they booked you, you started doubting yourself, 'Geez, am I funny enough to do this?' I never really had confidence. When I was a stand-up I was acting as well and I never really had the confidence in myself as an actor. I would go out thinking, 'Gee, I don't think I can do this,' and then I'd try to convince other people I could. But when I started doing improvisation with the Second City troupe in Chicago, I really gained confidence in myself and started to do what I wanted to do rather than what I thought they wanted to see."

Stiles made the shift from traditional stand-up to improv with ease. "I didn't like the whole planning thing about comedy. I just prefer to go in and not think about it, just do it and then forget about it. I think comedy is something different for everybody. I do it as kind of a release now. I do Drew [*The Drew Carey Show*] everyday, so for me it's just more of a release than a mechanical, planned-out type of thing.

143

"I had an audition for—it might have been *Mad TV*—years ago, and I went and they said, 'Okay, we'd like you to do some characters.' I said, 'Well I don't really have any characters,' and they said, 'You do Second City don't you?' I said, 'Yeah, but I can't just do the Salty Sea Captain character that I do all the time, you know? I mean, you do a show and you forget all about it and you get rid of whatever you did and then you do another show. So I never really had a bag full of tricks and stuff. I think that the Groundlings troupe in Canada kind of teaches it differently. The people who come out of Groundlings are like Pee-Wee Herman and Elvira. They aim for their two or three characters—but I never really did that. I never had my main characters that I did all the time.

"I enjoy improv. We do it at the Improv every Thursday as a release. We don't get paid for anything. We just go down as a group, and it's the only time of the week that I actually get to do everything I want to do. When I go to my summer house up north, I don't do films or anything. My wife kicks me out of the house at least once a week to go up to Vancouver and do improv, 'cause I get a little edgy if I don't do it. But I love it. I live for it."

Anthony Clark's hometown charm endears him to audiences. "I'm from Gladys, Virginia. You ever heard of it? Well, let me tell you, if you have one year left to live, live there, because every day seems like a fucking eternity. So I grew up in the south and I was raised basically in a trailer park for most of my teen years. I didn't even realize we were poor until I went to college and I was like, 'Oh, my God, people are rich everywhere.'

"Coming out of Boston everybody was so hard edged. I think, at the time, I had quite the southern accent, so I was this innocent country kid looking at the city. There was always a uniqueness to it and an element of surprise. Someone described me as being able to get away with talking about anything because I had such a charming manner, but sometimes the punch lines are devastatingly black. That's the best comedy, the unex-

144

pected, where the audience sees the left hand coming, they see the joke, and then they get the right hand in the back of the head and they had no idea where that punch line came from. Sometimes, the weirder the better, if it makes no sense it's the funniest.

"I find humor in everything. I'm very observational when I'm at the mall or something like that. Maybe as the college kid smoking a little marijuana, all your friends around, somebody says something hysterical, then all of you start riffing on it, then all of a sudden you have five minutes on chicken. It's just that weird. Sometimes you read the napkins in your pocket the next morning and you think, 'I don't think that's gonna work, I'm not gonna open with that.'

"When a comic is nervous the audience gets nervous, they can feel it. But if you go up there really warm, like, I've done this a million times and welcome to my living room, nothing is gonna upset me, I think they feel that, too. I also think that every great comic has a uniqueness that is one hundred percent his own. I think if you were to look at my act on a piece of paper you would think, 'This will never work. This is really stupid stuff.' But it can never be stolen because I'm the one who makes it funny. I'm the key that starts the Mercedes Benz, and without it you have a Kia or the Aspire. Don't they have a car now called Aspire? It's Aspiring to be a Mercedes.

"I've been very fortunate that no matter where I've performed, from Seattle to San Francisco to Denver to Chicago to Atlanta to Austin, my act seems to be universal. It's killed in England, it's killed in Ireland, and I just think I'm goofy. I just think I walk out there and they hear my voice and I say something incredibly retarded and they go, 'Oh God.'" At least Anthony's audiences don't need to schlep to Gladys, Virginia to experience a funny country bumpkin. And I mean that in an endearing way, I swear!

Freddie Roman got his act together—eventually. "When I started, I tried different ways. For example, Woody Allen would do fantasies or routines based upon things that were not true. I'm the opposite, my humor is based on things that are true, on news, on my family. My daughter is thirty-five now, I started talking about her when she was two and I did a routine about taking her to a restaurant and going to the men's room with her. Now that she's thirty five, I talk about her being the mother of three children, and my humor comes from that.

"My humor depends on coming up with things an audience identifies with. I came about it through trial and error. I would do an occasional story, but I found that the strength of my performance came from material that was basically about my life. Sometimes a circumstance lends itself to improvising. The mike goes off, the lighting, it's too warm in the place, and that forces you to improvise, which I enjoy by the way."

Like Ryan Stiles with his improv, Jerry Stiller, working with wife and partner Anne Meara, experiences a slightly different view of the stand-up genre. "I don't know if Stiller and Meara ever had a style. Style is something that kind of evolves when you find yourself comfortable enough in front of an audience to talk to them in an honest way. It comes also from having worked in clubs for years. It took courage to connect with people we never met and get them to laugh by revealing things that were happening in our lives, sharing those with the audience. Once we got past the fear of doing that, they were on our side. Then we went into a couple of sketches and they saw what we could do in those tight five minute pieces. We got the laughs and then we could talk about whatever came into our heads.

"We used to watch the great singer Helen O'Connell when we opened for her in Chicago. Helen was a master. She would not only sing those songs, 'Amapola' and 'Tangerine,' she started talking to the guys out there. They were all stockbrokers who had had a tough day and she just chatted, charmed them, then segued into a number. You learn from people like that. You started to pick up the way they schmooze and you see how people like it. They seemed to say, 'Hey, we don't need 'a funny thing happened to me on the way to the theater tonight.'

There was a whole new level of intimacy possible in small clubs. As long as we could sustain the appearance of truthfulness, we did okay."

Stiller's persona sometimes met with resistance by audience members. "Sometimes intimacy could backfire. One night we were doing a Hershey Horowitz and Mary Elizabeth Doyle sketch, the Jewish boy and the Irish girl who meet through a computer. It was a tiny club, The Downstairs at the Upstairs, and as we were going through it I heard the words, 'Jew, Jew.' I said, 'Wait a minute, am I actually hearing this?' It was a guy, drunk at the first table. We went on with the sketch, which lasted for six minutes and he kept repeating, 'Jew, Jew,' sotto voce, under his breath, but nobody in the audience seemed to have picked up on it. I said to myself, 'Do I interrupt the sketch and deal with this guy?' We finished and went downstairs to the dressing room. I was in a weird state. Finally, I said, 'Anne, did you hear that guy? He kept saying "Jew, Jew." She said, 'Yeah, I heard it.' I said, 'I didn't know what the hell to do. What could I have said?' 'You should've said, 'Where? Where?' Of course, that was a line Godfrey Cambridge once used in his act.

"Doing stand-up, you never know what to expect. If you want to live a life of excitement, never be bored, try comedy. My advisor in high school said, 'You don't want to be a comedian, become a school teacher.' I said, 'I want to do this kind of work,' which led up to meeting Anne, performing together, staying married, and raising Ben and Amy. It's funny, where the trail has taken me."

Pat Cooper blazed a different sort of trail. "See, I'm a gambler, I play Russian roulette with comedy. I've done it and I keep doing it. It gets my rocks off. It's better than sex sometimes for me to do comedy. But I'm an observer. That's the secret, observe. You see a curtain, a picture, a carpet, a phone, you see something and you talk about it. My type of comedy is off the cuff, it's challenging. I don't know if you know this or not, but I challenged any comic in the country to take me on when I was on [Howard] Stern. I didn't do it once, I did it twenty times. He told me Sam Kinnison was the best. He said, 'I love Sam

JERRY STILLER

Jerry Stiller, along with his wife and comedy partner, Anne Meara, has played theaters and nightclubs around the country, filled with audiences clamoring for Stiller and Meara's unique cerebral-style humor. Jerry appears on the CBS sitcom *King of Queens,* and television audiences are still talking about his stint as the manic Frank Costanza on *Seinfeld.* On Broadway, Jerry has appeared in such plays as *Hurlyburly, The Ritz, Passione, Three Men on a Horse, The Three Sisters*, and *After-Play* written by Anne. His film appearances have included *The Taking of Pelham One-Two-Three, Airport '75,* and *Hairspray* to name a few. Jerry and Anne have written, performed, and produced award-winning radio commercials for Blue Nun Wine, United Van Lines and Amalgamated Bank. He recently penned his autobiography, *Married to Laughter, A Love Story Featuring Anne Meara.*

HERSHEY: I love you, Mary Elizabeth Doyle.

MARY ELIZABETH: I love you Hershey Horowitz.

HERSHEY: Will you marry me?

MARY ELIZABETH: Yeah, I will. I will.

HERSHEY: No, no. It'll never work.

MARY ELIZABETH: What do you mean it will never work?

HERSHEY: It's impossible.

MARY ELIZABETH: Of course it will work.

HERSHEY: My father's a Jewish bagel maker. Your father's an Irish cop.

MARY ELIZABETH: What difference ...

HERSHEY: What do you mean, what difference? It's like hot pastrami on white bread.

Mary Elizabeth: Oh come on, it doesn't matter.

Hershey: What do you mean it doesn't matter?

Mary Elizabeth: We love each other.

Hershey: Love, schmove. It's a world of hate.

Mary Elizabeth: Look Hershey, it'll work out. The families will go crazy for each other.

Hershey: They'll go crazy. That's what they'll do.

Mary Elizabeth: Oh come on. I'll grab your mother. I'll hug her and kiss her. I'll say, Mrs. Horowitz, you're terrific. I hear you make the best mashuganah ball soup in the world.

Hershey: It's matzo ball soup, yeah. That's it. That's it. You tell her that.

Mary Elizabeth: I'll say, gee, do you know where we're going. We're going to Israel on our honeymoon. We're going to live on a knish for a couple of weeks.

Hershey: A kibbutz. Kibbutz!

Mary Elizabeth: Then I'll go to your father, and I'll say, Mr. Horowitz, look at it this way. You're not losing a son, you're gaining a shiksa.

Hershey: No, no, no. I'll go to your father. I'll wear a green tie. I'll say 'top of the Irish to you sir.'

Mary Elizabeth: It's 'top of the morning.'

Hershey: Top of the morning, to you sir! Sure, it's a great day for the Jewish ...

Mary Elizabeth: No, Irish.

Hershey: ...the Irish, when a fellow like you can get a fellow like me for a son-in-law. H-O-R-O-W ...

Mary Elizabeth: Beautiful, beautiful.

Hershey: ...I-T-Z spells HOROWITZ.

Mary Elizabeth: He'll love it, Hershey.

Hershey: And I'm gonna tell him, 'we're gonna go to Ireland on our honeymoon. To kiss the Kelly stone.'

Mary Elizabeth: No, Blarney Stone. What difference.

Hershey: Whatever I have to kiss, I'll kiss. I have a surprise for you.

Mary Elizabeth: A surprise for me?

HERSHEY: Take out your hand. Close your eyes. When I say three, tell me what you see.

MARY ELIZABETH: Alright.

HERSHEY: One, two, three. Do you like it?

MARY ELIZABETH: What is it?

HERSHEY: It's a bagel.

MARY ELIZABETH: A bagel?

HERSHEY: Yeah, I mean, I figured until the best thing comes along ...

MARY ELIZABETH: It's beautiful.

HERSHEY: I'm so glad you like it.

MARY ELIZABETH: It's my first bagel.

HERSHEY: Oh golly. Let's run away together. Get married right now.

MARY ELIZABETH: Honey, there's no ...

HERSHEY: Let's not waste any more time.

MARY ELIZABETH: We don't have to rush. We have the whole summer to plan.

HERSHEY: Alright.

MARY ELIZABETH: Let's get married in the fall.

HERSHEY: You got it, pick the day!

MARY ELIZABETH: October.

HERSHEY: October, great!

MARY ELIZABETH: October the 4th!

HERSHEY: Rosh Hashanah.

MARY ELIZABETH: Russia-who?

HERSHEY: Rosh Hashanah. That's the Jewish New Year. 5729. It's a High Holy Day.

MARY ELIZABETH: Ah, Happy New Year.

HERSHEY: Yeah ... It's impossible on that day.

MARY ELIZABETH: Alright. Sorry, I didn't know. How about the following week?

HERSHEY: Beautiful!

MARY ELIZABETH: October 12th?

HERSHEY: Yom Kippur.

MARY ELIZABETH: What?

HERSHEY: That's the night before the Day of Atonement.

MARY ELIZABETH: That's no good. Even I know that.

HERSHEY: Look, look. It doesn't have to be that long. Let's do it in August.

MARY ELIZABETH: Yeah August!

HERSHEY: August 15!

MARY ELIZABETH: Oh, August. That's the Feast of the Assumption.

HERSHEY: The what?

MARY ELIZABETH: The Assumption. Besides, it's my uncle's anniversary.

HERSHEY: Oh really?

MARY ELIZABETH: Yeah, he's ordained twenty-five years, a Benedictine Monk.

HERSHEY: Well ... congratulations. Look it doesn't have to be in August. What about November? November the first?

MARY ELIZABETH: Oh, that's All Saint's Day.

HERSHEY: All Saint's Day?

MARY ELIZABETH: Yeah ...

HERSHEY: Well, what's that?

MARY ELIZABETH: You know, I mean it's a special day, my mother has a special devotion ...

HERSHEY: Oh, I didn't know that. It's like All Souls Day, right?

MARY ELIZABETH: No, that's different.

HERSHEY: What's that?

MARY ELIZABETH: Halloween.

HERSHEY: Oh. Oh, right. It's not important ... What about the springtime? March?

MARY ELIZABETH: Mar ... Oh, March is no good. You're running right into Lent, Ash Wednesday, Easter. How about April or May?

HERSHEY: May is no good.

MARY ELIZABETH: Why?

HERSHEY: Now you got Pesach Purim and Shi Lewis.

MARY ELIZABETH: Honey, it doesn't matter.

HERSHEY: Nah, it doesn't matter. The important thing is that we love each other, right?

MARY ELIZABETH: Flag Day. Arbor Day. What's the difference.

HERSHEY: The important thing is that we love each other.

MARY ELIZABETH: And that we are gonna be married.

HERSHEY: Right.

MARY ELIZABETH: And Hershey?

HERSHEY: What?

MARY ELIZABETH: One day we'll have a baby.

HERSHEY: Yeah.

MARY ELIZABETH: Yeah, a little boy.

HERSHEY: That's right.

MARY ELIZABETH: And do you know what we're gonna call him?

HERSHEY: What?

MARY ELIZABETH: Benjamin.

HERSHEY: Benjamin?

MARY ELIZABETH: Yeah, isn't that beautiful?

HERSHEY: I was thinking of Sean.

MARY ELIZABETH: Ah, sweetheart.

HERSHEY: Sean Horowitz. After my great, great grandfather.

MARY ELIZABETH: Yeah?

HERSHEY: Shlyma.

MARY ELIZABETH: That's beautiful.

HERSHEY: I think so.

MARY ELIZABETH: We'll call him, Sean Benjamin.

HERSHEY: Sean Benjamin! Wonderful!

MARY ELIZABETH: Oh, I can see him playing on a floor next to his little sister, Esther.

HERSHEY: Esther? That's beautiful.

MARY ELIZABETH: Yeah, Esther Bridget.

HERSHEY: Esther Bridget?

MARY ELIZABETH: Yeah, and before long, there'll be little Timothy. Timothy Tevia.

HERSHEY: Timothy Tevia? Isn't that sweet ...

MARY ELIZABETH: And Danny. Danny Dovedol.

HERSHEY: That's nice too.

MARY ELIZABETH: Yeah. Michael Moishe.

HERSHEY: Yeah, alright ...

MARY ELIZABETH: Aloysius Matel.

HERSHEY: Sweetheart, this is ...

MARY ELIZABETH: Xavier Itraq.

HERSHEY: Sweetheart, this is a three room flat.

MARY ELIZABETH: Honey, what difference.

HERSHEY: I mean ...

MARY ELIZABETH: Shirley Chivoun.

HERSHEY: See, at first I thought we'd be a little conservative.

MARY ELIZABETH: Yeah?

HERSHEY: Maybe a dog.

MARY ELIZABETH: Honey. Whatever.

HERSHEY: Yes, yes. Alright.

MARY ELIZABETH: The important thing is the wedding.

HERSHEY: The wedding! That's the important thing!

MARY ELIZABETH: I want a big wedding.

HERSHEY: I want it to be the biggest wedding that ever hit East 42nd Street.

MARY ELIZABETH: And I want all your relatives ...

HERSHEY: And I want all your friends and relatives ...

MARY ELIZABETH: Music ...

HERSHEY: I know just who I want.

MARY ELIZABETH: Who?

HERSHEY: Lenny Hershkowitz and the orchestra.

MARY ELIZABETH: Who is that? I never heard of them.

HERSHEY: He plays great Kisotskis, Russian Chairs, Freylechs ...

MARY ELIZABETH: What's that?

HERSHEY: What's what?

MARY ELIZABETH: The one with the echs?

HERSHEY: You mean Freylechs?

MARY ELIZABETH: Yeah, what is that?

HERSHEY: You know, Freylech, (singing) die, die, die, die, die, die ...

MARY ELIZABETH: It's very catchy. Honey, I was hoping we could get my cousin to play for us.

HERSHEY: Your cousin?

MARY ELIZABETH: Yeah, Tommy Tooey and his Donegal Five. They are great!

HERSHEY: Tommy Tooey?

MARY ELIZABETH: Oh, they're terrific.

HERSHEY: Do they play the Katasky?

MARY ELIZABETH: Well, they play the Knights of Columbus.

HERSHEY: All right, great, great. Hey wait a minute, we'll have alternating orchestras.

MARY ELIZABETH: Great!

HERSHEY: And in between we'll have Peppy Melito and the Rumbas.

MARY ELIZABETH: Great, then we don't offend nobody.

HERSHEY: Right, beautiful, beautiful.

MARY ELIZABETH: Food, food, it's very important.

HERSHEY: Hey, listen, I got a great idea. I know just who I want. Joel Nussbaum, a friend of mine. He works at Moscowitz and Luperitz, a caterer on Second Ave. He can get us 2,000 cold cuts for $85.

MARY ELIZABETH: Cold cuts?

HERSHEY: Cold cuts.

MARY ELIZABETH: Oh, honey, I don't think cold cuts are right for a wedding breakfast.

HERSHEY: For what?

MARY ELIZABETH: Well, for a wedding breakfast, cold cuts ...

HERSHEY: Well, I thought this thing would be held at night, I mean ...

MARY ELIZABETH: Oh that's silly, the ceremony's 11:30 in the morning by the time we leave the rectory it will be 12:30 ...

HERSHEY: By the time we leave the what?

MARY ELIZABETH: Well, the rectory, Oh honey, I forgot to tell you, we can't get married in the church because we're different faiths. But Father O'Grady will be happy to marry us in the rectory, isn't that great!

HERSHEY: Father O'Grady?

MARY ELIZABETH: Yeah, he's a great guy, he plays the piano, all the kids love him.

HERSHEY: Sweetheart, I thought Rabbi Finegold ...

MARY ELIZABETH: Bring him along!

HERSHEY: No, wait a minute, wait a minute ...

MARY ELIZABETH: No, I mean it, I want him sitting right there right in front.

HERSHEY: Look, I don't think you understand ...

MARY ELIZABETH: Look any rabbi of yours is a friend of mine.

HERSHEY: Look, wait a minute. No, I thought that Rabbi Finegold would perform the ceremony at the temple.

MARY ELIZABETH: Temple? But Hershey I can't get married in a temple.

HERSHEY: And I can't get married in the rectory.

MARY ELIZABETH: Yeah, but you see I thought that you ...

HERSHEY: I thought that you ...

MARY ELIZABETH: Yeah, but I love you ...

HERSHEY: Yeah, I love you.

MARY ELIZABETH: Well, I guess I better give you back your bagel.

HERSHEY: Look why don't you hold onto it. You never can tell. Maybe someday two people like us who want to get married, can just get married.

Kinnison. I think he's a genius.' I said, 'Well, I hope Sam
Kinnison marries your daughter. Oh, now he's not a
genius, I see. You like to hear about Sam Kinnison bang-
ing other girls. I'd like him to bang your daughter!' He
didn't know what to say. That's Pat Cooper. I got the balls
to fight you back.

"You're telling me that Sam Kinnison or Andrew
Dice Clay or Richard Pryor or any of them, could go to
Utah, where they don't know any of us and they don't
know shit about comedy. Send them to a Mormon festi-
val—no act. If you have a half-hour off the cuff, then
you'll see who's great. Go ahead. I'm on national radio,
'you're all bullshit artists.' Not one call. But you know
how many comics called and said, 'You know, Howard,
I'd bet on Cooper.' I may be full of shit, but they know
I've got the balls to do it. You have to prove that. A man
sings through his nose, he becomes a star. If you sing like
Perry Como today, you can't get a job. That's controversy.
When I went on Snyder's show, I told off everybody.

"I started out, I did thirty minutes, opened up for
Steve and Eydie or Tony Bennett. Then they started to
push me. They started to think that I wasn't a human
being and I said, 'Hey, wait a minute, I don't need this
aggravation. I'll always get a job, and if I never get a job,
I'll go back to brickwork. What is this, to be abused by
people? Who are these people?' And I said, 'I'll straighten
their asses out.' I don't do that in my act. I'll do it on a
Roast. I'll do it with you or on a radio show. If a guy says,
'Pat what's your opinion of ... ?' I'll say it."

"Everybody likes to see the other guy in an awk-
ward position," says Stewie Stone, "it makes them feel
better. It's like Alcoholics Anonymous, it works because
when you realize everybody's as screwed up as you are,
you're not the only one in life, it helps you get over it—
Over Its Anonymous. When you can see somebody in a
worse position in life than you are, it's funny. They're
slipping. There but for the grace of God, I'm slipping on
the peel.

"Then there's self-deprecating humor where you
poke fun at yourself, which I do a lot. I don't do jokes per

se, I talk about my life and basically find humor in the pain I'm living with at that moment. As a kid I grew up in Brooklyn. I wasn't the biggest kid on the block, so if I made the big kid on the block laugh he wasn't gonna beat me up. Or, they wanted me to hang around. So I found as a kid, and most comics find this, the macho people want to laugh, and they always want the funny guy around to break the ice.

"I talk about my life growing up in Brooklyn, 'cause I think basically a joke's a joke, and what makes one comic different from another is the way he perceives life and the way he deals with it. Buddy Hackett is a prime example. Buddy Hackett is, I think, one of the funniest men ever. I always remember as a kid watching Buddy at the Concord, or Alan King. Those were the guys who I loved. Lenny Bruce doing social commentary and Phil Foster. I mean, Phil Foster, who later was the father on *Laverne and Shirley,* was my idol because he grew up in Brooklyn and he sounded like me.

"Freddie Prinze walked up to me one day and said, 'I'm in show business because of you.' I said, 'Why?' 'Because I went to the Copacabana in high school to see Gladys Knight and the Pips, and you were the comic and you talked about Brooklyn and you didn't use great English and you sounded like me and you looked great in that black tuxedo. And I said, 'Hey, I could do that.' I said, 'Terrific, I sounded stupid so you figured anybody could do that.'

"I talk about remarrying my ex-wife. I talk about having my daughter. I talk about the problems of not having a baby. I talk about physical problems you have as you get older. I used to talk about dating, they used to bill me as the single Alan King. I talked about picking up girls in laundromats. I would do the jokes about not having enough laundry so I'd say to a girl, 'can I share a dryer with you and watch your clothes go around with mine?' I'd pick them up walking the dog. I did all that stuff and then I went into the marriage stuff as my life changed. When I was starting, no one wanted a young comic. Today they want a nine-year-old comic, but in those days people thought you couldn't be funny unless you had experience, and you couldn't know what you were talking about unless you were thirty-five years old.

"I do reveal. It's cathartic. I've been in therapy my whole life and my therapist once said that I don't come for therapy, I come for dialysis. I get all that crap out of my system. I remember once going to see Richard Pryor with a friend of mine, a manager at that time who managed Sonny and Cher, named Denis Pregnolato. Pryor went on and did an unbelievable routine about getting divorced. When he came off Denis said, 'That was hilarious,' and Richard got mad. He said, 'It's okay for them to laugh but you know the pain I'm in. How dare you? You know what I'm really feeling.' So, in comedy, there's a release of pain. He was mad that his friend laughed at his pain where everybody else should laugh, but knowing him you shouldn't laugh. That was very interesting."

Stone admits that finding your voice, your career even, doesn't happen overnight. "It takes years. It takes waiters walking across while you're on. It takes opening for a star and they don't care that you're there, don't ever want you there." We want you, Stewie!

While Jeffrey Ross admits that he doesn't like to talk about his gimmick, he managed to rise to the occasion. "Fortunately at this point, I don't have to have a gimmick, and I try not to analyze what I do. I seem to be getting better and better at analyzing what other people do, because I have experience writing and producing, doing different things. I rarely watch tapes of myself, 'cause I think it'll mess me up. Some people call me laid back. I hear mean. Last summer after the Belzer Roast, *New York* magazine called me the meanest man in comedy, which I found funny 'cause we only Roast the ones we love.

"They call me a throwback now. I guess that's true. Whatever I am now, I always kind of was. I don't know if it's confidence or this brash sort of behavior on stage. I never really showed fear and I don't know what's going on inside. You can't hurt me. If a joke doesn't work, I don't collapse. I did do that in the beginning, I would have bad shows and I'd fall apart on stage, but once you do that a couple times you don't ever let it get to you again.

"At first it was just fun, it was like playing in a band, which I did in high school and college. You're out at night with some sort of purpose. I used to hate bars in college. I hated going to clubs. I could never meet women that way and suddenly, here's a reason to go out at night and talk to people. I was always a night creature anyway. My dad was a night guy. He was a caterer, parties all weekend—tuxedos. I guess I've always been a creature of the dark time of the day and it was just a thrill to be getting on stage and saying whatever I wanted.

"I'm at this restaurant—I would never hang out by the door, 'cause I couldn't bear to watch people pay admission to see me, even if I was just emceeing for someone else. It made me too nervous to see the money changing hands. I just couldn't deal with it. So I would hang out sort of in the corner. There was no dressing room or anything like that. I'd just eat my free dinner. I couldn't have the steak. This woman comes up to me. I see her husband putting on his coat, like fifteen, twenty feet away, she says, 'I don't mean to bother you, I just want to tell you that my husband has cancer and I have not seen him laugh like this in a year. Thank you for doing such a great show.' I was like, 'Jesus, wow, this actually has some sort of purpose in life.' I couldn't even imagine that equation had something to do with what I was doing, but that's when I realized it.

"For most of the people who came to my shows, they weren't even my shows, I was just one of three or four or five people on these programs. They were there to get drunk. They were there to heckle, 'cause it was free with their dinner. They were there to cruise women. They were there for a million reasons. I just couldn't imagine that any of them were worthy, and somehow I realized that comedy does have some sort of meaning in the world. It cheers people up. It makes people feel better. It can be satirical; it can be social commentary; it can be medicine.

"My whole life I'd been taking care of sick people, especially in my early years in comedy. I had an aunt, a sister, and a grandfather all sick at different times. It was a joke among my friends in New Jersey, none of them would live with me, 'cause everybody who did died. Maybe my comedy came from a dark place at that point. Then I realized that it wasn't all about me, that there were actually nice people who I was making laugh.

"There is definitely a considerable amount of editing at this stage in my career, because I'll do a show at midnight on a Friday night at the Laugh Factory for college kids and Mexican teenagers. In Hollywood that's who shows up on Friday night at midnight. I'll be talking about Britney Spears and I'll be talking about Compton-Online, 'You got mail, bitch.' Then I'll be on a plane at 6:50 a.m., for a Saturday night gig at Mar-A-Lago in Palm Beach, and there's Donald Trump and it's basically the same jokes and the same attitude, but I'm rewriting the references and taking out the curses while I'm saying it. That's really challenging.

"I do find, the less you memorize your act and the more you re-remember it, it's funnier that way, 'cause it's like you're making it up on the spot. I have jokes that I'll do forty different ways in forty different shows, so it's organic to that room and that audience. 'I've seen younger faces on cash,' is a line I wrote for one of the early Roasts I did. Now, I don't do that joke very often, but just to give you an example, if I'm at Mar-a-Lago talking to a country club, high-end crowd, I might say, 'Hey, you guys are great, the other day I was at so-and-so club, and man, those people ... they're, like, dead. I've seen younger faces on cash.' Or maybe I'll be at the Comedy Cellar on MacDougal and I'll point to the table in the back of older people and I'll do the joke so the kids around them laugh. The less I rehearse it, the better for the joke. It's kind of in my Rolodex and however it comes out, it comes out."

"I talk about how everything that I've ever been punished for, expelled for, hit for, is what I seem to get paid for today," laughs Howie Mandel of his ever-evolving stage persona. "When I was younger, I was really nervous and really scared. I was on stage and I was showing it. I was showing it physically and verbally. I remember standing there and just realizing I didn't have a plan and saying, 'I don't know what to do. I don't know what to do.' They started giggling at my nervous contortions and I really didn't understand what everyone was giggling at and I asked them, 'What? What? What are you … ? What's going on?' And that became my catchphrase, 'What? What?' with the hands—I talk with my hands.

"I was just nervous and it was exaggerated and I was standing there and I didn't care if I made a fool of myself. And that's when it clicked. I'm not really that manic anymore because in reality I'm not that nervous anymore. So for me to go up on stage and go, 'What? What?' And stand there and look a little epileptic like I did then, I'd be putting on an act. I think people would know it, and I don't think it would be as entertaining. But at that time it was somewhat entertaining and it caught people's eye and I looked different and I sounded different. I used to take a bag of garbage up there with little toys and things. Somebody gave me a rubber glove and I didn't know what to do and I pulled the glove over my head and I inflated it and the audience laughed at that, I don't know why. I don't even get the joke today, but people still request it and ask me to do it." If only he could see what that looks like from the audience's perspective, then he'd get it.

"I was doing three hundred cities a year, touring constantly, and I didn't prepare, because my act was just drilled into me. I had tried and proven pieces that always worked. Eventually the fear totally went away and I was just out there reciting and as the curtain opened and the spotlight was on me, I couldn't tell where I was. Every place is exactly the same and every night is exactly the same and I think it became apparent in my performance that I was bored. That I wasn't excited. There was nothing exciting about it. There was no challenge so it didn't feel like there was any real skill. When I thought of an idea and I went out there with just something that hit me during the day and they would laugh at it, it was great.

But then, if I was doing it everyday, there was no excitement left. I think subliminally the audience can feel that.

"When there's a few thousand people in a room, people yell, 'Hey Howie!' People will yell out at a concert. A lot of people ignore it. I was just so bored sometimes that I would stop and say, 'What?' and then a conversation opened up. And I realized that the most fun I had was when I talked to the audience and opened it up. That became the key to me being excited again. I don't know where I'm going and even if I'm going into the toilet there's something exciting about that. I'll talk about the fact that you just dragged me into the toilet and I've got to try to get out of the toilet but the audience knows, and I know that they're watching something that hasn't happened before, may never happen again in that way. We're all in the moment. There's something exciting about that and it has kept my performance exciting, so that I look forward to the next night and I look forward to people yelling out. I look forward to opening up that wall. So they can talk to me and I'll talk back, about being married and having teenage kids and all that. I've just grown up. I'm a lot more comfortable. I feel a lot more comfortable. I think I look a lot more comfortable on stage. And one night I may be uncomfortable and that will show too. I don't know. It's not a conscious evolution. It's just, from the moment I get on stage I act the way I feel.

"Somebody who I watched and loved and admired and was inspired by was Steve Martin. Steve Martin is actually a very serious, brilliant man but I think his sensibility and his sense of humor are such that you can't tell somebody the next day what he did. In reiterating it, it doesn't sound as funny as it was. And I think, by the same token, people were laughing at me and it wasn't so much that I didn't have jokes or written material, but I was a character. Now, in these years, I'm not as manic and probably a lot more of what I say can be repeated the next day, because I talk about what's happening.

"I've been with my wife for twenty-eight years and have children and inevitably, to this day, people come up and they go, 'It must be crazy living with him. He must be nuts.' People want to believe that that's you, and it is me, it's certainly a part of me. I think if you meet somebody for an hour or two hours, there's no way you know them. Even if they're at a party you don't know them. You have a good time with somebody, you don't know what they're like when they're agitated, when things aren't going well for them. You don't know. So that is a slice of me on stage. People want to believe that that *is* me. And they don't want to think that I'm just a guy out there telling jokes. They want to think that I'm the crazy man. They want to think that that's me.

"Inevitably people come up to me, and they'll say, 'What's wrong? You're Howie?' And I go, 'Yeah? What do you mean, what's wrong?' and they go, 'Well you're not smiling.' People think you should be smiling because you're a comedian. I'd come out of an elevator in a building and they'd go, 'Why aren't you smiling?' And I'd be like, 'Because I'm alone in an elevator and I believe that if I was alone in an elevator and the door opened and I was standing there smiling, you would think I was retarded, and if you didn't know me you probably wouldn't get in with me. That would be scarier than me not smiling.'

"People like to believe that the persona they see on stage, the persona they see in movies and in soap operas is the person. They don't want to think that you're in that kind of control where you're putting on a character. I wasn't putting on a character, I wasn't holding back, and I don't hold back how I feel. Those are my opinions. When you get on stage every night, you have to recreate it and make it seem new and fresh, and I have my ways of doing that. And therein lies a little bit of trickery and maybe skill, but these things are honestly come by.

"In so many art forms it takes a long time for people to get on the bandwagon, or get it. A lot of painters die penniless and poor. It was the same painting throughout their life and nobody seemed to jump onto that bandwagon or really get it. I don't think you have to turn yourself inside out to do your art, because your sense of humor is a sense of you. That's who you are. It's not a part you played in a film, it's just you, without any other tool—without paint, without a costume, without a sound—it's just you out there. You look at Richard Pryor, when he recreated the characters that touched his life and touched his upbringing. Ultimately, if you really look at his life, he started off somewhat tragic but he found the humor in it and that's what got him through it and that's what everybody seemed to relate to."

Who knew that the very things that horrified you in high school would come back to reward you in a career in comedy? That finding a personality that doesn't coincide with your peers could be a gold mine? Along with coming up with an act that is as individual as your fingerprints, you also have to subscribe to the Sally Field testimonial: You have to get people to really like you. Standing up just might be the easy part—it's standing *out* that will make or break you as a comedy star.

CHAPTER 4

IT WAS THE WORST OF TIMES

...And hurt like the dickens

George Bush vomited on the Prime Minister of Japan. Rob Lowe videotaped a sex romp, only to one-up himself performing a duet with Snow White on an Oscar telecast. Pee Wee Herman was caught with his pants down. Ronald Reagan fell asleep during an audience with the Pope. Robert Downey, Jr. woke up in his underwear in a stranger's house. Chevy Chase had a talk show. Everybody has a worst moment, that instant when all the world's a stage—and your zipper is wide open.

For stand-up comedians, those moments seem more painful, albeit funnier, thanks to their personal slant on the situation. It's waking up and realizing you really are at that party naked—and the last time you'd been to the gym, dot.com companies were thriving.

Comedy, as a career, may not always be fun—but even in the worst of times it should always be funny. Let's face it, that person sliding across the newly waxed floor gets laughs every time—from the people watching. If you're brave enough to stand up again then you're ready to take your humiliation to the stage and make an ass of yourself on a much grander scale. It's not what happens to you when you fall, it's how you tell the story about it after you get up.

Any teacher will tell you to learn from your mistakes. Well, class, the professors of comedy are about to enlighten you on the art of the jackass.

For Howie Mandel that worst moment came at a private event. "Somebody asked me if I would do a benefit for Holocaust survivors and I said, 'Sure, why not? It's my heritage, I'd be more than happy to.' As it turned out, this event was a very religious event, which I didn't know. I had said, 'Yes I will do this event,' thinking I was going to raise money for Holocaust survivors, not thinking for a moment that I was doing a show *for* Holocaust survivors. So I looked into the room and there were maybe a hundred elderly people—with their parents.

"There was a podium and a piano and they had brought in this rabbi from Israel and he started talking. He said, 'In 1941 in a certain town in Poland, six hundred women were taken and raped and then burned … we must never forget. And then a few months later another town and another European city, children, babies, were taken and killed … we must never forget. And then in June of so-and-so, something else happened, and the Holocaust grew and we must never forget. And by April 1945, six million Jews had perished … we must never forget. In 1979 this young man came to The Comedy Store and on a dare got up on stage and somebody saw him and he got on *Make Me Laugh*. In 1982 he started on *St. Elsewhere*.'

"My introduction—the Holocaust, he attached it to my resume. There was not even a bridge between the Holocaust and my career. My career was part of the Holocaust as far as these people were concerned. Then he said, 'And now, Howie Mandel.' While there was still sadness and tears in their eyes, I entered the stage and started to do my act. To silence, except for the people sniffing—a lot of sniffing and wiping tears.

"After about ten minutes, some woman started banging her fork on the table really hard—some eighty-year-old woman—and I said, 'Excuse me?' She goes, 'Young man, young man. Enough with the jokes, sing already.' Then I look to the side and I see the woman

HOWIE MANDEL's career has encompassed virtually every area of entertainment, including television, film, and the stage. He has also performed as many as 200 concert dates a year. His stand-up career started at LA's The Comedy Store and led to his first television appearance on the comedy game show *Make Me Laugh*. He later starred on television for six years as Dr. Wayne Fiscus on the award-winning NBC drama *St. Elsewhere*. His Emmy Award-nominated children's series, *Bobby's World,* ran for eight seasons on Fox. Howie has done countless comedy specials and hosted his own syndicated talk show, *The Howie Mandel Show*.

who hired me is giving me the wrap-up sign, that they're very tired.

"Then some guy turns around in his wheelchair, a ninety-year-old man, and starts making his way to the door. He hadn't oiled the wheels so for the next ten minutes you just heard the squeaking and the silence and the echoing of my humor. So not every night is a gem. I think every comedian has and will continue to have war stories, and the beauty is, the glass is half full. The bad moments will always provide us with stories and reference points to create more humor."

Who says comedians of different generations don't experience the same problems? "One summer, I get booked for Passover week at a bunch of the resorts in the mountains," says Freddie Roman. "Now, Passover week the crowds were very old. I mean old, and I was booked at Singers Hotel, in Spring Valley, New York. I get on the stage and ... can't relate. They were so old that they didn't understand me. Hated me. Not a laugh. Finally, after thirty minutes, a lady in the back of the room raises a hand, she says, 'Mister.' I say 'Yes.' She says, 'Can you sing a song?' I said, 'Darling, I don't sing.' She says,

'Then can you let us go to bed?' That was great and she was right, I was punishing them by making them sit there."

It seems appropriate to follow Roman, a major headliner in the Catskills, with George Wallace's first Catskills experience at the Nevele Hotel. "I was just starting. I was actually doing stock jokes. I don't know how much money I was getting, but I was up on the stage for forty-five minutes—I didn't get one laugh. That's worse than any funeral. I just stood up there and kept talking. I thought, maybe it would get better. Maybe there was a chuckle here and there, but you know when you're bombing. I choked. When I drove back across the Tappan Zee Bridge, I thought, I oughta drive off this damn bridge right now. But the lesson I learned there was that anytime I go on stage, I don't ever worry about bombing. It'll never be that bad. It'll never be as bad as it was at the Nevele. I went to the Nevele about three years later and one of the old waitresses tapped me on the back and whispered, 'You're much better this time. We loved you.' You have to go back and finish it—I knew what I was doing then.

"I could go on stage with those same stock jokes and deliver them better now. You gotta know you're in control. It was the first time I was in an all-Jewish audience. The Jewish audience and the black audience are the toughest audiences in America 'cause they know all the jokes. They create comedy, without a doubt. Well, not totally, but I guarantee you, Jews and blacks are up there.

"I have a passion for what I do, I know I can make these people laugh. I can't wait to get back on stage and the next night, after the Nevele, I was back on stage at Catch A Rising Star and people were laughing again. 'Okay, wow, boy, this is okay. I'm getting back on the horse.'"

Here is Lily Tomlin's Upstairs, Downstairs moment. "Irv Haber, who owned the Upstairs, wanted me to come back to the revue and I said I didn't want to. I wanted to do a single in the bigger downstairs room, because there are no places to do comedy except those kind of Vegas-y clubs. So I said to Irv, 'I can do it, Irv, you'll see, people will like me,' stuff like that. So Irv booked me and he gave me a two-week date and I opened for a singer named Tony Darrow, for two weeks. I can't tell you how much the audience did not like me, did not relate to me. There was no place to go, there was no dressing room or anything. I'd have to leave and walk out through the bar to get out and I'd go down to the deli nearby just to get out of the club. I didn't want to have to face all of those people because they were just absolutely, overtly hostile.

"I'd go down to the bartender and get a coke after the show, and he'd say, 'So, you wanna be in show business, eh kid?'—that kind of thing. One day, I was down at the deli and a friend of mine who had come to the show was with me and this other couple was there as I walk in. They were saying to the waiter, 'Oh, this girl she's just—ugh—we just couldn't stand her,' or whatever. They were saying something really hostile about me. They said, 'We had to leave. We just left.' So as I walked in they said, 'Uh, oh'—because they knew I heard everything they said—they tried to cover. They said, 'Oh, we enjoyed you,' or something like that and I think I said something like, 'Oh bullshit.' I was just so absolutely crushed and devastated."

Even Rita Rudner's *bad* moments are cute. "I did a charity event where I could either have sound or lights but I couldn't have both at the same time because the generator couldn't take it. I chose the sound and no lights and I had to cut it short."

Every comic eventually hits that all-time low that for some could mean the point of never returning to the stage again. For Jerry Stiller, comedy put food on the table and supported his family, but it wasn't all rosy. When the good times falter, that's a problem, he admits. "It was in Cleveland—we came in with my father-in-law and Amy, my daughter—into a place called The Club Sahara. The audience just wasn't ready for us. While we were in front of them, doing sketches that had gone over very well at the Blue Angel, this guy was playing his transistor radio, listening to the Cleveland Browns ball game. I couldn't interrupt because we were doing sketches, six minute sketches. Finally, out of exasperation I said, 'Would you shut that thing off?' and the guy said, 'I'll turn it down!'

"When the show was over, the owner came into our hotel room and said, 'How dare you insult my audience like that?' He looked at us and said, 'I hired two people, now I got four people, gypsies! What kind of an act is this? You call this an act?'

"Here I was thirty-seven, thirty-eight years old. I was so wiped out that I walked out of the hotel room, went down to the parking lot, and I lay down on the hood of a car and I started to cry. I thought, 'What the hell? I bring my wife, my kid, my father-in-law here. What am I doing? I don't belong in this business.' I really wanted to give up the whole thing at that moment. But my father-in-law came over—I'll never forget him, Eddie Meara—he came over and he patted me on the back and said, 'Everything's gonna be all right Jerry.'"

Even the MTV generation has its lows. Just ask Jeffrey Ross. "In 1992 the Boston Comedy Club on 3rd St. [in New York] was my home club, my room. I would emcee there all the time. My manager owned it, and MTV was auditioning people for the *MTV Half-Hour Comedy Hour,* which was *the* show for a guy in his 20s to go on. Your college price would go up if you made a good tape on MTV, it was the coolest market. It was within my reach—whereas clearly Letterman and Leno weren't. I really, really, really wanted it, more than anything. If I did that I wouldn't have cared if I did anything again almost, it would be the coolest thing I could do. I had a really prime spot on the show, I followed a guy who was too nerdy and too goofy to ever get on the show. He was doing political humor, it just wasn't gonna work. I was like, man, if I don't kill after this guy....

"I went up and I don't know what I did wrong, exactly. I tried opening with a joke that I probably shouldn't have opened with, and my whole attitude was probably wrong. I remember, three jokes in, not getting any laughs. Boom—no laugh, joke—no laugh, joke—no laugh. I basically dropped the mike on the floor, did two more jokes without the mike, that didn't work and walked off stage with my glass of water still in my hand. Walked right out the door, threw the glass against the wall of the comedy club, walked to my car, and drove back to Jersey. I was like, Jesus, what the hell am I doing with my life? This is crazy. I don't have the skin for this. Even in success, what am I actually amounting to? A couple of stupid jokes in Greenwich Village? What is this gonna get me? Where is this going? This is stupid. This is a meaningless way to spend your life. I went to college. I don't think I ever fell apart like that again, though —never let the audience get to me like that again, and it made me so strong.

"I basically begged to get another audition a couple of days later. I said, 'I'll host the auditions for the same show up at Stand-Up NY,' which was a better room for me—a little more sophisticated room, uptown. At that point my humor wasn't as universal, there was a difference between uptown and downtown for me; whereas now you can drop me anywhere and it doesn't matter. I emceed for the same people to get on the same MTV show, but I changed my attitude and I relaxed. If you relax and slow down and show some confidence, it works. I did well and she booked me."

There's always a light at the end of that tunnel of dark tales though, unless, of course, you're Pat Cooper and you're in a bad marriage. "I had one of my worst times the first time I played the Copacabana. My ex-wife hands me a summons before I go down the fucking steps. I grab the fucking thing, and she says, 'That's for you.' Before I'm going down. My first time at the Copa. 'Ladies and Gentleman, Pat Cooper!' I open the summons and I read it out loud, on stage, 'The first part, the second part, and the third part. Now what part am I? The first part, the second part, or the third part? I want to know what the hell part I am?' So out of a tragedy, I was fucking hilarious. That's me. I got lucky maybe, I don't know. Wow, I worked twenty fucking times after that because of that."

photo by Richard Lewin

PAT COOPER

Pat Cooper has been entertaining
audiences with his "comedic
anger" for over four decades. He
has appeared on stages from come-
dy clubs, to major theaters, includ-
ing the legendary Copacabana,
Westbury Music Fair, Trump's
Castle, Caesar's Palace, and the
MGM Grand Hotel. Pat's numer-
ous television appearances include
*The Ed Sullivan Show, The
Tonight Show with Johnny Carson*, and *Late Show with David
Letterman*. He is a frequent popular guest on Howard Stern's
radio show. Pat has several successful comedy albums to his
credit including *Spaghetti Sauce & Other Delights, You Don't
Have To Be Italian To Like Pat Cooper*, and *Pat Cooper's
Classic Routines*.

"MAMA"

FROM PAT COOPER'S ALBUM
YOU DON'T HAVE TO BE ITALIAN TO LIKE PAT COOPER

Mama. The worst thing in the world is to tell your mother you
don't feel good. I went home one night, I said, "Mom, I got a
cold. I don't feel good." She said, "Take your clothes off."

"C'mon mom. I'm thirty-nine years old." She said, "What hap-
pened? You grew something else since the last time I saw you?"
You answer her, not me.

Unbelievable. Mama ... what a wonderful word, ladies and
gentlemen, I always repeat it because it is a wonderful word.
What enjoyment does my mother have? She goes to church. All
the years that I know my mother, every Saturday, confession
with her girlfriend Angie. One Saturday, Angie couldn't go to
confession, she had bursitis of the shoulder. She called Mother,
"Oh Mom, s'cusa, I cannot go to confession, I have a bursitis in
the shoulder." My mother says, "Don't a getta nervous. You
tella me the sins an' I'm gonna tell 'em to the priest." My moth-
er doesn't talk to Angie anymore. "That son of a gun, what a
swindler, she don't tell me those things."

Mama ... I said, "Mom, what do you think about the priests getting married?"

"As a long as they marry the nun. Otherwise there gonna be sexcommuncation." Unbelievable. These women are so delightful. No education but they're the smartest women in the world.

Mama, Mama, Mama, Mama ... Another thing I gotta tell you that really fascinates me. Every time I leave the house she goes, "Where you goin' Patsy?"

"I'm goin' to work."

"You have a car?"

"Yes."

"You have a St. Christopher statue on a top of the dashboard?" I said, "Mom, I got fourteen St. Christopher statues, I can't see where I'm driving anymore." I said, "In fact I got four St. Christopher's looking backwards. In case the cops come, they're gonna warn me."

"DRAFT TIME"

FROM PAT COOPER'S ALBUM
MORE SAUCY STORIES

I remember 1951 and I'm thirty-nine years old, we got drafted to go to Korea. Six hundred Italian boys in New York City, 599 went to Fort Dix ... I went to South Carolina. Nobody told me that the southern people didn't know what an Italian looked like, what he was all about. I used to lay down in my bunk, they used to pass my bunk: 'That's an Italianioyoyoyoyoyo— feel his skin, I think he's greasy.'

And I remember one morning I'm standing at attention and the sergeant says, "Where's Pasquala Capitutio?" I says, "You mean Caputo?" He said, "I said that, where's Capitutio." He said, "Would you tell your mother please, don't send no more pepperini and provalonie in those boxes. All the oil's going all over the mail envelopes."

They ate anchovies—they thought it was worms. Thank God my mother used to send me jars of marinara sauce, thank God. I used to put it over the grits. I thought it was rice. I didn't know what it was.

Freddie Roman also worked the Copa. "I'm booked at the Copacabana by Marty Erlichman, who managed Barbra Streisand, and Gary Puckett and the Union Gap, a very hot singing group at the time. They had six number-one records in a row. He had seen me one night in Florida where I killed them. He said, 'Would you like to open for Gary Puckett?' I said, 'My God, the Copacabana, I'd love it.' 'Ok, you got the job.'

"Opening night at the Copa, I've got on a new tuxedo, new patent leather shoes. At the Copacabana you had to walk down four carpeted steps onto the dance floor and the emcee screwed up and said, 'Jules Podell welcomes you to the Copacabana for the spring revue featuring the comedy of Freddie Roman, and starring Gary Puckett and the Union Gap. And now please welcome the comedy of Gary Puckett.' Well, now I'm flustered a little bit and I walk down the steps and I have these new shoes on and I go from the carpet to the floor and my feet give away from under me and I slide under a table. People are screaming. Fat Jack Leonard is sitting at the table with Red Buttons and he says, 'Who do you think you are? Jack Durant?' Durant was a comic who used to open by coming out and doing a pratfall. I get up and I have no timing, no nothing, I'm scared to death. I do thirty-five minutes of material in fifteen minutes and I walk off. It was a horror."

Freddie, who is famous for his Catskills humor, has had to deal with anti-Semitism at times, "We were on the road with *Catskills on Broadway* and we got to the Colonial Theatre, in Boston—sold out the whole week, every show. It was a marvelous engagement. Thursday night, the third night we were there, full house. I come out to open the show and I'm talking about ten minutes and I hear out in the audience, 'I didn't pay fifty dollars to hear a Jew.' And the audience heard it, and I just let it go for the minute, I didn't say another word. And he's telling his wife, loud and drunk, 'This Jew bastard. I told you I didn't want to pay fifty dollars.' I said, 'Sir, just go to the box office and tell them I told them to give you your fifty dollars back and get the hell out of here.' The audience stood up and cheered. So he said, 'No. Now I won't.' So they called the police and the police came and took him out and the wife stayed. She wanted to see the show."

Jim Gaffigan was solar systems away from both the Copa and the Catskills for his greatest moment of discomfort. "I did one show at the Uptown Comedy Club, which was on 125th Street, in Harlem. You know, I'm pretty much a Midwestern guy and I had probably been doing stand-up for three years or so and I went up there and it was an all black audience and the show was called 'New Jack Comics.' This is when New Jack City was kind of big. It was definitely an urban pre-hip-hop audience, but there was not a white person in the place. They announced me as 'Our next comedian is, like, a white guy,' and the audience started booing me before I even walked out, and it looked like somebody tried to trip me.

"I also had a situation where I was dealing with a heckler and I actually was doing really well. Then afterwards he stood up to go to the bathroom and he had a gun under his jacket. I was like, geez!" But that's nothing for this pro of bad moments. "I've had crowds of two hundred people boo me."

Just to set the record straight about rough moments though, Gaffigan is tough. "I've never been a crier. You have to build a resilience to it, particularly at the beginning. That's where stand-ups are really insane. Because it's one thing if you're at a certain level and you go up there, maybe you'll have a rough moment here and there, but years two and three, when you are finding yourself, you go up and bomb all the time. It's not like singing. Say, someone sings off key, people get real quiet and you hear them whisper. But if you're not a good stand-up, people are mean to you. They're like, 'Hey, you suck.' You definitely start to think, 'Okay, I'm a lunatic,' but it's okay. It's a challenge and it's probably a power trip."

We'll get to taboo topics up the road, but it used to be that you couldn't talk about religion or politics without causing a major war. People have evolved, however, and gotten much more impassioned about more relevant

JIM GAFFIGAN

Jim Gaffigan is an actor/comedian who appeared on *The Ellen Show* on CBS. He also starred opposite Christine Baranski in the CBS sitcom *Welcome To New York*, playing a character loosely based on himself. Jim has also made guest appearances on the series *Law & Order, Law & Order: SVU, Sex and the City, Third Watch*, and Comedy Central's *Dr. Katz*. Along with working on the stages of all of the comedy clubs on both coasts, Jim has brought his stand-up humor to *Late Show with David Letterman* and *The Late Late Show with Craig Kilborn*. Jim's motion picture credits include *Three Kings, The Thomas Crown Affair, Personals*, and *Entropy*.

Isn't it strange that when you're single all you see are couples, and when you're part of a couple, all you see are hookers?

If you're Hispanic and you get angry, people are like, "He's got a Latin temper." But if you're a white guy and you get angry, people are like, "That guy's a jerk."

It's hard to get a woman buzzed on a date when you don't drink. "Yeah, I'll have a glass of water and what do you want? A shot of Jägar? Ten of them?"

People always know someone who looks like me: "Hey, I know someone who looks like you!" I never know what to say. "Well, tell them 'hi.' I share their pain. Tell 'em to get Rogaine."

I wish I was a film director in everyday life so that when someone was telling me a boring a story I could just go, "And cut!"

"But I wasn't finished."

"We got it, that's a wrap. Trust me, you were great."

I think I'm lactose intolerant 'cause whenever I have five milkshakes I feel sick and I think it's the lactose.

Sleep is too important. Have you ever been invited to something:

"Hey you wanna help the homeless?"

"Yeah, I'll help the homeless."

"Meet us Saturday at 7:00 am."

"Uh, forget the homeless. They're homeless in the afternoon, too. I think they're big brunch people."

My favorite animal is the manatee. Have you seen this animal? The manatee is endangered with extinction and I think it's 'cause it's out of shape. It looks like a retired football player. You ever see it on the Discovery Channel? It's always, "I'm bloated—too much pizza." And the manatee is also called the sea cow. That sounds like an insult, it's almost as if the manatee was introduced to the ocean and the other animals were like, "Who's the new guy?" and the manatee was like, "Oh, hi everyone. You can call me the manatee."

"Yeah right, sea cow—fat ass."

"Uh, the name is manatee."

I would love to see the manatee on a talk show like Ricki Lake:

"Ricki, I'm here 'cause I'm endangered." And one of those rude people in the audience would be like, "Yeah, I want to say something to the sea pig."

"That's sea cow."

"Whatever. Sea pig you think you're all that 'cause you're a fat seal. You gotta get yourself a job and an education."

"I live in the ocean."

"You live in the ocean 'cause you ain't got no job. You gotta go to Weight Watchers, some program."

"I have a layer of blubber to keep my body warm in the water."

"Whatever, talk to the hand."

"I don't have a hand."

Doesn't it look like God didn't finish the sea cow? He was like, "Let's see, start with blob of shit here, blob of shit here—What? Is the phone for me?"

topics—like sports. Don't even try to go there, or you run a risk that Red Buttons had to face. "I'm working in Boston one night, at the Latin Quarter, and the Yankees had just defeated the Boston Red Sox for the playoffs in the American League. Foolishly, I did a joke about the Yankees. Some woman ringside got up and at the top of her lungs said, 'Red Buttons, go and fuck yourself!' But loud. Everybody was stunned, including myself, and I said to her, 'Thanks Madam, I was looking for a new shtick for my act.'"

Buttons also shared this red-faced moment: "I was working Bill Miller's Riviera and there was a guy sitting ringside, with his back toward me, and I became very, very annoyed. I went to work on this guy all through my act and then the guy turned around and he had no eyes—he was completely blind! Little moments." Like this one: "I'm working out in New Jersey on a New Year's Eve—now I make sure I don't work that day anymore—and some drunken broad—some mobster's wife—walks up on the floor and puts a cigarette out on my tuxedo." Red's situation was not lost on the broad's husband though, who thew some bucks his way saying, 'Hey, Red, we're sorry, buy yourself a new tux.'

"It's like winning the Academy Award, you're in shock. Nightclubs are always treacherous. I was never comfortable in nightclubs 'cause there was always talking. You're in there competing with guys who are looking to take some girl to bed, and when you're doing comedy, that's a terrible obstacle to overcome."

Hearing no laughs is bad enough, but when the audience is literally surrounding you, as David Alan Grier discovered, the silence is compounded. "Every comic has bombed, and if someone says they never bomb, they're lying. I remember, I was playing Cleveland on New Year's Eve with Jamie Foxx and we were in this rotating theater-in-the-round. We were on tour and we had this opening act that went way too long—there was the emcee, then the opening act, then Jamie went on, it was already after midnight. They had a twenty-minute intermission, so by the time I hit the stage it was like one-fifteen, one-thirty in the morning, and I proceeded to die the death of an overfed goldfish. The stage was slowly rotating around and around.

"All I could think was, 'Alright, I'm contracted to do forty minutes, so I was just like, fine, let me just do this—'Hey, have I told you about my shoes? Why I love my shoes'—'Boo, boo. Shut up. Get the fuck off stage,' and it was just going around and around. I finally finish my act, I go off, and when you fail, the stench of failure is worse than cancer, nobody wants to be near you. So the fat security guard hustles me into the limousine and of course nobody's there except for my wife, who gives me that mom hug, which just makes you hurt more. The next morning my agent called and I picked up the phone and we laughed for a good five minutes.

"That was pretty much the worst professional bombing. It becomes a whole Theater of the Absurd, because everybody boos except one person in the back row who yells out, 'We love you David.' Then they boo him and it's just like, why am I alive?"

Stewie Stone has experienced everyone's worst nightmare. "Everybody's fear is walking out on stage and discovering that your fly is open. Everybody checks his

photo by Richard Lewin

STEWIE STONE, a former drummer, honed his Brooklyn-style humor in the popular resorts of the Catskills. His frank observations and often self-deprecating jokes keep audiences laughing wherever he performs. He is one of the more popular entertainers working in Las Vegas and Atlantic City. Stewie has toured with many great singers including Paul Anka, Frankie Avalon, Engelbert Humperdinck, Frankie Valli, Ben Vereen, Bobby Vinton, and Dionne Warwick. He has performed at many Friars Club's Roasts as well as produced and toured around the country with the Friars Frolics.

fly, it's called a bird check. I was working the Hilton, in Las Vegas, with Engelbert Humperdinck, and unfortunately Engelbert passed a kidney stone which sounds like a terrible thing, but when a star is sick, everybody has to go to the doctor with them. When I worked with Sonny and Cher, she had a cold, I had to get B-12 shots with them. I'm not sick, but you have to go with the star—I'm getting shots, they're getting shots.

"So Engelbert passes a stone and we have to do the show that night because he had canceled a lot of shows and they said if you keep canceling we're gonna get mad at you. They didn't want to understand that he was passing a stone. So we all sat in the doctor's office looking at mesh, looking for the stone, and he passed the stone just as we had to get to the theater. We ran back to the dressing room and I shaved and showered and ran on stage and I'm thinking, 'Thank God we're doing this,' and I'm wondering, because they're laughing in spots, 'Why are they laughing? I'm not that funny.' People are going, 'Look down, look down,' and my shoes are not untied. I looked—you turn around and zip up your fly. It is the most embarrassing thing, or tripping and falling on stage, or something stupid. Or you walk on and you can't find the break in the curtain to get back and they're yelling, 'Get off!' 'I can't!' Those are embarrassing moments.

"Years ago I worked in Lake Tahoe with Dr. Hook or some rock group, and I'm going on and they're snorting coke and smoking pot and yelling, 'What is he doing here?' Then the guy who hired me has the nerve to tell me, 'cause I worked at Tahoe all the time, he says, 'Wear a tuxedo for this show.' I come up in a tuxedo and these are all kids in torn t-shirts. The funniest thing when you work at rock attractions, they come backstage before the show and they have gorgeous suede jackets and gorgeous Gucci shoes and alligator boots, and they take off these clothes and put on ripped jeans. It's like a whole different kind of show business."

Carol Leifer can relate to opening for rock bands in Tahoe. "My worst moment was opening for the Beach Boys at Harrah's, in Lake Tahoe. I got the gig because Carl

Wilson, one of the Beach Boys, saw me on Letterman in one of my early appearances. I was doing TV at the time, but I wasn't that experienced with a casino kind of crowd. Especially a crowd going to see the Beach Boys, young and drunk and ready to party. It was thrilling to get this offer to open for them. I did Christmas week, but it was very tough 'cause I just did not have the chops to deal with that casino crowd. I remember, it was a New Year's Eve show and there were these drunk frat guys right in front who would not stop chanting, 'Reefer, reefer,' like my last name. They were literally pulling on my mike chord and there was no one from the casino policing the room or watching. I'm actually trying to wrestle the mike out of these guys' hands. I would have to say it was the worst experience I ever had."

Maybe music and comedy don't really mix as well as people think, seeing as Joy Behar's worst moment is rooted in that situation as well. "My worst moment was when I opened for Buddy Rich, the drummer. I was very, very green and it was at the Bottom Line. There were a lot of drummers from Queens in the audience, and they had their sticks with them. They were waiting to see Buddy Rich and I came out and they were banging their sticks, 'Get off. We hate you.' I was like, 'Look, I'm getting paid to do ten minutes here, Buddy's in the back snorting some coke.' I just made it up. I said, 'I have to do this time so just shut up.' It was horrible. But that was a situation where I really did recognize that it was not my fault. If they're not listening, if there's some big distraction going on like drumsticks, then how can I blame myself? I know it's not me. They weren't there to see me. I never have a bad time if they're there to see me. The ultimate goal of all comedians, I think, is to have their own audience."

Seems like Shecky Greene was working at Tony Soprano's Bada Bing Club long before HBO was ever conceived. "When I still wasn't sure that I wanted to work in show business, I was working in a place called the Cuban Village. The outfit was all hoodlums. I was getting a hundred and ten dollars a week and later on they brought in

CARROT TOP, whose real name is Scott Thompson, is a rare breed of comedian known as a prop comic. Currently seen in AT&T commercials nationwide, he is also widely successful touring various theatrical venues as well as the college circuit, performing to sold-out audiences at campuses across the country. Carrot Top, with his signature red hair, has made several appearances on *The Tonight Show with Jay Leno* and *Live with Regis & Kelly*, among other programs.

'hostesses.' I went to one of the guys and I said to him, 'Bob, I can't work here anymore.' He said, 'That's ten dollars off your salary and every time you open your mouth it's another ten dollars.' I thought he was joking, came my check, it was a hundred dollars. Following week I said to him, 'Bob, this is getting … I'm gonna quit.' 'You quit, we break both your legs and it's another ten dollars off your salary,' and they took another ten dollars off my salary. I was lucky enough to come to work one Saturday and somebody had died in the club and they closed it up. Otherwise, I'd still be there, on North Avenue, in Chicago, and I would probably owe them thousands and thousands of dollars."

You just know there's going to be bad days in the life of a prop comic, and Carrot Top confirms it. "I've been at shows where the power went out and I had to just sit there for twenty minutes with my bullhorn and tell my jokes. Luckily I had a bullhorn, see, most comics would have to stop. I had a bullhorn right there, so I pulled it out and said, 'Okay, I don't have a microphone.' I did the show for twenty minutes with my bullhorn until the mike came back on. But that still sucked.

"In Birmingham, Alabama, about eight years ago I was performing at the Comedy Club and there was such a bad snowstorm that they shut down the city and they cancelled the show. We were at the hotel and the snow caved in the roof of the Comedy Club, something hit a burner, and burnt the whole club down. So my whole act went up. All my props, all my stuff. My whole entire life. The whole club, the whole strip mall, everything burned down with my stuff. That was kind of weird. I was gonna do *The Tonight Show* on Monday, two days later, but I couldn't go on, and Jay Leno's like, 'Ah, Carrot Top's stuff burned down in the Comedy Club.' So that was kind of a low point in my life. I thought, Jesus, I gotta rebuild the whole damn act. I gotta go back to Wal-Mart and start buying crap. I gotta steal another Crime Watch sign. That sucked. But it made me strong, I came back and rebuilt, actually came up with better stuff."

"I think my worst moment was one of the first times I was on television," says Richard Belzer. "I forgot half of what I was gonna do and I just did four minutes instead of eight. When I came off stage I felt terrible and they said, 'Great.' Nobody noticed, but for me, personally, it was a huge deal to do that on television.

"There was a night where I got into an actual fight, a guy pulled me off the stage—at The Comedy Store in Los Angeles. That was pretty amazing, 'cause that's like breaking the fourth wall, it was pretty wild. I wasn't even talking to the guy. I was saying something to someone else and this guy said something and I said, 'I wasn't talking to you.' He grabbed me and pulled me off the stage and then I got away from him and picked up the mike stand and started swinging it at him. I didn't hit him. It made all the papers."

Kevin Meaney's act is apparently much more risqué than he knew. "I did a show in Boca Raton, Florida, for a corporation that said, 'Now, remember, there's no profanity in the show.' They were really uptight about language and offending anybody and I assured them, 'I'm not going to offend anybody. You got my tape, you know what I'm doing.' So this woman sitting in the crowd— she's all tight assed—and one of my lines goes, 'Why do you do this to your father and me? Get the puss off your face!' The tight-ass says, 'We talked about language, what were you talking about up there—'what's the puss?' Were you talking about pussy?' I said, 'What are you talking about, that's an expression that my mother used about my *face.*'

"I had a gig at the Bank of Boston, I was just starting off," says Meaney, about another embarrassing occasion. "I was doing stand-up maybe two years at the most, and I made a grand entrance—in a golf cart. I drove in, 'Look at the golf cart, it's in the dining room, this is exciting.' I get up and I start doing my show and I'm getting laughs. The president of the bank is sitting way in the back, there's like five hundred people in the room, he stands up, 'You! Get off.' Everybody knew it was him, because they recognized his voice. Nobody turned around to look and I'm up there, 'Me? You want me to get off? Ha, ha, okay, okay, funny guy.' 'NO, YOU GET OFF, NOW.' And it's like you could hear a pin drop. It's their boss talking and I just kind of slithered off the stage, feeling like I did something so bad."

W. C. Fields detested working with kids and animals, and David Brenner knows why. "I'm doing a concert somewhere in the Midwest where they have these theaters that have like three thousand people under a shell and another three thousand people in the grass behind it. It's sold out, packed with five, six thousand people, and I walk out and in this covered, domed area is a huge bird. It almost looks like an eagle but it's a black bird. It must have been the biggest raven or crow—I don't know birds, to me sparrows and parrots, that's it. So it's flying in there. Well, what do you think they're going to look at? You can see people looking up and this bird is flying, I mean really flying. So what do you do? Your show's over. It's like having a child or a dog on stage. It's over, nobody's gonna watch you. So what I did is, I became the bird. I cupped the microphone and I said, 'Oh man, look at all those people. Oh, I gotta go to the bathroom. Oh, there's a bald head.' Whatever the bird did, I did commentary for around eight to ten minutes. Finally, thank God, the bird left the premises—he did an Elvis, 'the bird has left the building.' Then I did the rest of my show."

The great thing about comics is they always have a postcript. A few years after the bird incident, Brenner recalls, "A man stops me in a restaurant. 'David Brenner,' he says, 'you know, I gotta tell you something. I saw you outside of ... ' wherever it was—Minneapolis, or whatever the place was—'and all these years I keep telling people, I don't know how you trained that bird to do that.' What are you going to say to the guy, 'You know you're an idiot mister?' I said, 'It wasn't easy.' That's all I said, 'It wasn't easy.' "

"The worst gig I ever had was for a group of Hassidim," says Susie Essman. "Some café in Borough Park decided they wanted to present comedy. The people were just appalled. They were appalled by me—and I was clean. I kept it clean, 'cause I knew. But the very existence of me offended them—that I was a woman, that I was a Jewish woman. I think if I was not a Jewish woman I wouldn't have been as offensive to them. But the fact that I was a Jewish woman, up there on stage performing, was so offensive and I could not get one chuckle. Not one. I worked them, I did. I was dancing the horah up there. I didn't care about the money, it's like get me out—and at the same time I felt like, okay, these are deeply religious people. I don't want to offend them; I don't want to insult them. I respect who they are.

"I remember once I had to do a private party in New Jersey somewhere, in some restaurant, and I get up there and sitting right in front of me is a priest. I just looked at him and I said, 'Now what the fuck am I gonna do with the priest sitting in front of me?' He laughed and it broke the ice. I mean, I had to mention the priest sitting in front of me.

"The only other time I remember really, really dying—the priest I didn't die with—was the Hassidim, and once in Montreal, in an Orthodox Jewish synagogue. They had me performing, not like in a little game room in the back, but in the synagogue where the Torah was, which was an inappropriate venue for comedy. They're Canadians, what the hell do they know?"

Anyone who is planning on getting up on stage, ready to rock the world with her jokes, had better prepare herself for her own private Armageddon. For the day you die up there—and you will—Essman has a soothing comment for you: "It's horrible."

Okay, that wasn't so soothing.

"It's the worst feeling in the entire world."

No, really, she is sympathetic.

"It is the worst feeling in the entire world and you don't forget it."

Let's face it, you will not be in a very good mood afterward, so just listen to her. "I remember my bad sets better than my good sets and everybody, I think every comic is like this. You just remember that feeling. You feel humiliated. You feel like you want to die. You just want to die."

Interesting business, this comedy stuff, where one man's nightmare is another man's Emmy Award. Gilbert Gottfried has never held back when it comes to trying to get laughs, so there might be a moment or two that didn't go all that well. "Everything's the worst. My entire career's the worst." It's tough pinning down the baddest of the bad moments but Gottfried rises to the occasion. "I was a presenter on the Emmys and I said, 'I can really sleep better at night knowing that Pee Wee Herman's been arrested. If masturbation's a crime, I should be on Death Row,' and I launched into this whole routine.

"They'd given me the names to announce, and they said, 'You've got some extra time here, so just have some fun.' I thought, what's more fun than masturbation? So I did that and you'd think I showed kiddie porn or something. They bleeped it on the west coast. The producer of the Emmys made a public apology. There were people writing in, saying this is the most offensive stuff that has ever been on TV. The Emmys has never invited me back. Then, like a month or so later, *Seinfeld* did a whole episode on masturbation and that gets considered to be a classic moment! So you never know.

"The interesting part about that, everyone was talking about how shocking it was and every news show, magazine-type show, magazines, and newspapers all did the same thing—they said, 'This was shocking and offensive and totally inappropriate and horrible and here's an example just so you'll know.' And they'd run the bit from beginning to end. Actually, more people saw it because it was censored. But, of course, the public needs to know so they can warn their children."

Now what the hell do you follow a Gilbert Gottfried masturbation story with? Hey, how about another moment from Rita Rudner? "I think one of the hardest things is being booked on a television show for the first time and getting bumped—not getting on, after you got all ready. That's what happened to me, both on Letterman and Carson. Because when you're a new comedian, you get five minutes and if someone talks through your segment, that's it and you just leave. They try and re-schedule you, so it's very anti-climactic and that's difficult. That happened to me quite a few times but you just have to deal with it.

"You're petrified. You're gearing up for it, you've been to the clubs every night for years, you've finally gotten your big break, and you sit backstage and the show's over and you didn't get on. I mean, Shirley MacLaine talked through my time the first night I was supposed to be on the Johnny Carson show. She just wouldn't stop talking and I thought, if she's so in tune with the universe, why didn't she know that she was talking through my segment? I love her. I think she's great. I didn't hold it against her."

Dick Capri's cool countenance makes any bad moment seem—well, like he couldn't give a rat's ass. "There are a lot of times where you go out and if it goes very badly it is because the situation is no good—bad mike, bad sound, audience can't hear you. They're not there to watch you. They don't give a shit. I've done shows where, as I walked toward the door leaving, they say, 'You stink.' I say, 'Oh, thank you very much.' I brush everything aside. I always feel they are wrong anyway. It's not an easy job. If you feel funny in your head, no matter what the audience is like, if you're working well and you walk off stage and you say, 'I did it right,' even if they didn't react the way you expected them to react, as long as in your heart you know you did a good performance, then you don't feel bad about it."

Norm Crosby likes to take his awkward situations to the high seas. "I was on a cruise one time, and there were born again Christians who were actually standing in the front of the casino telling people not to go in because it's against God's law to gamble. The Captain had to come down, there was almost a riot. We're on a ship in the middle of the ocean, on a cruise, and they're telling people, 'Don't go into the casino, don't gamble.'

"My show was the next night after this confrontation, and the cruise director said to me, 'Wow, it's gonna be rough.' I started to play with them. I said, 'God bless you. We need people to uphold our morals. Whatever happened to decency? Young kids move in together, they don't want to get married. Senior citizens in Florida move in together, they don't want to get married. The only people who want to get married today are homosexuals and Catholic priests.' They stood up and applauded. I had such a good time with them. I was doing all my bible stuff. 'Peter wrote a note to John, John gave it to Matthew, Matthew gave it to Luke and Luke gave it to Abraham—because they couldn't read Hebrew.' They screamed; they became my friends."

That's the ticket, make friends with your audience. Too bad this advice came too late for Ryan Stiles, though. "I've had a lot of bottles thrown at me," says Stiles, who, at 6'6" makes a pretty easy target. "I'm talking about Canada. You're doing a lot of shows for lumberjacks and the pool table gets shut down so they have to listen to the comic, and they're not too pleased about it. I had a guy threaten me—if I did another show, he'd drag me behind his truck. Stuff like that. Well, that second show—I didn't do that second show, I went home that night. I lived in the middle of nowhere so it wasn't worth it for twenty bucks. I snuck out and left."

Sometimes, though, money talks—and Jeff Foxworthy will tell you why. "In the first year that I did stand-up, there was no money. There was never any money. I think the second month I did comedy, I made twenty dollars. I agreed to do somebody's company

DAVID ALAN GRIER, before turning to stand-up comedy, began his career as an actor, earning a Tony Award nomination for his performance in the Broadway show, _The First_, a musical about baseball pioneer Jackie Robinson. He continued on Broadway with _Dream Girls_. His extensive film credits include _Jumanji, Boomerang, A Soldier's Story, I'm Gonna Git You Sucka, McHale's Navy,_ and _Streamers,_ among others. On television he is best known for his work on the Fox TV series _In Living Color,_ creating such memorable characters as Antoine Merriwether of "Men On ... " He also starred with Delta Burke in _DAG_ as well as appearances on Comedy Central. As a stand-up comedian David has played all of the comedy clubs around the country.

Christmas party and they told me to be there a little before nine. Well, they didn't put me on till about eleven, the place wasn't even set up to do comedy. It was like a disco, and a guy walked out and stuck a microphone down in the middle of the dance floor and the mike cord was about three and a half feet long and he's like, 'Hey everybody, shut up a minute. We got a comic, his name is John Foxberry.' Nobody quit talking, these people were polluted. It was one of these open bars. They kept doing whatever they were doing, and I quickly discovered that if I took all the tension out of the mike cord, I started getting feedback.

"So I'm out there plowing away, I think they were paying me fifty bucks but I needed it. I needed the fifty bucks and I was supposed to do twenty minutes, and for the first five minutes nobody paid any attention. Then I started to get a small group of them listening and I forgot about the mike cord problem and it was like, ' ... and by the time I got to the store and picked up the carton of milk … bbbwewwwaaaaaaa.' These people were like, 'Oh, the hell with this, I'm not listening to this.'

"I did the twenty minutes, said, 'Thank you, good night.' Not one person applauded because I don't think anybody realized that I had been doing comedy. Except for a group of guys—remember the old discos with three levels where you could look down on the dance floor? Well, there was a group of drunks on the top level that were dipping their napkins in their drinks and trying to hit me on top of the head. So I'm doing stand-up that nobody's listening to and dodging these wet napkins splattering on the dance floor. I walked through the crowd and you'd think somebody would say, 'Oh, sorry man, these guys are a bunch of assholes.' Nothing. I just walked over to the guy in charge. I'm as embarrassed as a human being can be and I said to him, 'Listen, can I just please get my check and go?' He's like, 'Oh, sorry man, we don't have any money. I don't know who's got a check. I don't have one.' I was so humiliated I said, 'Okay. Alright. Thanks,' and I just left. Left with no money, no dignity."

Ah, dignity. If you have any intention of following in these guys' footsteps, you may as well remove that word from your lexicon. Just hold tight to that moment in your life when you walked into the job interview with dog shit on your shoe, or dragged some toilet paper onto the bus, or had those poppy seeds lodged in your teeth for your first encounter with Mr. or Ms. Right. That way, you'll be prepared to plod through that stand-up gig in front of a roomful of strangers, hold your head up high, and make an ass of yourself. And maybe, just maybe, you'll make 'em laugh.

CHAPTER 5

PUTTING IT TOGETHER

...And praying they know
it's comedy

Martha Stewart might be able to help you turn that dead pet turtle into a pretty wall sconce with just a little découpage and glue, but she's not the only gifted one around. Stand-up comedy requires some semblance of preparation. There are tricks, tools, and timing to be honed, sought, and sweated over. Austrian philosopher Ludwig Wittgenstein once remarked that, "Uttering a word is like striking a note on the keyboard of the imagination." Stand-up comics could say the same thing, sort of. Of course, their version would most likely read something like, "Uttering a joke is like the perfect A-flat on a whoopee cushion." The trick is making sure that the whoopee cushion is in place before you sit down.

Once you've actually made it to the stage, unless you're Larry David and decide the audience isn't worthy, you're there for the duration—so you might as well know what you're doing before you get there. Preparation is essential to a comic. "I don't prepare," says David Brenner. Okay, scratch what I just wrote. David Brenner knows a lot more about this than I do. You'll see that there are a wide range of opinions, though, so read on.

"What would scare me, is if I were prepared," explains Brenner. "That would scare me. After my first time on *The Tonight Show*, a friend of mine, George Schultz—he started the first comedy club in America,

photo by Steve Sigalofs

DAVID BRENNER holds *The Tonight Show*'s record for number of appearances—a whopping 158. *The Book of Lists #2* recognizes this stand-up comedian as the "Number one most frequent guest on television." He is constantly touring the globe with his slice-of-life routines and hilarious observations. Before stepping onto the stage, Brenner enjoyed a successful career behind the scenes as a writer, producer, and director of television documentaries, heading up the distinguished documentary departments of both Westinghouse Broadcasting and Metromedia Broadcasting. His autobiography, *Soft Pretzels with Mustard* was a national best seller.

Pips, out in Sheepshead Bay—who was a fan and mentor, said to me, 'That chunk you did on buses was one of the funniest things I've heard. When did you write that? I never heard that.' I said, 'What bit on buses?' I didn't know what he was talking about. That night, when I watched a tape of myself on Carson, there was the bus routine. I'd never heard of that bus routine, but there it was.

"What I've had to do all through the years is carry a tape recorder and record every show I do and then the next day I have to listen to the tape to get the new jokes that I wrote. Well, now I'm able to memorize most of them. But that's how I work. I just go into what is natural. I've been that way since I'm two-and-a-half-years-old. Since I first spoke. So, for me to prepare to be funny, when all the years prior to that I've never prepared, is ridiculous. I mean, why would I be prepared?

"I'll have a topic—an article about Enron or something—and either I'll just flip it because nothing happened, I didn't hear myself saying anything, or the next thing I know, I'm saying something and I'm trying to memorize it so I can do it again. But I want to say just one thing: I'm not making a qualitative judgment. The guy who sits down at his computer and writes jokes and nurses them and changes them and flips them and does all these other things, the guy who approaches it scientifically, he's just as good as I am. Just because I'm a self-motivated, one-man improvisational group doesn't make me any better qualified as a stand-up comedian than the guy who writes the jokes in longhand or at the computer. It's just a difference in style.

"Don't forget that I have trunks full of material that I can slip into at any given time if the spurt is just a spurt instead of a deluge. If I'm not being creative in a big way, I can always go to some pieces. When I did television, I had a rule that I would not repeat the same material for a minimum of a year. Other guys, if you see them on TV and then you go to the club to see them, it is the same six minutes every night from then on.

"I couldn't do that. As a matter of fact, one time, my father called me up and he said, 'You know you are *TV Guide*.' I said, 'What do you mean I'm *TV Guide*?' He said, 'I'm sitting with the *TV Guide*. You are on *Hollywood Squares* every day—you're the center square, right? (I used to take Paul Lynde's place when he got sick or took a vacation.) They have a big ad for you. You're on Merv Griffin. You're on Dinah Shore. You are co-hosting [Mike] Douglas all week, and you're hosting *The Tonight Show* all week. You're *TV Guide*. This is David Brenner Week.' Then he called me after my Friday-night hosting of *The Tonight Show* and he said, 'I gotta tell you something, what's amazing is, I watched every show, you didn't repeat one joke on any of those programs.'"

Gilbert Gottfried also subscribes to this simple method of stand-up comedy: Just wing it once you get there. "I've always been bad at writing it down. It's like something comes to me on stage—sometimes I remember it afterwards, but I've never really written stuff down. I do try to. What's tricky about not writing it down is that you can lose a joke. If the joke is, 'I ate the entire chicken,' and instead, without thinking about it, you say, 'I ate

GILBERT GOTTFRIED

Gilbert Gottfried headlines at comedy clubs across the country. He is also a frequent guest on *The Tonight Show with Jay Leno* as well as a regular on *Hollywood Squares*. Additionally, Gilbert was nominated for a Cable Ace Award for hosting his own series *Up All Night* on USA. Gilbert has made a series of offbeat film performances including *Beverly Hills Cop II, Problem Child, Problem Child II, The Adventures of Ford Fairlane*, and Walt Disney's *Aladdin*, where he voiced the character Ayego the Parrot. Gilbert has appeared on Comedy Central in the *Friars Club Roast of Hugh Hefner*.

GILBERT GOTTFRIED'S PRETZEL ROUTINE
BARRY DOUGHERTY & GILBERT GOTTFRIED

BARRY: Right now I'm flying on a plane from LA to New York and I just finished opening up the little pretzel packet the flight attendant doled out as the appetizer to lunch. There's a routine in here somewhere, seeing as I can't open the packet. I'll admit I stopped going to the gym but I'm still pretty good when it comes to opening up tiny plastic bags. In any event, I've just apologized to the man seated next to me seeing as he's now removing pretzels from his shirt ... and jacket ... and hair. I'd like to say my pretzel packet exploded from an unforeseen force but the truth of the matter is, it just sort of all got away from me during the struggle. There are pretzels everywhere which explains why the letter "H" on my keyboard is stuck—pretzel salt has lodged between the H and the J.

I'm considering going up to first class and asking Gilbert Gottfried if he can do three minutes on my pretzel ordeal. Yes, as it happens, Gottfried is sitting in first class—to clarify, I'm in coach. I bet he doesn't even have pretzel packets to open—or maybe the flight attendant opened it for him.

You see, it all starts with a situation, then an observation, and then the bit. I did indeed ask Gilbert for a routine, only not at that exact moment. I waited until we had lunch a few weeks later as opposed to barging into first class. You can't just do that these days.

In spite of his fear of this now becoming known as his pretzel routine, here is Gilbert Gottfried's Pretzel Routine:

GILBERT: So I'm on a plane and they hand me a tiny bag of pretzels. Who cares that I asked for an afternoon flight leaving Monday and they booked me on an evening flight leaving Friday? I've got a tiny bag of pretzels. Why complain that to go from New York to Chicago I have to change planes in Peru. I now hold in my undeserving hands a tiny, stale bag of pretzels. So what that I have no idea what part of the planet my luggage will end up in; and what's so bad that I'm in a seat that's so small and crowded that the only way I can squeeze in and out of my seat is with a shoe horn. I have a bag of pretzels. Oh, how delicious. I look forward to eating them, savoring the three-and-a-half pretzels packed in there and then picking at the grains of salt at the bottom for dessert.

My only problem now is opening the bag. I start tugging on the bag; they're impossible to open. The plane I'm on is totally unsafe. It feels like it's made out of Styrofoam, but my bag of pretzels has a state of the art security system. I politely ask the stewardess if she has a chainsaw. I give the bag one final tug using all of my strength, the bag finally breaks open with torrential force, the pretzels shoot out. One knocks out the pilot, the other rips off the wing of the plane. We start hurdling downward, about to crash into a pygmy village in the Congo, which I'm very happy about, because that's where my luggage is.

the whole chicken,' and for some reason 'entire' was the thing that made it really funny and 'whole' gets nothing, you're screwed.

"Your mind wanders up there sometimes. You find yourself thinking about whether you're gonna have a hamburger later that night, or where you put your green sock … then you think, 'This is the part of the bit that never gets a laugh; this part gets the laugh and I should really work on that part.' It's only when you're on stage, while you're doing it. A lot of times too, if you start going into a bit that's kind of wrong, it's like when you're driving on the highway and you miss your exit and it's gonna be a few miles before you hit the next exit. You can't turn around in the middle of a long bit, and you're thinking, 'Ugh, now I'm stuck. There's only so much I can do with this, and the crowd's not buying it. I can't back out now, I missed the exit.'

"Scientifically, if someone doesn't like you, it's always the guy sitting way up front or in a part of the club that has the most lights. The negative people always sort of position themselves in a place where you can see—everyone can see—they've got their arms crossed, giving you an angry look."

Well, maybe there's a reason for that.

For comedy perfectionist Phyllis Diller, preparation involves more than just knowing her jokes. "The room matters, and after all these years in the business I know what the room should be like. It should not be square, it should be oval. Oval is the greatest. Like an actual old-fashioned amphitheater. It should be tiered. The closer the people are together the better the show will be. The seats must be red; the whole thing should be red, red to dark red, to wine. Now, you can't work a blue room. The blue room where I learned this used to be in the Roosevelt Hotel. It is elongated, it has posts holding it up and it is blue. It's called the Blue Room and nobody can work there, because I've gone to see other people there and thank God I was there to help them. It's not a comedy room. Red is your color for comedy and, remember: oval, close together, good sound.

Cary Hoffman

CARY HOFFMAN is the owner of Stand-Up NY comedy club in New York City. Cary's club has a reputation for showcasing some of the hottest up-and-coming stand-up comedians in the business. Along with running the club, Cary also manages many of the comedians showcased in comedy clubs around the country. When he is not delving into comedy, he is also performing himself, as a singer—but not just a singer, an interpreter of Frank Sinatra. Sounding uncannily like the Chairman of the Board, Cary takes his show on the road with a trio of musicians bringing back the sound and style of Sinatra.

When you are sitting someplace all by yourself, you get self-conscious and you don't want to laugh out loud. The best comedy room in the whole world, on the planet, is Harrah's Sammy Davis Jr. Room, in Reno. It seats five hundred. It's oval, it's dark."

Cary Hoffman, who makes sure that his Stand-Up NY comedy club is laugh-friendly, also weighs in on the nature of a good comedy venue, talking about the layout of his club—long rows of tables, pushed close together. "It's the easiest way to squeeze in the most people. If I took that space, which is less than two thousand square feet, and did it as a restaurant, I'd fit seventy-five people. I get much more in there now. Laughter is contagious. You're sitting next to somebody, you're touching them, and all of a sudden you feel their body shaking. Either they're having sex or they're laughing, and both are nice—but I can only charge a cover charge for the laughing."

Once the room has been assessed, Diller moves on to the business at hand—comedy. "I was always such a fan of Bob Hope, and I think that my delivery is pretty much copied from him. It's all about knowing where to put the pause. It's amazing how sometimes putting a pause in a sentence assures you of a laugh. It's something you can tinker with all your life and I still am. I'm tinkering with it. With everything, unless I've already got it figured, I'll still be tinkering on the last show of a run. This is true of Broadway shows, too. On the very last show, they are still talking about what would have been better."

With Diller, practice makes perfect. "A concert pianist wouldn't dare not work for a month. She has to practice four hours a day, even when she hasn't been booked. With stand-up comedy, how you gonna rehearse? You have to listen to tapes or study, but I have to admit, it bores me to listen to my own tapes. I'm going to have to get better at it. I'm gonna have to force myself. A lot of people practice at little clubs and try to get it back before they go to the paying jobs, or to work out new material." So how does Diller work it out? "A line at a time, an idea at a time, a bit at a time. Sometimes it's just a line, sometimes it's a whole bit. Sometime it's just a great line and with that line, other lines come to you. It all just happens in my head. It's just natural for me. I'm sort of really a light touch with everything."

Susie Essman concurs with Diller's assessment of what works. "The venue's important, the vibe in the room, who goes on before you—everything like that is important. But basically, in a split second, there's a little file cabinet in my head, a little Rolodex, whatever the hell it is, that I go through at rapid speed if something's not working and I gotta call out something else. Sometimes nothing works. Sometimes, no matter what I call on, they just will have none of it.

"I prepare differently to do a Roast than to play a comedy club. When I do a Roast, I'm extremely well prepared. I think that's a mistake a lot of people make. If you look at the people who do well at the Roasts, prep is everything because it's difficult. First of all, you're doing it in a ballroom, which is impossible. It's an impossible room. There's zero intimacy in that room. Because they're televised, you have to be so prepared. Now, as prepared as I am at those kinds of things, I still improvise within a set—but I can do that because I'm so prepared. I know exactly what I'm doing. The trick is to make it seem like I'm saying it all for the first time, that's a little acting trick.

"When I go on stage in a comedy club I'm not prepared at all. Unless I have new material that I want to work on, then I'm very focused on the new material. Usually, I jot down a premise and it's in my head, just sitting there, and I go on stage and do it having no idea what my punch line will be, and I find my punch line on stage. It's really scary. I think that doing the rote material is the bane of every comedian's existence. That's always the hardest thing. What happens, for me at least, is that I get addicted to killing. So I kill so much, I have such a high kill ratio, that I get addicted to it. I don't want to throw new stuff in that's not necessarily gonna work, but until you put the new stuff in front of an audience, you just don't know."

Essman has a philosophy on trying out new material. "I like to do it as much as possible, but I don't. It depends on how much I'm performing and how lazy I am, and what's striking me and what else is going on in my life. There are so many people who haven't seen me. But then there's the 'greatest hits' theory. Sometimes when I do a headline set, like at Caroline's, people come who have seen me many times; they are upset if I don't do certain things. I'm going this week to see Barry Manilow—now, do I want to hear him sing all new material, all new songs? No, I want to hear the songs I know. I go to hear the Rolling Stones, I want to hear "Satisfaction," I don't want to hear a brand new set. So, in a way, you kind of have to look at it like that. But every time I do a headline set I see a lot of people who have seen me before, and I feel like, 'Oh, they've all seen this already. I can't take this.' I get nauseous. I don't have enough new material. There are people like Richard Lewis who have new material every night. I don't work that way.

"Because I play with the audience so much, it's always a different show. Because I don't just do my material, it's always different. I rely on that, maybe a little too

SIMON SAYS ...
MAYBE NOT

Neil Simon is considered to be
one of the more prolific authors
of our time. His Broadway
resume consists of such shows as
*The Odd Couple, The Sunshine
Boys, Barefoot In The Park,
Brighton Beach Memoirs, Biloxi
Blues, Plaza Suite, Broadway
Bound,* and *The Good-bye Girl.
Lost In Yonkers* earned him the
Pulitzer Prize, as well as one of several Tony awards. Neil also
wrote the screenplays to many of his popular plays which
were successfully made into movies. He has authored his
memoirs in the book *Rewrites.*

I asked the comedians if they subscribe to Neil Simon's theory
about what words are funny. I even devoted a sidebar to their
answers. Then I decided to ask the master himself where he
really stands on all this wordplay nonsense, and how it all
began. That's when I realized I should have asked him first.

"I heard it once from Abe Burrows, who wrote *Guys and Dolls*
and *How to Succeed In Business Without Really Trying,* among
others. I was working on a radio show in New York and I think
he made some kind of quip like, 'Remember boys, words with
K in it are funny.' But I figured out that words with a K in them
are funny, because in the days of vaudeville there were no

heavily. That spoils me a little bit and makes me a little
lazy, so that I don't write as much as I should. I'm still
giving them a good show. It depends what head I'm in,
sometimes I'm not in a stand-up comedy head. I'm think-
ing about other things, and my creativity is going in
another direction. The news, my mother is an endless

microphones. So words with consonants became much clearer to the audience. If you had a lot of vowels the words were hard to pick up, and I think it's as simple as that."

Oh dear. That's it? But what about certain days of the week? Or numbers? When Simon wrote *Laughter on the 23rd Floor*, he must've chosen twenty-three because it's funnier than just three, right? "I don't really think comedy works like that. I use numbers but there's no secret about it. I don't think there are any numbers that are funny.

"There are certain things, certain words that are funny. The K thing is the best example because when you hit the right words they sound funny whether there are microphones or not. I think it's what the comedian is talking about that's really funny.

"There's a certain music to writing anything, even Shakespeare, but I think the music of comedy is an important issue. When I write a play, sometimes I'll go back and take a word out of a sentence, not because there are too many words in it but because the rhythm of the sentence is better without it. I try to get rid of all the words that I think are unimportant. Sometimes there are people who speak in longer and more graphic sentences, so I use that. I do most of these things by instinct; I don't have a little monitor there that watches over me.

"Maybe I'm naturally funny, maybe I'm not. I don't know. I don't think it comes down to the sound of the words or the length of the sentences. I think it's a situation and the words follow ... but you can't simplify it down to funny words and sounds. It's all minor stuff."

Now he tells me.

source, conversations I have with people, things I see on the street, these are all just sources of material."

So how do the people who become fodder for comic material react to Essman's act, people like her mother? "I don't let her see me live too much anymore. She's seen me on TV a lot. She thinks that the mother that I do is just somebody I made up and has nothing to do with her. It's really interesting. She thinks, 'That's not really me, that's just part of her act.' That's fine, let her think that. When I talk a lot about ex-boyfriends—and most of the ex-boyfriend stuff I do is a composite—they all think it's them. They all want it to be them, and they all want me to talk about them. It's fascinating. I'll get a call from somebody I haven't seen in years or run into them on the street and they'll say, 'I saw you on TV and you did that bit about the blah, blah, blah. That was me you were talking about, wasn't it?' And it usually wasn't!

"Relationships—since I've had so many of them—are never-ending sources of material. What goes on between men and women is just endlessly fascinating to me. If I say a line like, 'Did you ever run into your ex-boyfriend and think to yourself, "Was I in a deranged, psychopathic dementia?"' Everybody has had that experience, where they run into somebody—'What was I thinking?' Male, female, gay, straight—everybody's had that experience. I mean, sex is one of the driving forces in our lives. Why nobody can talk about it, I don't know." Go see Susie ... she's prepared to talk about it.

Jim Gaffigan may not say too much about sex, but here's how he works on his act. "It varies. I try and write. I go through periods where I'm not writing that much. Like, I'm working on a TV show, I'm studying a script a lot, but I might have an idea floating around or have an old idea in my head. Some of it is kind of organic in that I get up there and start talking about a topic, and I just have a point of view on it. Like I watch the Golden Globes and I think, 'This is so silly.' Then I think, 'Alright, the foreign press votes for this. Geez, this just confirms my belief that the foreigners are dumb.' I might not even do that on stage, but that'll be an idea that's floating around. I also have to put that in the context that I'm a white guy. If I say that on stage are people gonna think I'm just a xenophobic prick. So then I'm like, maybe I can't do that.

"You can't get up there and be in a bad mood, unless you're a bad-mood comic. But if you're a bad-mood comic or a social satirist, if you're having a really good day, you gotta get up there and bitch and moan. It gets to a point where I'm more adventurous than not. Some comics get up there and want to mix it up because there's really no fourth wall in stand-up, so they really want to delve out there. There's something immediate about that, that and the crowd loves it, but I would prefer to use jokes and build jokes. Coming up with a new joke is very rewarding.

"I'm always trying to come up with another Letterman set, whether it's on technology or being from Indiana. So I think in the context of five minutes, which is, in a way, completely different from a live set in a club. When you're on the road a lot, you're thinking in the context of forty-five minutes, and you're also thinking about not burning yourself out. I did a Comedy Central special that they're airing to death, so I'm trying to come up with new material. I've done a lot of Letterman appearances, a lot of Comedy Central, so now I'm trying to go beyond that. You can always get up and do safe stuff that you know is gonna work, but you're not really growing then.

"Sometimes I think, 'Okay, how did I come up with that joke? I had a bagel then I had two cups of coffee, maybe if I have a bagel and another two cups of coffee, I can come up with another joke.' Anything can work in a certain situation, so a joke might be very funny one day and never work again. There might have been a certain level of intimacy with the audience, or something going on in the world that day that made it make sense. That's why topical jokes are great, but they have a short life span. I try to stay away from topical stuff 'cause it's kind of frustrating, there are tons of people writing for Jon Stewart and Letterman who come up with great topical jokes."

Richard Belzer's a topical guy. "I don't sit down and write jokes too often. I have an idea, I make a note, and then I go on stage and write it. I improvise. I write on my feet, which is probably the hardest thing to do for most comedians, but for some reason it's the only way for me. I do sit down and write jokes sometimes, but for many years I'd just go on stage with an idea and start talking about it. I had set pieces that I worked around.

"There was a time that I had twenty-five minutes of good material, which is a lot to have. I had a twenty-five minute act and I had it down and it was a pretty good set. Then I decided, I'm gonna do the last bit first—I tried, like a Rubik's Cube, to change it in every way, and it worked however I did it. Then I became so confident with this twenty-five minutes that I would do a set piece and then I would improvise, knowing that I could go back to the set piece if I had to. The improvisational stretches got longer and longer and I did less and less prepared material as I felt more comfortable on stage.

"There were nights when I would do over an hour of unscripted material, much to the chagrin of other comics. I was notorious but I was the emcee, so sometimes it took me forty minutes to bring somebody on 'cause I was improvising."

"It all depends on the situation," says Jeffrey Ross. "Last night at the Improv, I prepared by smoking some pot with my buddy Ralphie outside, wandering on stage, and doing whatever came to my head. That's Thursday night at the Improv, after working an eleven-hour day on *Watching Ellie*, that's how I prepare.

"For a Roast, or for *The Tonight Show*, that's a whole other story. It's like when you're a senior in college and you learn how to prepare for different things quickly. The Roast used to take me months to prepare for, now I can do it in a couple of weeks. I sit down almost every day, preparing, trying jokes out on people, that's really big. I have certain people I go to and try them out on, and if they say they're funny, I know they're funny. If I can get Buddy Hackett to laugh, I know the joke is a winner. If I can get certain buddies to give me notes and shortcuts and variations, that helps. I hate preparing. I really hate it. I hate rehearsing. I hate preparing, so I don't do talk shows very much, because you have to prepare."

Ross, like every other comedian, can only tinker so much before taking that joke or bit to the stage. "I think it's on a case by case basis. Sometimes, I know the joke works before I try it, I'm getting really good at that. Stuff that's for my act, I used to try it a lot of times, a lot of different ways. Now if I do it a couple times and it doesn't work, I realize it's not gonna work. I hosted the Writers Guild Awards at the Beverly Hilton. I had the best writing staff in Hollywood working with me. I had the guys from *Dennis Miller Live*, Chris Thompson, who's a top sitcom show runner—great guys giving me jokes, helping me write. I had to go up in front of the hardest audience I had ever performed for, the Writers Guild.

"I looked at them, there's Alan Ball, Arthur Hiller, Larry Gelbart, and Blake Edwards. Then there are the people I just wanted to look good in front of, like Phil Rosenthal and Ray Romano and all the network people. I'm going up and doing jokes I've never done out loud. I'm not there to do my act. If all else fails, I could bust into it, but I really wanted to try doing the material that I had created for the event, to see if I could do that, and that's really intimidating. I realized a couple of years ago, if I think it's funny, it's probably gonna work. You become a pretty good editor. I did great, but I was over-prepared. I was so over-prepared that the material was written word-for-word up until two hours before the show. So I'm reading it off a TelePrompTer. You have to really learn it to make it look natural but it's there up on the prompter for me to read.

"The biggest laugh I got was a joke I told before I even looked at the prompter. As I was walking out on stage, I thought of something: The president of the Writers Guild West made a ten-minute speech—it was black tie, at the Hilton—and she walked off. The offstage announcer ... 'Now, your host for this evening ... '—the orchestra kicks in—it's me. I walk out and I say, 'That's great, thank you Dorothy. I think I speak for the entire membership when I say I think we could have read most of that shit in the newsletter.' I just said it, and it got an applause break, and then no matter what I did, it worked. So I was so prepared and had it so down and tried to be really ready that I was able to improvise fearlessly, 'cause I knew I could go right to the prompter.

"That opening joke defined my voice for them, and they knew it was improvised 'cause I didn't know what she was gonna do or say. I knew I had a good opening joke to go to, so I knew that I could do an off-the-cuff remark. If I didn't really know my script, I might have been afraid to try that 'cause it might step on something else I was gonna do or I wouldn't have a good transition. The more you prepare, the more you can improvise."

"I used to tape myself and listen to the tapes," says David Alan Grier. "I don't ever tape myself now, which means I lose probably a third of the best jokes I ever had. It just doesn't work for me. Now, I just perform. I make notes after I'm done, and a lot of the stuff just comes out of the notes and the areas I want to hit. At home, I'll write out as much as I can and then read it over and edit it and then try it out. Usually the material is over-written, and I have to take away things and find the essence and where the joke is, but I find that out by performing.

"If a lot of comics come on and everybody hits September 11th, one after another, then maybe I'll go to another subject, because the audience is getting tired. But I've also been in audiences where, like, nine guys hit the same area and then all of a sudden a comic comes on with a fresh perspective and a different point of view and it's hilarious. It's like you've never heard it before. That's really what you want to do."

Jeff Foxworthy tests the waters before he sees if his material will fly. "I've never been a guy who would sit down and write a complete bit and go on stage and do it. My wife can always tell when I'm gonna try out something new because I'll throw it into the conversation during the course of a week and just see if it gets nibbles, if people chuckle at it. If they do, I probably have five lines, and I go out on stage and, somewhere in the middle of the act, I just throw it in. If three out of the five lines work, I keep those three and go back the next night and add three more. Especially when I'm working every night I can see, over the course of a month, a bit grow into a ten-minute routine.

"Now, because I don't do it every night, I just do it on weekends, and in front of six thousand people who paid a lot of money, I better be funny. I can't just go up there and try new stuff every night. That's why I love going to the little clubs to work out. I guess because I've gotten a little braver, I'll go out and do stand-up for ten or fifteen minutes and then go, 'Alright y'all, I been working on some stuff.' And I'll pull my notebook out and just stand there with a notebook going, 'Is this funny or not?' And if they laugh at something I put a checkmark by it and if they don't, I wad it up and throw it in the trash can. I think audiences love being a part of that. I know that at the end of trying all the new stuff, I can fold the notebook up and do another forty, fifty minutes of comedy and make them laugh and say good night.

"In my mind, my act has always been like an encyclopedia in that there's a certain place I start and a certain place I finish and if I get tired of doing things, I chuck them out. Whatever I stick in, there's a definite place that it goes. It goes behind something and in front of something, so if I do a two hour set, maybe that's the whole set of encyclopedias."

Foxworthy remembers everything, so be careful if you happen to spill your family secrets, they just might wind up on stage. "One of the things that I love is that we all think our family is the biggest bunch of idiots on the planet, and if you went into the house next door, they would be sitting around the kitchen table talking about their family being idiots. I love when people tell me the dysfunctional and idiotic things that their family has done. We all need to hear these things so we feel better about our own families. It's like going to the state fair: You can walk around for five minutes and feel, 'You know what, compared to these other freaks, we're all right.' I really get off on real-life stuff and real people who aren't comics."

"You start to see how your act becomes certain blocks of things," says Carol Leifer. "I have pieces about growing up. I have pieces about traveling, pieces about dating. At a certain point, the act becomes so known to me that I don't have to think about memorizing it per se. But at the same time, when I go out there I want to make it sound like I'm just thinking of it, 'cause if the audience senses you're doing it by rote, they lose interest quickly. So now when I do new material, I kind of put it in between established things that I know will work. I usually write it down and practice it at home a couple of

LISTEN AND LAUGH

In Neil Simon's *The Sunshine Boys*, the characters engage in a hilarious discussion of what is funny—certain sounds, certain words—ideas to which many comedians either consciously or subconsciously subscribe. Every comic seems to agree with Simon, but the funniest word choices tend to vary.

RED BUTTONS

"Orange is not funny—banana is funny. There are certain things. It's unconscious though, it becomes unconscious when you're doing your act, to include those words. Unconscious or not, those are the things that have been set down, like in cement, and everybody talks about it. Neil Simon will tell you that, so it must be true."

ANTHONY CLARK

"You try to pick funny words to describe things. I'll tell you a joke of mine, just so I can say a few funny words. The joke goes like, 'Yeah, I been partying quite a bit. I been livin' la vida loca. I been hanging out with Ricky Martin, or the Rickster as I prefer to call him, and a lot of people only speak Spanish to you when you're hanging with the Rickster and I think that's cool. I took three years of Spanish in high school and all I know how to say is, "There's a cow on my patio."' Then I look at the audience and I go, 'El Toro on my pateo.' And then I go, 'I don't know if it's ever gonna come in handy but if I'm ever down Mexico way, and there are cattle on my porch, I'll know exactly how to report it.' Then I wait and go, 'To the federales.' And it's just words, just stupid, chosen just to say in Spanish 'El Toro' and then in English, 'on my' and then go back to Spanish for 'pateo,' as if that will pass for Spanish."

RICHARD BELZER

"Certain numbers, certain words, certain letters, absolutely, there's no question they're funny. Like, Joseph Heller's, book, *Catch 22*—that's funny. Is 'Catch 37' funny? He tried out different numbers and there's no explanation why twenty-two is funnier than thirty-seven, is there? I think with true comic intuition some part of your brain makes you say a word and then you realize it's funny, rather than sitting down and laboring over each word, going through the dictionary and saying 'aardvark' is funnier than 'antelope.' It might very well be true, but I think it's more intuitive, at least for me. I'm just lucky that way, I guess."

JEFF FOXWORTHY

"I remember, backstage one night at the Comedy and Magic Club, sitting around the green room and Leno and Shandling and Seinfeld are arguing about whether green or blue is funnier. And part of your mind goes, if the audience could see this they'd think that we're insane, but to the comic it is very important, and they were right, one is funnier than the other. I still do that. I've just started writing with my brother a little book of short stories and we were writing a thing last night about people who trade for everything. There are some people who never spend cash, they trade. He was saying his father-in-law was like that, that he could start with a picture frame and end up with a Ford pickup truck through a series of trades, and I sat there and thought, 'You know what? *Birdfeeder* is funnier than *picture frame*.' He was like, 'Yeah, you're right, birdfeeder's funnier.' Why is it funnier? I don't know, it just is.

"I wrote a joke one time around the word Yahtzee, just 'cause I thought it was such a great word. 'The closest I can imagine my father ever had to an orgasm was when he got Yahtzee'— Yahtzee's just a funny word.

"I think February's a pretty funny sounding month. April's too pastel. Gotta have a little bite to it. October's kind of funny. See, people would listen to this and think you're insane."

RITA RUDNER

"Comedy is like poetry, it has to have a scan to it. There are some stock comedy words I'd stay away from because I've heard too many people use them, like 'Winnebago' or 'Food Chain' or something like that. But if I can find a new comedy word that no one else is using, those are my favorite comedy words. I have to test it. That's the only way I know if it's funny.

I say it to the audience, and if they laugh I leave it in, and if they don't laugh I either try and fix it or I don't say it again. They're my boss; they pay me; I work for them."

CAROL LEIFER

"The 'K' sound, the 'KAH' sound is funnier, I think that's true. There are certain things that are funnier than others. If you need a car name for a punch line use, 'Buick.' Buick is funnier than, I don't know, Pontiac or whatever. If you have to have a newer car, 'Geo' is funny."

FREDDIE ROMAN

"When I heard that line in *Sunshine Boys*, I said, 'That's so true.' There are words that are funny. Words that have soft starting letters, 'S', they're not funny. 'K' is great. 'T's are fine and I can't explain why. I do a joke about going to the bathroom and if you use the word 'pee,' it's a guaranteed laugh. If you use 'tinkle,' it's cute, nobody cares. There's a definite correlation between sounds and words."

GEORGE WALLACE

"I think seventeen is funnier than eighteen. I don't know, I really believe in that odd number."

JOY BEHAR

"As a comedian, you do it automatically, you pick the right word. I think it's part of the ability to do comedy. There are certain countries that are funny, like Chechnya. I have a joke, it's a silly, stupid joke but it's about how, when you get older, your body starts to fall. I say that at this point, my nipples are facing Venezuela. Now, why did I pick Venezuela? I didn't pick Chile. I didn't say my nipples are facing Chile. That wouldn't have gotten a laugh. Of course, the word 'nipples' is in there. But if I go up there and say, 'Well, I don't know about you but my nipples are facing Paraguay,' it won't get a laugh, but Venezuela works everytime."

DICK CAPRI

"Some words are funnier than others. Like car is funnier than automobile. Certain words are always funny—'belly button' is always funny. 'Kumquat' is always funny. 'Barracuda' is funny. If you say, 'I was out with this girl the other night, what a barracuda,' people laugh. I have no idea why.

"There's a great classic story that Rich Little always tells about numbers. He did a great impression of Jack Benny and he finally meets Jack Benny, and he said, 'Mr. Benny, I do an impression of you,' and Jack Benny said, 'Well, let me see you do it,' and Rich Little put his hand up on his face like Jack Benny did and he had four fingers up on the side of his cheek, and he said, 'Ya know ... ladies and gentlemen.' And Jack Benny said, 'That's not correct, I don't use four fingers, I use three.' Rich Little said, 'Why do you use three?' and Jack Benny said, 'Because three is funnier than four.'"

PHYLLIS DILLER

"The funniest word should always be the operative word at the end of the joke, and the joke should always end with an explosive sound like 'BOP!' Everybody knows that. You shouldn't use pretty words, you'll never hear a word like mellifluous. Short and tight, tight, tight. Short words, as few words as possible to get the joke. Some words are funny. Look at Rickles with 'hockey puck,' there's an example.

"Music, all comics are musicians: Jack Benny, Henny Youngman, Morey Amsterdam. Johnny Carson with the drums. Phil Silvers with the clarinet, Woody Allen with the clarinet. It's because you need an ear. You're not writing for the eye, you're writing for the ear, and there must be a cadence."

JERRY STILLER

"Neil Simon said K's are funny: If you want to congratulate somebody you say 'kudos.' There's something funny about the use of words that sound like pictures, that demonstrate something rather than describe it. You don't do it deliberately, you find it as you do your work."

SHECKY GREENE

"We talked about this just yesterday, somebody said the word cucumber, I said cucumber is not funny. But if you say, 'We had a pickle.' See, a pickle automatically makes you think of a delicatessen. 'The man brought us our sandwich and didn't bring a pickle!' — But a cucumber ... cucumber? You don't eat a cucumber in a delicatessen, you eat a pickle, what's a matter wit' you?"

SAMM LEVINE

"Everybody says 'puke' is funny, I don't think so. I think 'vomit' is funnier than puke. That's just me. Every time I have to use a word for upchucking or throwing up, I always go with vomit. That's my word, 'cause it's an underused word but everybody knows what it means.

"Funny number: eighty-eight. Eighty-eight's hysterical. I don't know why—number of keys on the piano, I don't know— eighty-eight's a funny number. Ah, the *Sunshine Boys*, words with a 'K' are funny, um, yeah, although by that standard, puke would be funnier than vomit. I think I found the exception to the rule. I go my own way."

LILY TOMLIN

"Words create a rhythm, they create surprise. Language certainly is an element in structuring something. You might have a very funny thought but you have to work at a bit to craft it so

times so I don't forget it when I get up there. I usually tape my performances because I'm a big believer that if you hear it and it did well that night, you can figure out what they responded to."

Leifer doesn't mind giving jokes their due, but realizes that sometimes enough is enough. "You can't really give jokes too many chances. If things don't work three times, then they're just not happening, or you need to find a different angle. I started doing this joke recently:

you get the very best out of it. What day did they say was funny? Thursday? Well, I'm laughing but I don't know why. It's funny that we all think that Thursday is funny. Monday isn't funny, I guess."

STEWIE STONE

"Threes. Threes are funny. My wife and I fight all the time about this, she'll say twos. The rhythm is not right with two. 'K's are funny. Certain names are funny. Buddy Hackett for years used the name 'Schweid. Dr. Schweid.' He always used Schweid and that was the guy who owned the Pines. He hated that guy and for some reason the venom came out of him with that word. I still laugh at him to this day when he says Schweid. I don't usually get involved with days. Certain months are funny: February. 'Cause you could bite into it: 'February.' It's how you attack it. Comedy is basically a feel, it's a rhythm and a feel. Doing your act is almost like a song."

NORM CROSBY

"Certain cities are funnier than other cities. A guy says, 'I come from Hoboken.' That's funnier than saying, 'I come from Detroit.' Over the years, through trial and error, you learn which words are funnier than others. Then again, you can't depend on that for your laugh. Once you start thinking about stuff like that, you handicap yourself; because it ties you. You say, 'Wait a minute, should I say this, should I not say that?' You're better off to just let it flow."

'I walked into a men's bathroom and observed, "What's with all the ice in the urinals?"' The punch line was like, 'Are you hiding extra beers in there?' In doing the joke, what people really responded to was the ice. The part about the extra beers wasn't really working, but the ice got a really good laugh. So in listening to it back, I'm on the path to a good joke. I just don't have it yet." What I want to know is, how did she know about the ice in the first place?

We knew this was coming from Howie Mandel. "Absolutely no preparation. I think everybody needs to do what they do. I need adrenaline. I have my little tools and tricks and skills that make it seem fresh every night. One of those tricks, and it's not much of a trick, is to go in with absolutely no prep and let the audience interrupt or veer me off course so I don't know where I'm going. And that triggers my adrenaline, and my nervous energy seems to work for me. I can't be totally comfortable. I have to be a little nervous for the act to work. I need my heart to be beating to be interesting, I gotta be on the edge.

"I don't think about anything. I stand backstage kind of blankly and nervously and then when they say, 'Ladies and gentlemen, Howie Mandel,' and the curtain opens up and I hear the crowd roaring, there's that adrenaline and I realize I have no plan. I usually begin my act by just screaming along with the audience. I do a lot of screaming and people laugh at that. But while I'm screaming, inside my own head I'm thinking, 'Oh shit. What am I gonna say?' and I just scream until I think of something, and it works for me.

"As I got more and more successful I found out what worked. Whatever works I'm gonna do again. People want me to put the rubber glove on my head, so I'm gonna. I'll close with that 'cause it's a big laugh. And they like when I do the Bobby voice—which is this little boy voice that I do in my act—so I'll do that, and eventually I've filled up an hour and a half. I have an hour and a half of stuff."

Having hung out with Howie backstage at one of his concerts, I can attest that he just sort of hangs around. He ate a turkey sandwich until someone mentioned it was Passover, then he spit it out and just ate the meat—no prepping. Personally, I wanted to study jokes or something. I felt that somebody in the room should be preparing. Then he went on stage and screamed—go figure.

"I do it like sectional sofas," says Rita Rudner, designer of jokes. "I have lots of jokes about different subjects and depending upon what night it is and who I'm speaking to, I move them around and arrange them in different ways. In the middle, I add new jokes, I add a new piece of furniture, a coffee table. And if the coffee table is good, then I leave it in. When I introduce new material I put it in between material that works. I move jokes around so it's not always the same thing. I'm able to try new things but I always have things that work."

When you start your career in puberty, it's a given that changes will be made along the way. Just ask Samm Levine. "I used to go over my set list again and again and again. On the way to the club I would go over it in my head, exactly what I was gonna say, exactly what I was gonna hit. Then I realized, that's not a good way to do it because then you fall into a routine, you can't adjust for laughter. You can't figure out if the crowd is really liking a particular topic you're hitting on or if you should use the "B" material that you haven't used before on that joke. I used to be very set on what I was gonna say and a few years ago I pulled back just a little bit. I learned to linger with a joke.

"I went up to Seattle and on the plane on the way there, I wrote some Starbucks jokes. I mean, I didn't really write them, I just had a vague concept about jokes that I wanted to tell. When I got on stage, I really had only one Starbucks joke—and the crowd loved it. I mean, Seattle, I thought they were tired of Starbucks. I guess all the comedians had that same fear so everybody was afraid to tell their Starbucks jokes. They might not have heard one in a year and they were just ready to hear one. In all honesty, it was not that good a joke. I talked about the first guy to ever walk into Starbucks and said, 'I'll just get coffee with cream.' 'Okay that'll be seven hundred dollars.' What does that guy do? 'Seven hundred dollars? You have a smaller swizzle stick?' 'What for sir?' 'Well for seven hundred dollars, I'm assuming the sweetener is actually cocaine!' I just ran with that. I just ran with the concept of the coffee costing too much and people overreacting, and Seattle being affiliated with coffee. 'How does that feel? Like Los Angeles being affiliated with murder, you guys are affiliated with coffee and Bill Gates. Good for you!' They weren't good jokes, but I could feel the crowd responding."

George Wallace's routines are tailor-made. "If I'm in Las Vegas, I'm gonna do Las Vegas jokes. Last week, I was working for Ford Lincoln Mercury. I was up in front of the top one hundred Ford dealers in America, in Phoenix, Arizona. So I sit down and study, 'What do I say to these people?' I walk out and I go, 'What a pleasure to be here with you, you guys got me in this nice hotel, this nice room, first class everything. The top one hundred Ford Dealers of America. Who's the number-one person here? Who's the number one Ford Dealer in America?' A guy raises his hand. 'Sir, it's a pleasure to meet you. It must be great to be number one in America. You've done well. But you're not the guy I want to talk to. Who's number one hundred? Who's the guy just barely made it in here?' They died. 'Now you know you're not the real number one hundred, you know, somebody couldn't make it. You're not supposed to be here.' Number one hundred raised his hand. They laughed. They went crazy. So you break it down. What do you do? Where are you from? That way, every show is special."

When you're the Dean of the Friars Club and you've been making people laugh for most of your adult life, not to mention hanging around in an atmosphere that just reeks of laughter, your preparation pretty much consists of making sure your alarm clock goes off in the morning. Notes Freddie Roman, "In the theater for *Catskills on Broadway*, you know what to expect, so there's very little preparation because they are paying to see the Broadway show and that's what you are gonna do. But, perfect example, last night I did a 70th birthday party for a man who's a big fan of mine. It was a surprise party and I was the surprise. He's a very wealthy man and they had a hundred movers and shakers there, and I actually spent a half-hour yesterday writing some things down that I knew they would identify with. In a unique situation like that, you do prepare a little more." If it's not unique, then you just be your naturally funny self and wing it, the way Freddie does.

It's a given that Ryan Stiles, in his improv mode, has to wait to be given a scenario before he can go into his hilarious bits. He can't really practice his act ahead of time. "You totally make your mind blank, that's why it's great. I had to go into my son's class for one of those parents' things. I went in to teach his class improv and they were incredible improvisers, because they have no preconceived notions about how things are or should be. Their minds are blank and that's the way you have to be in improv. You can't go in thinking, 'Hey I'm gonna do a scene about a fighter tonight,' you just don't do that. Because, if you start doing that, you're not listening to what other people are saying to you and that's where all the comedy comes from."

Before there was improv, though, Stiles had his stand-up act to put together. "I didn't use cards. I kind of wrote everything on my hand so I could see it as I was adjusting the mike. I wrote some stuff at home. Mike McDonald is a comedian I worked with in Canada. He thinks that a lot of good stuff comes to you when you are sleeping. You dream funny lines, write them down, and then you wake up in the morning and look at it and it's like, 'The dog is barking.' You thought it was hilarious in the middle of the night, but you never know until you actually try the stuff out.

"My problem was, I never wrote enough stuff so I ended up doing my favorite bits and the stuff that worked, but I always admired guys like Leno who would go up with a new thirty minutes every night. After a while, you're working for people who've seen it a million times, and you're going back to play the same clubs all the time. It's not like a rock concert, where everybody wants to hear *Brown Sugar* and if you play new stuff they get pissed off. Comics are exactly the opposite, if you do the same joke twice they get mad at you."

Joy Behar has to be funny every morning on *The View*, and when she's not being funny there, the audiences in comedy clubs expect to see a perfect act. "I always think I'm gonna forget everything. I wonder if Baryshnikov wonders, 'Am I going to be able to leap in the correct way?' The art of performing happens in the moment, so you don't know what's going to happen out there. That's why it's so frightening. If you're an artist and you paint a picture, you see it every day, how it's

IX-NAY ON THE RISQUE

Leave it to comedians to either stop at the edge of a cliff, or keep on forging ahead. They may know their boundaries but that doesn't mean they're going to adhere to them. Stand-up comedians have never been squeamish about crossing certain lines, but what limits are there in this profession? What, if anything, is taboo?

JEFFREY ROSS

"Is anything taboo? I think that has to be qualified. Certain areas are taboo for certain audiences. I've gone up in front of people with spina bifida for a benefit and made jokes about handicap ramps. With the right comic and the right style, they're gonna laugh harder at jokes or material catered to them. Audiences don't like to be pandered to.

"I remember one time about ten years ago, I was opening for Ray Romano. He was headlining in Poughkeepsie, and they told us not to curse. Here's the nicest, sweetest most wholesome act there is, Ray Romano, and he cursed three times, he couldn't help it, because they told him not to. He doesn't even have that in his repertoire. He got heckled and he would go, 'Fuck you,' 'cause they told us not to. There's something in the comic mind that is mischievous. I'm sure if they made an announcement before the Friars Club's Hugh Hefner Roast, 'No jokes about 9/11,' there would have been twice as many because we're used to working on our own terms."

RED BUTTONS

"I think having taboos is dangerous—it becomes censorship. Even self-censorship is very dangerous. I think everything's on the table in comedy, but taste plays a great big part."

RICK NEWMAN

"Hardly anything is taboo. After September 11th, there was a moratorium, that period of time where at first all comedians didn't want to get up on stage. It seemed so shallow, it wasn't important. But that began to change and a lot of them said, 'It's what I have to do for myself and the audience, to get up there and be funny.' Then they began to talk about September 11th and the audience began to respond in a favorable way. I think hardly anything is taboo. I can't really think of anything and certainly after X amount of time, nothing's taboo. Whatever happens, you've got to get back to living and laughing. You just do."

GEORGE WALLACE

"A big taboo in my community, the black community, is: Don't do jokes on Malcom X or Dr. Martin Luther King. I'll touch anything else."

SUSIE ESSMAN

"There are topics that I don't talk about, that are taboo for me, but it's not a judgmental thing, it just not what I feel comfortable talking about. I don't like to talk about child molestation, for example. I don't find that funny. Somebody else could do a joke about it that's funny and I could laugh. In general, I don't think there are any topics that are taboo in comedy, that's what makes comedy. Here's an interesting thing, all totalitarian regimes, the first thing that goes is humor and comedy, because comedy is, by its nature, subversive. Because of that, there really can't be any taboos or limitations on it. The minute you do impose limits, you're denying what comedy really is.

"Historically, the court jester was the only one who could make fun of the king in a certain way. We're needed as the thorn in the side of society because somehow when you say something and it's funny, it's more acceptable. When somebody's laughing, there's a window, there's an opening there to stick in some new ideas or some new thoughts."

KEVIN MEANEY

"I don't think anything's taboo. It's up to the individual. Who's gonna edit you? The audience is gonna be the final judge, so if it is taboo, the audience is certainly gonna tell you that they don't like what you're saying and you'll learn soon enough what's taboo."

JIM GAFFIGAN

"Comedians are not well known for their boundaries. Jackie Mason was irreverent in talking about goyim versus Jews. If we look at tapes from the '80s, there's some very funny stuff, but, from a 2002 perspective it's very homophobic. Or it's very sexist. But during that period it was far out.

"It's really easy to make a joke funny by saying fuck, it's a lot harder to do it without it. So sometimes you'll be like, 'Alright, there's a fuck in there now, but I will eventually get rid of it.' Irreverence is like liberty, it's constantly evaluated and constantly readjusted. Probably in ten years if a comedian goes on stage and says, 'I'm gay,' the audience will go, 'We don't give a shit.' People like Don Rickles, the insult kind of guys, I'm sure he's probably been like, 'What the fuck? I could say that two months ago, now I can't?' "

DICK CAPRI

"Sometimes you gotta be careful with religion. There are certain things—pedophilia—you can't talk about that. Sick things."

CARROT TOP

"Certain things are taboo. For instance since September 11th, I'll talk about Osama bin Laden or Afghanistan and stuff but I don't really talk about the event. I don't bring up the actual day and what happened. There are certain things that revolve around death that I kind of stay away from. There are a lot of comics who totally get away with it. Chris Rock can get away with a lot more than Carrot Top can. My crowd, it's all ages and they think I'm silly. If I go too far they're like, 'This is Carrot Top?' I have a character that allows only so much. I'm clean and I'm silly so if I got up there and started talking about abortion, the crowd would go, 'Oh my God, this is not the guy we saw on Regis.' "

JERRY STILLER

"We never went into four letter things. We just never went that way. People would come up to us sometimes and say, 'You're clean, you're not blue,' so it was kind of a reputation thing.

Henny Youngman would never say an off-color thing on stage, even Berle wouldn't do it, really. There was a certain kind of a line people knew we would go right up to but never cross over."

JOY BEHAR

"No subject is really taboo, but it has to be approached topically. There are certain topics that I don't think are funny—AIDS, abortion—they're not funny to me. But people who say stupid things about them, that's funny ... it's open season on them."

JEFF FOXWORTHY

"I think what's taboo depends on the comic. There are a lot of things that are taboo for me—rape's not funny. I don't like things that hurt people. Somebody can say, 'Well, the redneck jokes,' well, that's self-inclusive. It's not 'laughing at' it's 'laughing with.' But I was never very much into the mean stuff."

CAROLINE HIRSCH

"Years ago, Andrew Dice Clay was at Caroline's and he was doing some AIDS jokes that were really not appropriate and I didn't like that. I told him, 'Please don't do that. Just don't do it.' But it's a freedom of speech issue, and you really can't say no. It's about freedom. Sometimes I cringe."

STEWIE STONE

"You wanna know something? It's how you feel about it. You can almost spot how comfortable a guy is with a dirty word. When Richard Pryor was in his prime, you heard the content of the humor and the feel of what he was saying, so all those dirty words never meant anything. But another guy'll say something and I'll be offended by him. I'm always offended when women are dirty, 'cause it's still somebody's mother or sister or aunt. Maybe I'm old-fashioned.

"I don't get involved in politics, 'cause I'm very involved offstage in politics. When I go on stage it's not my job to persuade the people in the audience to be liberal. I'm a liberal and if I talk about being a liberal, right away I lose half the audience.

If it's entertaining, whatever you're talking about, the people will go with you, it's not taboo."

RICHARD BELZER

"The Holocaust. There's nothing funny to me about the Holocaust or molesting children. I would never go near them. Those are probably the only two things that are off limits, for me anyway, and I think for most people who give it any thought. Sam Kinnison did some very rough stuff—some of it was profoundly misguided. I was close enough to him to talk to him about it, like his homophobia, which I found profoundly repelling and totally unnecessary and vicious. He did start to change his ways a bit after a time, but some of his politics were naïvely right wing. To his credit, he listened to me and realized that.

"One thing that I'm really allergic to, gay-bashing jokes. They make me fuckin' sick, and some comics do them, just reflexively, and I can't take it. There are funny jokes you can do about gay people and heterosexuals and about sexuality, without dehumanizing people. But that's a fine line to walk."

GILBERT GOTTFRIED

"Just a week or so after 9/11 at the Friars Club Hugh Hefner Roast, I said, 'I got to hurry up, I got a flight to LA tonight. I couldn't get a direct flight, they have to make a stop at the Empire State Building.' The audience was quite shocked and quite offended. You do that same joke a month later, it'll probably be fine. It's all about how audiences react, though. I'll do a joke about Jackie Onassis and the audience will laugh, then I'll do a joke about Coretta King and it's like, 'Oooh, he shouldn't have done that.' So you never know. It's always odd when you're on stage and a joke that always worked, they start going 'Oooh,' or hissing. Sometimes I wonder if they're really offended or if they didn't quite get the joke."

going, is the lip looking like a foot ... but we don't know. We don't know. We're up against the fear of the unknown, really. The only way that you can prepare is to say to yourself, 'You've done this a hundred times, you will be able to do it again. The audience will not hit you. You'll be fine and you will in fact remember everything,' even though that's a tough one.

"I'm very strict. I like to add new stuff all the time. Every single set has to be different, and I do what Lenny Bruce used to do: I never do it in the same order. So if last time I talked about my family at the beginning, this time I talk about the Hasidic Jews, start with that. I have to see the audience—what's the make-up of the audience? Are they young? Are they middle-aged? Are they old? Are they Jewish? Are they gentile? Are they black? Are they white? Who are they? And then I see where I'm going to start. I jump all over the place and that's part of the reason I'm scared that I'm gonna forget, because it's not a script."

Being a seasoned pro is a far cry from those first tries in the comedy spotlight. How did Behar gather her material early on? "I decided, well, this is the way you are funny at parties, by just saying crazy things and having fun. So my conception of being a comedian was to create a party for myself. Now, how do I get material to create the party? I was always too scared to just make it up on the spot. So what I would do, wherever I was, if I said something funny or spontaneous and people laughed, I would write it down. Then I'd try to recreate it, try to make it what we call now 'a hunk.' So let's say I said something funny about dieting and people laughed, and the next day I said something funny about my Italian family, and these were different situations. I would add a funny line to the diet section and then to the family section, and I'd start to develop these hunks. I'd only get to do five minutes at a time, 'cause none of the clubs would let you stay on longer than that. This was a blessing because I don't know what I would have done if I had to go longer. But even after you've accumulated material, of course, you're not confident. Is this gonna work again? Am I going to be able to get it to work again?

"Your brain has to be like a computer. At this point I have probably a couple hours of stuff and I have to decide which pieces I'm gonna go to, and then within the pieces there are ad-libs and there are topics that I cover in different ways. I can still talk about President Clinton, for instance, because I'm talking about him historically now. So I'm adjusting the act all the time."

With that adjustment comes the comic's age-old dilemma: Just how long do you give a joke before you realize it's just not that good? "I'm not like Joan Rivers. I heard she used to fight with Edgar all the time because he'd say, 'Lose it, Joan,' and she'd go, 'No. I'm going to try it again.' She's more dogged about it, I guess. Usually, I know if it's gonna work. At this point I can tell you if it's gonna work or not, because I can see the structure of the joke and the timing, and I can see where it's gonna fit in the act. But if I'm wrong, I lose it.

"I'm very diligent. When my boyfriend, Steve, says something funny, I'll take note of it. When I say something funny, he just laughs, and I say to him, 'Why don't you write this down? Or, 'Why don't you say to me, "You could use that?"' He's just enjoying it. So he's not working as hard as I am.

"Last week some woman stopped me on the street. 'Darling … ' and this is something that happened and I've been using it … 'Darling, you look so wonderful, do you mind if I talk to you for a second?' Well, I was in a hurry. 'I just think you are just so adorable and so delicious and you girls on *The View*, the way you banter … Can I ask you a question?' I said, 'What?' 'Do you have a good dentist?' So I said to her, 'Well as a matter of fact I do' and I gave her the name. I said, 'Star uses him. He's fabulous,' and I was trying to walk away. 'But darling, I have to tell you, I love the give-and-take that takes place on the show, the way you play a tennis match up there, it's just fantastic. Does Barbara use him?' I said, 'I really don't know if Barbara Walters uses him because I'm not that familiar with Barbara's dental habits.' 'Oh, but she's wonderful too. I go back with her, I love her, but you girls, I mean Meredith and Star and you, the way you throw that ball around. Does he do partials?'

Now this *happened* to me on the street. I had to talk about it on stage."

"I know what I'm gonna do basically, I've been doing it for a lot of years," acknowledges Stewie Stone. "Somebody once said to Alan King, 'You change your material all the time?' He said, 'No I change my audiences all the time.' You know what you're gonna do. I don't like to prepare. I write an outline, I put down three or four words, and that'll get me into what I'm gonna do. I like to flounder into it because I feel it's "realer" for me to do that than to sound like Winston Churchill, 'Ladies and gentlemen!' I'd rather fumble my way into it and find things out. That's my way, I'm visiting with the audience, I'm talking to them. I'm not above them, I always like to walk around the audience before the show, I like to be one of them."

Stone's fodder for his act comes from his everyday observations. "Shopping—malls, Gap, I've been in every Gap in America. Banana Republic, I'm very big in Banana Republic. When you're on the road you play golf and shop, there's really nothing else to do. After twenty-five years it becomes almost boring, and the exciting thing is to put yourself up the stream without a paddle. It's interesting doing a show at the Friars Club, where you're ad-libbing and kidding around. How will I get out of this one?

"Basically, the most trouble you get into is ethnic. You have to spot the ethnic crowd and if you're working all to one minority and they're not there that one time, you can't do those jokes, people are not gonna laugh. If you're in Florida it's easy to do Jewish jokes. If you're in Montana you know right away, I'm not gonna do that. You have to be smart enough to pick and choose."

Then there's the method comic, embodied in the newer, younger, yet equally funny breed. David Mishevitz is one of these. "I keep a recorder handy in the car and if something particular pops into my head, or something gets me mad on talk radio or something, I'll get the set up or the premise line out to it. I do write set up-punch line when I'm sitting down, and then I try to create around it when I'm on stage. So when I'm writing,

ABC's OF L·A·U·G·H·S

Apparently, stand-up comedy is as easy as ABC. Listening to the comedians, it's obvious that many of them subscribe to the Sesame Street system of laughter. Who knew that comedy could be FUNdamental?

Jeff Foxworthy

"I start at A and go straight through to Z. If I'm doing a twenty-minute set somewhere, I still start at A and end at Z but it may be A, G, T, Z. I'm probably more structured that way than some guys are. When I watch other comics, especially people that are new at it, I get frustrated when I see people bounce around because segues were always real important to me. I think good stand-ups are good at segues. That was always the hardest thing about writing a *Tonight Show* set or a Letterman set because you only had six minutes and if you wanted to talk about your new baby and your wife's cold rear end and the fact that your parents are insane ... how do you tie those together? That was the art, creating those segues. It's always been important to me to have a way to get from point A to point B to point C and get to the end of the night and people don't know how you did that."

George Wallace

"Most comedians do a show A to Z. A to Z. That's the best way to do your show and sharpen it every night. A to Z. I can't do that. I go from G to C and then B to R."

if I have a joke, I have to get up and walk around and talk about everything that's around it—the particulars, what would this character say, who else is there? I don't have all of that written out, but I do like to build around some kind of structure."

Some comedians just can't let go of jokes all that easily, even when they're just not working. Mishevitz is one of them. "I'll try to rewrite it or put it in a different situation or follow it with something different. But if I really like it, I just throw it out there. I don't use one

Susie Essman

"I'm not one of those stand-up comics who gets on stage and goes from A to Z and does her act. I never know where I'm going."

Norm Crosby

"You have to keep changing your act. You can't depend on a set, rote, mechanical A-B-C-D thing that you did last week or two weeks ago. I don't do an ABC, it could be GBFL one night, it could be MNPQ the next night."

David Brenner

"Some comedians have an act, I've never had an act. They start at A and they go through Z and I start one night at C, and go to M, then go to N, and then T and then the next night I start at B and go to Z and go back to T. That's how I work."

Pat Cooper

"There are natural comedians and there are mechanical comedians, and there are comedians who don't belong in the business. A lot of mechanics study their timing and then if you interrupt their timing, they gotta start back from the beginning again because they're in a line of A, B, C, D, E, F, G. If you interrupt them at G, they got to go back to A, they lose their place."

---

that's not getting any laughs at all, though. I've written a joke and never came up with a tag or a good punch line for it until two years later. I never throw anything away. You never know. If you're just riffing or something, it could find a way in."

Like many professions, comedy has it's own quirky vocabulary that the neophyte might want to brush up on or they'll be as lost as I was talking to these guys. Take "tag" for instance. What the hell is that? According to Mishevitz, "It's the tag to a punch line or an addition to it. For example: My cousin married a sugar daddy, but he's on a tight budget (that's the setup); that makes him a sweet and low daddy (that's the punch line); but they treat each other as equals—(that's the tag)." Who knew comedy was so complicated?

Kevin Meaney prepares his potpourri of laughs in a variety of ways. "I don't sit down and write it out—well, some bits I do. I'll write out what this character would say, but now that I have my daughter Kate, I really like talking about potty training and stuff. It's silly potty talk, but it's like this really good chunk that I have now. After I say something funny, I write it down so I'll remember it. Like, the diaper package says, 'Holds up to thirty-five pounds,' and that's just funny in itself. You think, 'Thirty-five pounds of what?' so you don't even have to say it and the people get it. 'She sleeps through the night, as far as we know—we drink a lot.' It's a regular setup-punch line joke. Then there's this video out about potty training with a clown, and children are with the clown. 'I don't want my daughter with a clown going to the bathroom!' It kind of writes itself. Sometimes it's that easy to write something—clown and children in the bathroom, that's disgusting—that's a bit. You kind of present it in a dramatic fashion for the laughs. So I just approach it like that, it's more organic than what people like to see, the personal aspects of my life. Personalizing your humor, that's the hard part. You can write a bit—'How 'bout the weather today?'—whatever, you can have a set up and a punch line, but you have to personalize it.

"You just practice. I don't practice in front of a mirror but I have to rehearse some things. The mirror is twenty-three years of audiences. You learn over the years, not in one show or one year or two years. I learn even now, I think, 'Look at that, I got a laugh doing that.' If you get up on stage and do something like I have, for twenty-three years, you ought to get somewhat good at it—one would hope. It's fun to practice in front of an audience and kind of goof things up, I mean, it's comedy.

"I always add to my act. That's what I have, I have an act and I can always add to it. I don't write a new act per se, I add to it. The act is always there. Pretty much anybody would say that, even Jay Leno. He has an act when he goes out to do a corporate date or Vegas or something like that, and he's pretty much still doing the act he's been doing for twenty years. He'll add jokes that worked on *The Tonight Show* or something, but pretty much he still does his act and that is something that nobody can ever take away from you."

How does a superstar of comedy like Red Buttons prepare? "I keep it up to date. I'm writing every single day and I'm so happy about that. I feel wonderful about that. I feel very productive. If I read the paper that day, I got something. Every single day I got something. Newspaper, magazine, and just living. I don't do mother-in-law jokes. I don't do the old family material. I come out of a sophisticated Broadway, Copa mentality—it's smart material. That's my grab bag. I don't analyze it, not that I know of. Now I just walk out and do it and I get a pretty quick idea of what is a funny line or not a funny line."

Now, you just know that a prop comic isn't going to pop on stage unprepared. "It is a lot more involved than people think," says Carrot Top. "I've got a big stage show and I've got all the stuff behind me that I kind of pick and choose among as I go. I change the show, like, I'm in Pittsburgh tonight and it's St. Patrick's day, a big parade down here, so I'll do a whole bunch of stuff about St. Patrick's day and about being in Pittsburgh, and about the Steelers. I try to localize my act, which keeps me on my toes but also keeps the crowd involved. 'Oh wow, how did he know that? How did he know to pick on X,' whatever. Like, at Foxwoods, I talk about gambling and about the Indian reservation. Whatever is going on in that particular area.

"One of the first things people say to me is, 'How did you know to pick on blankety-blank? Or how'd you know about Smashville?' I just kind of ask questions. I usually go out during the day and check the city out and get some ideas. I see if there are any landmarks or anything that's funny. I'll ask people questions and get informed by the local crew as to what's happening in town. And I'll add something topical, about the war or

President Bush. I really like to be current, but it's hard, too, because sometimes the jokes are great and then they're gone. During the Olympics I had a whole bunch of stuff about the games, but they're done now so it's a lot of good material that I can't really use anymore.

"If I need a new prop, I'll go find it. And if I find a cool prop, I try to make something of it. Like I found a mini-toilet and I thought, 'God, this is so funny looking, what can I do with it? So I made a plate for bulimics. It's a plate attached to this toilet seat so you can eat and throw up at the same time."

Not all working comics make their entire living doing stand-up. Take Anthony Clark, for instance, who spends much of his time working on his sitcom, *Yes, Dear*. "I've done stand-up for about ten or twelve years now, no, more like thirteen, fourteen—Jesus, I'm glad I'm not a banker, I cannot do numbers."

Well, at least we know he can do laughs, and since that's what pays his rent, to hell with numbers. "Now, I haven't done it in about seven months because of the TV show, but I'm going back and performing at Carolines in New York and in Boston at the Comedy Connection. I haven't done it forever but I have a CD of a live concert I did in Boston. I'll just play that three or four times and then integrate my new material, all the stuff that's happened in the last seven months that I haven't talked about. I'll probably go on here in LA a few times and do ten and fifteen minute sets at the Improv to see if the new stuff works. What doesn't, I'll cut or rewrite, and what does, I'll try to find a nice spot for within my act."

How does one prepare a rant? In the case of Pat Cooper, "I don't. I cannot write a story on paper because if I read it a second time, I won't say it. I gotta either tape it or go up there and just throw it away and never say it again. I know I can't use it a second time. I've had guys take my material. I say, 'You don't have to take it, I'll give it to you, you asshole. It don't belong to you because it don't fit you. I can get away with it.' They look at me like, 'Well how come he's getting laughs on those words and I ain't?' 'Because you're an idiot.' Everybody drives differently—I'll give you the ingredients to a meatball

photo by Marty Brinton/CBS

ANTHONY CLARK is starring in the CBS sitcom *Yes, Dear;* having previously starred in the series *Boston Common.* He has brought his stand-up humor to such venues as *The Tonight Show with Jay Leno, Late Show with David Letterman,* and *The Rosie O'Donnell Show* as well as comedy clubs around the nation. In films Anthony has appeared in *Dogfight, The Thing Called Love,* and *The Rock.* He has also starred on Broadway in *The Grapes of Wrath.* Anthony studied acting at Boston's Emerson College, and became exposed to the same comedy traditions that influenced Jay Leno, Norman Lear, and Steven Wright. His blue-collar brand of humor won him the "College Entertainer of the Year Award" while at Emerson.

and I'll use the same identical ingredients, yours will taste different from mine. Same ingredients. It's something within the fucking air, within the fucking hands, within the love of wanting to make that meatball round or wanting to make it beautiful, love of cooking. I care about doing comedy.

"I never write anything down, but you gotta understand *me*, I do that because it works. I'm doing a thing in Philadelphia for corporate people. They call me up, I say, 'Listen, give me a list of names, who are the ball-breakers and who are the guys that you like to tease. Tell me their bad habits, if they like bowling, if they like to go to the track. Then I'll walk up there and say, 'and you, and you, and you.' And they go, 'Holy shit.' Taking the time to do that is even better than doing your act. I did a thing for judges at the Friars Club a couple of weeks ago. 'This judge over here, he's retiring,' I said, 'I'm glad you're retiring, because you look terrible in a robe'—whatever it was it worked for that moment. People say, 'Well, geez, Pat, oh, you gotta do that at the bricklayers convention.' I say, 'No. It don't work,' and that's observing. I have an act, I have routines, of course, but I'll always go out there and do ten, fifteen off the top. I gotta yell, I gotta talk to the floor, I gotta scream." And that's gotta make people laugh.

Norm Crosby is now going to tell us what he does to prepare. "I'll tell you what I do, see? I take a basic line or two lines or a little piece of business that I think is cute and I embellish it. So every night I find something to add to it. For example, I had a line, 'When Christopher Columbus landed he put the flag in the sand and he said, 'I claim this land in the name of Queen Isabella.' And the Indians were peeking from behind the bushes and one Indian turned to another one and said, 'Well, there goes the neighborhood.' That line became a routine on Christopher Columbus and the landing, and it segued into Thanksgiving with the pilgrims, and then drummers sitting around a fire banging drums at a witch doctor. There's a medicine man up there with the bones in his nose, and dancing and screaming, and one of the old ladies around the fire turns to the lady next to her, she says, 'That's my son, the doctor.' You can go anywhere with it. I added to it and it became a twenty-minute routine. I do that even now, just keep adding.

"Buddy Hackett, who really knows a lot about comedy, is a very brilliant comedy mind," notes Crosby, "He knows what's funny. He knows why it's funny. Buddy says when you walk on a stage, you say to a lady sitting in the front, 'I like your scarf. I like that scarf, I like the color—burnt sienna, that's a strange color,' and you talk about the scarf and you talk about burnt sienna. 'Vincent van Gogh used to use that color a lot ... ' and you get yourself out on a limb somewhere, where the audience is looking at you and you have no idea where you're going and you just turn around and make it funny and get back to a punch line somewhere and get the applause and the big laugh out of that scarf or that woman or the color, whatever it is. Then you're a comedian."

Says Crosby, "I think of funny things sometimes and I jot 'em down—could be in the middle of the night—I could be somewhere and see something and I say, 'Gee, that could be funny.' I prepare by learning who the audiences are, why they're there. I was primarily a club date act. I started in the business in Boston and I worked for a couple of years before I ever walked into a nightclub. I did club dates. I did banquet dates. I did conventions. I worked for club date agents, there were a bunch of them in Boston.

"Every major hotel in the United States of America, in their ballrooms, in their banquet rooms, every single night of the week, they have a party. It could be the Knights of Columbus, the Masons, the Eagles, the Kiwanis. They could be gynecologists, they could be dentists, they could be surgeons, they could be lawyers, they could be anything. And these people buy shows. There are certain agents who sell them a show for their affair—a singer, a comedian, a magic act, an impressionist, and those are the type of shows that I did.

"The way I would prepare was to find out who these people were, why they were there. If it's a Knights of Columbus, a Legion, or the Masons, if it was a ladies night, it's good to know that. If it was the President's Installation, it's good to know that. If it was somebody's birthday celebration, that gives you a direction. So you can bounce off of that and use it. 'Well isn't it nice to be here celebrating Joe's 50th Anniversary? ... oh, and Mary ... stand up, take a bow.' Now you're home free, you've won the audience.

"I would go into the convention hall before the show and pick up little pieces of literature from the different exhibits and booths. Let's say it was a gynecologist convention, there would be exhibits by surgical companies, rubber glove companies, medicine companies, bandage companies, 'cause they sell this stuff to the doctors. So you get little pieces of literature and you read some of the terms and you walk out on stage and you say, 'You know, the hemoglobin count is not necessarily the proper count, 'cause they don't have computers to count the hemoglobin and if the nurse isn't feeling well, it's not a good count.' You talk something ridiculous, but the fact that you mentioned terms that they are familiar with brings them right into you. You learn a few medical terms.

"If it was lawyers you'd pick up a few legal terms and get a couple of names. They're honoring Justice Berger, say. 'I remember Berger when he first started out—he was a criminal lawyer. I mean if you gave him a case, it was a crime.' Within five minutes you've got the whole audience in your pocket, then you segue into whatever material you want to do, and every once in a while you throw in something to keep their attention—a legal term, a medical term, a butcher term to keep the butchers happy, a grocery term if it's grocery guys—but each time, the audience thought that I wrote the act specifically and expressly for them, even though I did the same act. They heard little things, enough so that they said, 'Hey, he wrote that for us.'

"Even now, when I work in Atlantic City I talk about the beach and the horse that used to jump in the water and the steel pier where all the big bands played. When I'm in Vegas I talk about Vegas, the desert, the pioneers who fell in the slush and trudged through the cacti and slid into the arroyos because they were idiots. They didn't know the expressway came right from the airport. When I worked at Harrah's in Reno—people come to get divorced. It's the same principle as doing personalized things for club dates. You don't do a set, mechanical, rote act every time."

It's all good. Write it down, don't write it down. Memorize it verbatim, don't think about it till you're introduced on stage. Talk to the audience, ignore them. Do it in a red room, a round room, or an empty room. Practice in front of a mirror or your friends, or just wait for the audience to tell you if it's funny or not. As long as you know that once you get out on that stage you will make laughter happen, that's all you need. There are as many methods of preparing for your act as there are rock stars who overdose. What works for you is as personal as your own style, and once you find the formula, that's one less hurdle on the track to being a stand-up comic.

CHAPTER 6

TAKE OUR ADVICE AND JUST DO IT

...Or maybe you should consider cleaning bird- cages for a living

Don't you think that Wrongway Corrigan could have used some sage advice when he flew his airplane from New York to California—landing in Ireland? What about Liz Taylor? You'd think she'd welcome a tip or two from a marriage counselor once in a while. Perhaps Mariah Carey should reconsider paying the person who suggested she star in *Glitter*. Everyone needs advice along the way, and stand-up comedians are no different.

You've read their stories, laughed, and possibly even cringed along with these comedy pros. They have either opened your eyes to a bountiful new career or have you heading over to the DeVry Technical Institute to learn a real skill. If you still think that stand-up comedy is the only way for you to go, then listen up because they've got a few more tips here for the neophyte comic.

"All those self help books are the same book. It's like getting in shape: 'Oh, you know what this book says? I should do sit-ups.' That's interesting, I don't want to do sit-ups, though. Maybe I'll read THIS book." Oh dear, okay, maybe not the best tip for me to include in *my* book. Thanks, Jim Gaffigan, for that honest but purposely obtuse comment on help guides. "You can read about stand-up. I'm a student of a lot of things, too. I read all the books but in a way it comes down to doing it yourself." Now he's starting to make a little sense—the part about learning by doing, though—not what you can or can't get out of a book.

In any event, these are the people who have seen it, heard it, and been through it all, so they just might help you get your feet wet. They basically guarantee that you'll risk drowning, but lifeguards are standing by. Hey, don't worry. You'll do fine.

Gaffigan did say some other things worth repeating. "You have to write a lot, and that's advice I should take more often. You should perform as much as you can, I mean likability is important but people that really make an impact on me are great writers. Someone like Brian Regan may be talking about Pop Tarts in one of his stand-up routines, but the way he writes, it's brilliant."

Kevin Meaney suggests, "Be an emcee and you'll get lots of stage time throughout the night. You can go up there and hit them with a little bit of this, a little bit of that. The next time you bring up somebody else you can do a new bit; you can do little two-minute pieces before you bring the next comedian up. I think emceeing is very important in getting to a comfort level on stage. You have to be fearless. It's that type of a business—you can't show fear.

"If you think a bit is funny, you should continue to do it because it makes you laugh. I mean, my wife and my sister have said, 'I don't really like that bit about the liver, I don't think that's funny.' I could care less what my sister or wife think. They're not up on stage, what do they know? They'll say that it doesn't work, but you keep working on it. If you believe it's funny and it makes sense to you, you should continue to do it and eventually, hopefully, you can get the audience to see what you're presenting. Maybe it's one word that you didn't put in there at first. You'll find that eventually.

"The bar is always being raised—having to come up with a new bit—I love it when I come out with something that's so good that somebody says, 'God, why didn't I think of that?' It's all about coming up with new, innovative things to do. I'm thinking about doing something with file footage video. Showing Kennedy being shot, the Zapruder film right on the stage, and next you hear my mother going, 'Get in the house! Get in the house!' This is what really happened to me. The A-bomb goes off in Nevada, 'Get in the house—they're testing bombs!' I kind of have these visions of things to incorporate into a new show, stuff that I haven't seen anybody else do. I like that direction, it's funny and it also fits in with what I do. Everybody tries to come up with new things, but it's basically a set up and a punch line, and how well you can disguise that set up and how well you can disguise that punch line so that all of a sudden they're laughing."

Richard Belzer suggests you invest in a tape recorder. "When I started I was very big on recording my show every night and I recommend that other comics do it. I think it's invaluable, 'cause if you play back your set the next day, you'll hear things in it that you might not remember if you didn't. Your memory might play tricks on you and you'll think, 'Oh, that wasn't as funny as I thought,' or 'That was funnier than I thought,' or 'This could be said slower,' or 'This could use a little more set-up.' I used to have hours of sets and I didn't always listen to them, but when I did they were instructive. Often they were disappointing because what you think was a great set, the material cannot be repeated for some reason—the magic, the dynamics of the night, the physics of the night, some kind of weird science and the joke won't work. There were times where I did something that was really funny, I mean, killed, then I would do it the next night and it just didn't happen.

"I think comics, as a rule, will delude themselves if they didn't record. Sometimes they are really hard on themselves and they did really well. I remember when I emceed, a comic would come off and say, 'That was terrible.' I'd say, 'Are you kidding?' I was kind of the cheerleader. The classic joke, this woman comes up to a comedian in a nightclub and says, 'You were so funny, you made me laugh so much, I've never seen anyone so funny. I'd like to take you home right now and I'll do whatever you want. You can take me. You can have me. Whatever you want.' 'What show did you see? The first or the second?' That says it all. He's most concerned with which show it was, which was the better set.

"Try a joke out more than once. I used to have a rule that you give a joke eight or ten tries, maybe you need to get it on its feet and edit it or add to it, but trust your instinct. If you think something's funny, don't cut it because one time it didn't work. Give it a few times, I think that's really important. My main advice, and this might be hard for a lot of comedians, is to really try to tap into what it is about yourself that's funny. Try to find something in your own life and personality that steers the material. I think the best comedians are the ones that have a voice and they're talking in that voice, rather than writing traditional jokes and doing 'the straight man with lines,' as I call it. I mean, there are a lot of guys who write jokes and then go up and recite them and they get laughs. But to me it doesn't say anything about who this person is and why they think what's funny is funny."

Belzer is a master of incorporating the audience into his routines, something that not every comic is capable of doing. "Ninety-nine percent of comics are terrified, terrified. Even really good comedians don't want to talk to the audience. But I like the danger. It's something you cannot teach. You can't teach a jazz musician how to pick a solo, it's just so intuitive. You might have a piece of material about talking to somebody, a set piece that if somebody in the audience hints at something you can go into it. Like you say, 'What do you do?' The guy says he works in an office. Maybe you have an office bit, but try to weave set pieces in and around the improvising, rather than going out and just doing it cold. There are some people who can do that, just go out and bullshit with the audience and find stuff—but it's really hard."

"You gotta try it," says Rita Rudner, "You gotta go out in front of a bunch of strangers, because being funny for your friends is very different from being professionally funny at eight o'clock until nine-fifteen. To me, if an audience didn't laugh at me for ten to fifteen years, I would have given up. I was very lucky in that I was able to develop, not quickly, but within five years I was in television." So there's hope everyone, providing, of course, you're funny.

Freddie Roman tells it like it is. "There are nights it ain't gonna work and you're going to get rejected and you've gotta be able to overcome it and go back and do it again. For every one of those terrible nights there were fifty or a hundred great ones. So if you have the balls to stay with it, you get better. Just doing it time and time again, you get better. Then you gain confidence and all of a sudden you're strong.

"There are guys in the industry that were terrific to me, old-timers. Larry Best and Matt Robins, these guys were my idols going into the business. Then, the first time I ever did an important industry thing, *TV Guide* used to do a luncheon every year with awards and the dais was star-studded: Alan King, David Steinberg, Barbara Walters, all tremendous, and they just asked me to get up and do ten minutes and I destroyed them. David Steinberg was hosting *The Tonight Show* the next week and he put me right on with him and then the confidence started to come.

"The guy that's just starting out has gotta go to the comedy clubs because that's the venue today. There's no more Catskills for people to start at. The few big hotels left won't take chances. So the idea is to go to the clubs. They have these open-mike audition nights, and you do it and if you do well, they'll invite you back again. If you don't do well, find another club and try it again. You just have to keep going out and doing it. In today's world, originality is the most important part. Doing someone else's material does not make it anymore. There was a time when you could get away with it, years and years ago, but not anymore.

"You can sense it in the first two minutes you are on stage, whether they are gonna like you or not. I do a couple of jokes early on to test them, and if they react, I

know I'm home free. If they don't, then I gotta start work-
ing. For a young performer it's hard. Bob Hope would
walk out there for the last fifty years he was on stage and
the people loved him right away, before he opened his
mouth. A young guy comes out, they don't know you,
you gotta prove it to them."

Anthony Clark may not be a math wizard but he has
a pretty good head for tipping. "I don't really know why
anyone would waste forty thousand dollars to get an act-
ing degree. I mean, you can take acting anywhere, but I
have never ever been asked if I have a degree in acting.
Never, ever once. I think it's your body of work and your
resume. You have to start out at the very bottom and
that's the open-mike situation. Even though they're a
nightmare, if you're good enough you'll quickly proceed
into paid work and then into the live stages of New York
and LA, where maybe a manager or an agent with some
pull and some power will see something in you. That's
basically what happened to me.

"Start in a market where there's tons of stage time.
That's not as easy to do now as it was in the late '80s,
when I started. I think Boston still has a very vigorous,
healthy scene. I think Seattle, Chicago, and Denver have
great scenes. I think Houston has a great scene. I know
Atlanta has a great local scene. San Francisco has a great
local scene. If you think you've got it, go there and work
on it for a year or two. I would never suggest that anyone
start right out in New York or LA because every time
you're on stage it means too much. You're judged too
much. These aren't towns to get good in, they're towns to
be good in, to come to and go 'bang!'

"I think if I had continued to have bad shows I
would have gone more in the direction of acting because,
for me, to be an actor was the original goal. I think a lot
of people just adore stand-up and that's what they want
to do but for me, if it hadn't gone well it wouldn't have
been long before I moved on, because there is nothing
fun about going up there and bombing."

If you want to get to Carolines comedy stage,
Caroline Hirsch suggests you keep this in mind:

CAROLINE HIRSCH is the founder and owner of Carolines on Broadway in New York City. Carolines is one of the nation's premier comedy clubs and has helped launch the careers of such giants of comedy as Tim Allen, Sandra Bernhard, Billy Crystal, Pee Wee Herman, Richard Lewis, Jerry Seinfeld, and Garry Shandling, to name a few. Starting out as a cabaret featuring musical talent, Caroline eased the venue into comedy during the comedy boom of the early 1980s. She produced A&E's *Caroline's Comedy Hour* which won a Cable Ace Award for Best Stand-Up Comedy Series.

"Tenacity. You just have to be out there writing and appearing on stage. That's the process. There's nothing else, because you have to grow into it, and if you have talent, it comes out. It takes a long time. That's what you have to do, go up there every night, and get the material right and log the stage time. I gave Joy Behar one of her first, not a big paying gig, but better than Catch a Rising Star or wherever. I think she opened for Richard Belzer— and she wasn't the Joy she is today, this was fifteen years ago. God, has she honed her material. She had something, but she wasn't what she is today." What does Hirsch look for in comedians? "Their own voice. I think that's what makes people stand out. Their own take on a situation, how skewed it is."

Samm Levine suggests taking a sporting approach when you get out there. "Three strikes and it's out, that's the rule for almost any joke, three strikes and it's out. Try it three times, if you can't get two people to laugh at it get rid of it or change it so it's not the same joke anymore.

"Here is the same advice I give to people who say they want to be actors. It's hackneyed advice and everybody says it—be true to yourself. Don't let other people tell you what's funny and what isn't, because what's gonna make you successful is your individual sense of what's funny. If you're the guy who looks at it the way nobody else does, and you can make everybody else look at it the way you do, that's funny. That's why Steven Wright is so wonderful—because before him, nobody ever got up there and said, 'I bought a map of the United States. It's to scale, one mile equals one mile. Last summer I folded it.' Nobody thinks that way, and it's moments like that that bring the audience into your world. Don't let anybody change that world for you, 'cause that's what makes you special, that's what's gonna differentiate you from every other comic."

Jeff Foxworthy shares his practical approach. "Write everything down. Right now I've got a small notepad in my back pocket and a pen in my front pocket. Next to the shower, I've got a pad and a pen, next to the bed I've got a pad and a pen, I've got one in the console of my truck. I think a lot of people have funny thoughts but they don't learn how to catch them. Comics learn how to grab them and do something with them. Because, a lot of times when you laugh at somebody's material you're like, 'Oh I've thought that,' but you just let the thought go by. I find that if I don't write it down, twenty minutes later I'm wondering, 'What was that I was thinking about at the red light this morning?'

"My office is not for the faint of heart, there are folders and stacks of paper everywhere and I can tell you where I was when I wrote just about any particular joke. But now I'll find a stack, pull it out, and go, 'Oh that's funny, I could do something with that.' Maybe I didn't know what to do with it at the time I wrote it down.

"Look them in the eye. And even in those moments of panic you cannot let them know that you're scared or nervous. It's such a great feeling. The worst TV thing I ever did was the first TV thing I ever did, I got called out to do *An Evening At The Improv* back when they started shooting tons of those. It was one of those nights when they were filming, like, five half-hours. We were supposed to go on at ten and ended up going on at one in the morning, and there were fifteen people in the audience that they were begging to stay. I was the first guy up. Never had been on TV, and they told us beforehand, 'Listen, it's getting late, don't worry, we're gonna sweeten the show and put in canned laughter, so you just go up there and do your thing.'

"I looked like I'd just fallen off the turnip truck. I had this horrible outfit and I got up there and started into it, and these fifteen people had heard enough for the night. All they wanted to do was go home, and I was getting nothing, nothing. Two jokes in and I thought, 'Oh, this is gonna be awful and I'm doing TV.' I decided, you know what? I'm gonna look them right in the eye and I'm gonna take these incredibly long pauses to make it look like I'm doing well when they go back and sweeten this show. A buddy of mine in New York, who was a comic, called me four or five months later and said, 'I thought you said you died on that *Evening At The Improv* thing,' I said, 'Oh, it was horrible, it was just death.' He said, 'I am watching it, you are killing.' I said, 'Keep watching it and wait to see if they show a crowd shot.' Sure enough, a minute later he just burst out laughing because there's this roar of laughter and then they pan back and people have their elbows on the tables and their heads on the tables. But because I was standing there staring with that smile on my face, they had to put a big laugh in there. I walked away from it saying, 'I learned a little something tonight.'

"When I was doing my sitcom, we used to shoot next to *Seinfeld* and I remember talking to Jerry one day about the fact that, as successful as his show was, with a sitcom it's always rewrite it, rehearse, rewrite it, rehearse. ... Then you shoot it in two-minute segments and somebody takes it away and you're running on to the next scene and you finish that episode and you start the next episode the next day. The thing about stand-up, we both agreed, is that you know two seconds after it's out of your mouth that it's either funny or it's not funny.

"I've been very lucky and I've gotten to do a lot

of different things—write books, do sitcoms, I've got a country countdown show that I do on the radio. I draw, so I'm never bored. But if you put a gun to my head and said, 'You gotta pick one,' there would be no hesitation, it would be stand-up. I think there are some people, in their soul that's what they are. I never got into it to be in movies or have a TV show. I got into it because making people laugh just thrilled me to the soul and I'm not alone. Look at Carlin or Cosby. I was reading a few years ago that Bill Cosby is worth a billion dollars, and yet he goes out on the weekend and does stand-up. Well, he ain't doing it for the money. He's doing it 'cause he loves doing it. Leno loves it. Jerry loves it. Good Lord, Jerry doesn't have to work ever again, and yet right now, he's out doing stand-up."

Phyllis Diller has enough laughs under her fright wig to be called the Sage of Laughter. "Work hard. Work on your material. Material, material, material. Attitude. Get a stance. Don't just come out and talk. I'll give a perfect example. They know that I'm this housewife, domestic goddess—wish I had that. Anyway, here's an example of a person with an attitude: Richard Lewis. He's a sick man. Prince of pain. Wears all black. His hair is black. He's running all around. He's in a fetal position. See, the audience is being told, this is what it's going to be about, and from then on it's all laughs. That's his stance, his platform. Some of the new comics don't have any 'cause they're doing this and that and the other thing, but the quicker you can get your own persona the better your act will be."

"You gotta be prepared first," suggests George Wallace. "The only way a person can fail is if he's not prepared. I walk onto that stage, I know what I'm gonna do. I don't know exactly what I'm gonna do sometimes but I know it's in the computer." That computer, by the way, is in Wallace's head, lest you think he's lugging a laptop on stage. "I put a lot of data into this computer. When I get on the stage then it knows when to come out. But I am prepared. If you go out not prepared then people can just ruin your show.

"You try not to repeat words when you're telling a joke. Talking about a bus, you don't want to use the word bus until you get there. It's like introducing a person coming out on stage, you should not say that person's name until the end. Don't say, 'George Wallace did this, blah, blah,' just say, 'This man has done such and such....Ladies and gentlemen, I give you....' It's the element of surprise.

"All the new comics out there, stay the hell out of my business, get out of my space—unless you really have a passion for it. You wanna be a comedian, go up there and work to make people laugh. You've gotta be devoted to doing comedy.

"When he went on stage, Milton Berle didn't care what anybody did. That was his moment to take control, be in charge. But these comedy clubs are a little tough. You gotta worry that you're new, who's in front of you, the type of material you're using, and whether you're in the right environment. At that moment, you might be

GEORGE WALLACE began his career selling advertising but eventually moved on to selling out comedy clubs and theaters with his stand-up comedy routines. In 1995 he won an American Comedy Award as Best Stand-up Comedian. Some of his film credits include *Three Strikes, Little Nicky, A Rage In Harlem, Punchline, Postcards from the Edge* and *Batman Forever.* On television, George has appeared in *Seinfeld, In the Heat of the Night, The Fresh Prince of Bel Air, Arliss, Moesha,* and as Don King in the NBC special, *TV or Not TV.* His honest, tell-it-like-it-is humor has made him a stand-up favorite on such shows as *The Tonight Show, Oprah, Late Show with David Letterman, Rosie O'Donnell, Live with Regis & Kathie Lee,* and *Politically Incorrect,* among others.

creating who you are. They say that in comedy, it's a seven-year span before you even know who you are. So you're up there trying out jokes and that's what comedy clubs are for, to try out material."

For Jerry Stiller, who continually broke down that fourth wall with his partner Anne Meara, the audience-filled clubs became his classroom. "We didn't really get to be popular as nightclub comedians," says Stiller, "until we were able to go out often enough to feel at home on stage. And you know what home is like. You just have to keep going out and not giving up.

"You will not find success every night, even if you're at the top of the game. I've seen many great people not do well some nights. The crowd was there for some other reasons, they had other things going on. They wanted to play golf the next morning or they felt, 'Oh, you're a big shot, you're great on television but you're nothing here.' All those factors come in, it's just a question of whether you're willing to continue to do this kind of work, whether you like it or you're nuts enough."

You need to read your audience to know what will work and what won't at that given moment. Let Stiller clue you in: "Once, Anne and I had a date in Boston and we went up there with a piano player—we were gonna do Hershey and Mary Elizabeth and some pieces from *Fiddler on the Roof*. We got up there and it happened to be for the Road Builders Association. At that time the government had just taken away all the money for road building, and they were in a very strange mood.

"When we got up there, we thought everyone would know us. After we finished one sketch, the booker brought in a couple of strippers. I'll never forget it. They loved those strippers and they could not understand one thing we were talking about because they were all disrupted by the fact that jobs were lost and they were not getting anything from the government. You fly up there and you find, 'What is this? What kind of business am I in?' But you play the Blue Angel and they tear the doors down."

Red Buttons has plenty of experience to draw from.

"There are no sure things. I'm at a stage in my life in show business where I don't get nervous. I put myself in the place of a jockey, I'm on that mount, 'boom!' the gate swings open and I'm out there, that's the way I feel about it. It's just that little twinge, that little moment. 'Here you go,' they're pulling the switch and the floor drops out from under you, and it's a great feeling. It's a wonderful feeling, especially if you're prepared.

"The other important thing in our business is home-work. You gotta do your homework. You can't walk up there and depend on, 'Oh, I'm gonna go to the Roast and then I'm gonna sit and I'm just gonna ad-lib it. Very few people are able to do that. Steve Allen was one person who was able to do that. Steve would write the whole thing while he was sitting there—he was brilliant, but not too many people can do that. For most comedians, it's laborious. It's a job, and you figure it out and you do it, and you write and you rewrite and you take out. Then you take your little thing and you walk out and you do it. The trick is to make it sound like you're making it up, that's very important. If you make an audience feel, 'Gee, wow, did he just think of that?' it's wonderful.

"You find the best things on your feet, not sitting in a room in front of a typewriter. It's operating, it's being out there, it's having things come to you off the top of your head when you're loose, when you're free. A Broadway show, you rehearse five, six weeks and you go out there and you break it in in Boston, and you go to Philadelphia, or wherever, and it's a different ballgame. Most of the time, I sit there and I know I've got a Roast to do or something and I'll knock it out in the house but the first time I do it, it's right in front of that audience. Then you can forget about money, you can forget about every-thing, that's when it pays off.

"Make sure you're in it for the right reason and the right reason is just one reason—you love it. You have to do it no matter what. You have to walk through walls, you *have* to do it. You have to be unstoppable. You gotta be able to take no, no, no, no, no, and turn it into yes, yes, yes, yes, yes. In this business, you don't go in

JOY BEHAR, who began her career as a public school teacher, is a regular on the popular ABC morning show, *The View.* Joy spent several years on New York's stand-up circuit, winning several awards, before landing a job as the host of her own call-in radio show on WABC. On television she has appeared on *Politically Incorrect, Baby Boom,* and the voice of a neurotic patient on the animated series *Dr. Katz,* for which she won a Cable Ace Award. In films, Behar has appeared in *Cookie, This is My Life,* and Woody Allen's *Manhattan Murder Mystery,* among others. Joy is also the author of the book *Joy Schtick, Or What is the Existential Vacuum and Does It Come with Attachments?*

with prenuptial agreements; you go in knowing that it's forever, there are no deals. You stay with it, it's an everlasting love affair. Show business, I think, has more glue in it than love. With love you get divorced. Show business, that's it, you're stuck with it. When he was about ninety-something-odd years old George Burns was asked on an interview show, 'Mr. Burns, you ever think about retiring?' He said, 'To what?' That's the mindset—to what? No, I don't think I've heard of anybody retiring, not in the stand-up game."

Joy Behar knows from funny. "I've said this many times, if you're not funny, don't try to be a comedian. Everybody has something to offer to this world whether it's tending goldfish, running a bowling alley, being a CEO, interior decorating. Pick what it is that you are very good at and willing to work at. If you're not funny, why would you want to be a comedian? That's one thing.

"The second thing is that you really must feel the need to do it—really feel some kind of need ... to be adored, or to continue the party, that's my need. My role in my family was to cheer them up. It was post World War II and everybody was a little bit down. We didn't have any money. We lived in a tenement. My mother could have used a little Zoloft, but so could have everybody else in that neighborhood. I was like the walking, talking Prozac. I was also the TV set because we didn't have a television set until late in the '50s. So that's my role in life. If the situation is getting tense, I step in. I do it on *The View* too. I try to break the tension with something funny and I just keep on doing that. I don't really like conflict. I don't like people being mad. If there's tension of some sort, I'm very apt to say something to break it. It's one of my pleasures and it's fun." Joy is obviously a Libra.

Another Behar tip: "If you are good, if you are funny, move to a city where you can have a career. If you're gonna be in Duluth, fine, but don't expect anything to happen to you beyond Duluth. So move out of Duluth. Once you're in the business, you have to get on stage constantly. It's not one of these things where you do it once a month. You've got to get on five times a week, minimum, when you first start. That's all."

Rick Newman has seen a lot of comedians fly in and out of Catch a Rising Star. "You have to keep doing it. You can't go to acting classes to become a comedian. I'm not saying that it wouldn't help in some way, if you're telling a story, but you have to keep getting back on stage. You have no choice because a comedian has to use the stage the way an athlete uses the gym or exercises. The only way a comedian can become better is by working in front of an audience. There is no other way to get better at the art of comedy.

"The very first thing a comedian has to do is get two minutes of material that works. If he doesn't get those first two minutes, knowing what to do and how to get a laugh, then he can't build off of anything. And writing is so important, of course. This is no longer the day of using someone else's material. A record company or a network or anybody who's booking a comedian looks for the full rounded talent. Occasionally, another comedian will give him a line or he'll buy a line because something fits, but you have to write and then you have to be able to get up on stage.

"Stage presence is important, but stage presence comes from getting up night after night. Find something in yourself that is quirky but natural. And every comedian really has to be likeable. That X factor, a likability factor, is extremely important. You can be dark, you can be menacing, you can have an attitude, but you still have to be likeable. You have to get that audience, as a whole, to go along with your thinking and to respond with laughter. If you're working diligently, by the end of a year, a year-and-a-half, if you're still not able to get any kind of showcase anywhere, I think it's time to go back to driving a cab.

"Basically comedians, the ones who are really successful, are just funny, that's it. Somehow or other there's something inherent in their personality that makes them funny. There are comedy classes, which I'm sure you see advertised all over, and they teach you the basic steps. But you can't really teach someone to be funny. You can teach the structure or how to tell a joke or how to orchestrate and build a joke, but teaching someone to be a comedian is like trying to teach someone to be taller, you can't do it. Some of us get that as a gift. Some of us can write. Some of us can draw. Some of us can sing, but it has to be part of your persona."

I couldn't help myself, I had to ask Rick if he was funny, and whether he ever considered going into the spotlight rather than just turning it on. "No, no, no. As a matter of fact, I get quite petrified speaking in front of people. But there were times in the first year when an emcee wouldn't show up and I would have to emcee the evening, and I was terrified. I took the liberty—and who was going to argue with me—of stealing a little bit of a line from this comedian, a little bit of a line from that comedian, and somehow or other I could get through the evening."

Jeffrey Ross has a surefire tip. "Don't go on after me." But I suggest you follow his other learned tips too. "Here's some practical advice. These are things they taught me in my class in 1989." How cool is that? He had to pay for these and you just had get a hold of this book. "Take the mike out of the stand and put the stand behind you. Have freedom, then you can wave your arms, then you can move around, you don't have to lean on it. I sometimes lean on it like a crutch, but I know what I'm doing. I'm talking about a beginner who's gonna wind up fiddling with it like it's a security blanket and who's gonna let it get in his way. When you're ready to get off, you reach behind you and put it back. Unless you're really conscious of what you're doing on stage, get rid of things, make sure the stool's behind you, walk around, take command of the stage.

"Tape yourself. There's nothing worse than coming up with that great riff, then you come back and ask five people what you said and they all say five different things. Prepare. Over-prepare, if you're a beginner. Figure out what you wanna do, what you wanna open on, what you wanna close on, really figure it out and then forget it. Learn it, but don't learn it so much that you're stuck to it. When I do a Roast, I have all my jokes planned out. I know what I'm gonna do in order, but when Freddie Roman gets up and heckles me, I can't be so stuck to my script that I can't jump three jokes ahead to my Freddie stuff to get him. Learn your material and then forget it. That's the only way I can really put it into practical words or useable terminology.

"The more you prepare, the more you can improvise, because you can always go back to your script. Let's look at acting for a second. Say you have a monologue and it's two pages long, but the other actor does something, like drops a tray of glasses during your monologue. You gotta be able to improvise and if you know your monologue well enough, you'll be able to go in and out of it and drop a line of it and it won't fuck you up. But if you only kind of know it, you're not gonna be able to move out of it. It really works.

"Sometimes I'm on TV, I'll be on "Joy's Comedy Corner" on *The View,* and I'll do two jokes and get an applause break and she'll go, we have another minute, do you have another one? You gotta be on your toes. The

CAROL LEIFER is an internationally-acclaimed comedian and comedy writer. She spent three years as a writer and producer on *Seinfeld,* garnering both Writers Guild and Emmy Award nominations. Carol created and executive-produced *The Ellen Show* and was supervising producer on HBO's *The Larry Sanders Show.* As a stand-up comedian, Carol made twenty-five appearances on *Late Night with David Letterman* and starred in three of her own Showtime comedy specials. She made her television starring debut on the WB's *Alright Already* and was the co-executive producer of the ABC sitcom *It's Like, You Know.*

best comedy is not always done just standing up there at a mike. Sometimes I have to do my act in the form of an interview, on the radio or on Howard Stern or on Joy's show. I'm doing Carson Daly's new show, I'm not gonna be standing there by myself. I'm gonna be on a couch and he's gonna ask me about airline security. It's gotta be learned and rehearsed. I gotta know those jokes so inside and out that I can respond to any form of the question that he asks me. He might say to me, 'So, did they confiscate anything?' He might say, 'So, how was the flight?' He might say, 'So, what about airline security?' I don't want to step on what he's saying. You just gotta know what the funny part is, and trust that the punch line will land the same way, no matter how you get into it."

Carol Leifer knows funny, having been behind the scenes of comedy as well as in front. That means she gives good advice. "To be a serious, working comedian is really to commit at least a year. Go on every night, five nights a week at the comedy club that you work at or at other clubs, and judge yourself and really do it for a year. What makes you good is going on a lot and not judging yourself and putting up with the consequences even if you're not doing well, you're a comedian and that's how you learn. I know so many people now who take a comedy class and get a tape of themselves at the class and then it's like, 'Alright, can I get on Letterman now?' without learning the nuts and bolts of being a comedian. It takes a lot of time.

"I always get nervous before any show I do. I'm never one of these guys, like Jay Leno, who's eating a slice of pizza seconds before he goes on. The important thing is never to take it too seriously. It's a show and if they sense you're uptight, they'll be uptight. But that also comes with doing it."

"You know what's interesting?" inquires Gilbert Gottfried. "People come up to me, struggling comics or actors, and they say, 'Oh, I'm a comic' or 'I'm an actor' and 'Could you give me some advice?' I always feel, secretly, what they're saying is that they feel like they're struggling but they think, 'Hey, you just rolled out of bed one morning and had a career, can you now hand me a career the same way it was just handed to you?' I think they do think that. 'While I'm working hard, that guy just got movies and TV.'

"Whenever I give them advice I see them shut off 'cause it's not what they want to hear. They don't want to hear, 'You gotta work hard. What gets a laugh you do, what doesn't get a laugh you don't do. Gotta work hard and keep your fingers crossed.' No one wants to hear that. So when I give them advice like that, it's as if they are asking for ways of losing weight but they don't want to hear, 'Give up ice cream and cake and hamburgers and start exercising.' That's awful. 'No, that's not what I wanted to hear.' They want to hear there's some secret thing, there's something they can wrap around their heads when they go to sleep at night or something."

David Mishevitz may not have Shecky Greene's resume but he surely has been in the trenches long enough to know what to expect. Take, for instance, audiences. If he reads them before he goes out he might be thinking, 'Oh, they're laughing at everything so it's gonna be easy. Well, what if you go out with that attitude and

DAVID MISHEVITZ is a relative new-comer to the stand-up comedy world, having just left a position in the media buying department of BBDO West advertising. He writes his own material based on personal experiences and life's observations. He has contributed jokes to *The Tonight Show with Jay Leno* and is a paid regular at The Comedy Store in Los Angeles. David also does commer-cials and has provided voice-overs for such companies as Budweiser, Taco Bell, and Nascar.

they smell it on you? You can't get cocky. I'm thinking more about seeing who I have to follow and making sure I'm prepared to follow them, whether it's a younger guy or Andrew Dice Clay, who I did have to follow one time. What do you do after that? You can't be dirty. So it's more about trying to figure out how they are going to react to you. I've had easy crowds where I didn't put in all my effort because they were laughing at stuff that I think is just awful. It's just a matter of knowing what you are doing right then and there.

"Some people say you should go on the road, but is a one-nighter in Montana going to be any different from going on at one-thirty in the morning in New York, with four people who have been there since nine o'clock? Is that a big difference in how tight my material is going to get? I don't think so. Aside from a little bit of cash I might get, to help pay for stuff."

"If you don't feel funny in your head," advises Dick Capri, "if you don't feel that you have something to tell them and you're afraid that they're not going to accept you and you have no confidence in yourself, then you are gonna get stage fright. But if you feel that you are funny and you know what you're doing or you've done it many, many times and it always works, it's not nervousness, what it is, is adrenaline. Adrenaline will help you a great deal. If you go out and just say the words, they know you are just saying the words. If you don't feel the funny in your head and have that adrenaline going in your stomach and you go out and try to fake it, the meter goes down. Sometimes you get into a rut and you get burned out because you're doing the same stuff over and over. You need some pepper up your butt. You'll get a great audience and that will put pepper up your butt for a while.

"Repetition, keep doing it. My son is a comedian and if he has an audition or he's gonna do something, I tell him, work slow, because what happens with comedians, when they're nervous they talk fast because they are trying to get to the punch line quicker. That's the worse thing you can do. I've done thirty minutes of material in twelve minutes because I was nervous and I spit it out. The first time I worked Vegas, I was so nervous, I went out there and spit out this whole material in twelve minutes. I didn't even stop for laughs. My kind of comedy, you gotta talk slow. When you think you're slow, you aren't slow enough. It's like a golf swing, you got to do it slow."

Lily Tomlin is well aware of the pressures people starting out have to deal with, not to mention the unsolicited advice that is foisted upon them along the way. "When kids start out, I never interfere. People used to come to me and say 'you could be this or you could be that' and I knew that they could derail me. I didn't want to be derailed. I had to hold onto my material and whatever it was that I envisioned for myself. Whenever I see kids working, young kids starting out, I'm very reluctant. I don't want to interfere. I saw Bruce Springsteen at a very early point, before he was really famous. Remember how he'd jump off of things and play that guitar and jump up and down? That's what he's led to do, he can't stop himself from doing that.

"I don't know anything to tell anyone except that you learn by doing. Maybe you can learn by visualizing. Visualize yourself being hilarious. Athletes do it, they visualize making baskets and stuff and then they play better. I never cared about being famous—I wanted to make a living. When I worked in the coffee houses, I was happy. If I'd never left Detroit I would have been happy if I had my own coffee house and could do performances and experimental theater and other forms of entertainment, after-hours jazz. In those days we'd have poetry readings and folk singing and anything that people were interested in we put on the stage. We just needed a place to have an audience. You really can't do it without an audience. When I open *The Search for Signs Of Intelligent Life In The Universe* I say, 'I'm so glad to see you, there's always a chance you might not show up and without you there'd be little point in me being here.' Then I always say, 'I think most actors worry about playing to an empty house. I also worry about playing to a full house and leaving the audience empty.'"

According to Pat Cooper, "A great stand-up comic observes. Or, a great natural comic who don't wanna observe, he pays people to observe for him, and they give him one-liners, like Henny Youngman. Henny Youngman, in my opinion, was one of the best. But he had a writer. That's not to make Henny Youngman less, it was naturally he made those lines happen, that was him. If I said, 'Take my wife please,' I don't think it would have worked. But it worked for him. Young people gotta understand that.

"Today, you can be a semi-comedian and wind up making millions of dollars, but when I was around you had to put it out there. You bombed the Copa once, you never went back again, it was over. There were no second chances. Here, you get nine, ten chances—well, I had a bad day; it was too near Christmas (but it's in July?). Yeah, but, but—so everyone turns around and has an excuse and unfortunately, my era is over.

"Analyze what I say. Even the serious things, there's a touch of humor. Even in my anger, there's a touch of humor. When you've got that it will survive you, it will protect your hate. Because I don't have hate. Why? Because my comedy offsets that. I have anger, but

I don't have hate. So how do I protect myself from that hate? I have my sense of humor. I throw out lines. Comedy has saved me from the electric chair. Comedy has saved me from the gas chamber. Comedy has saved me from murder. I would have killed everybody, and I say that all the time."

Carrot Top has a somewhat different view of things, which is no surprise. "The only tips I can offer are what I was told, too. I never believed it until I started it, but it's getting stage time. The more time you get on stage, the more you get acclimated to what you're doing. I didn't even know what I was doing until like the fourth or fifth year, because you don't know who you are yet. I found my whole character of Carrot Top, the props, the whole idea of my shtick, my style, what I talk about, the content of what I talk about—that came about as I got more stage time.

"When I first started, I was imitating somebody's style until I kind of found out who I was. When I first started, people were like, 'You sound like Letterman.' I did a lot of Lettermanesque stuff and then I found out who I was and picked out what I was gonna do and how I was going to talk about it. Getting stage time is the key and I always say, just make people laugh."

David Alan Grier has some solid advice for anyone who wants to try the stand-up game: "Don't do it. Don't do it. I'm serious. You have a better chance at being an NBA superstar than being a comic." Oh, sorry, I thought I erased that part. But when I explained that might not fly in a book about being a comic, he offered, "My advice is this. You have to be talented enough to make it and stupid enough to keep trying. You have to define yourself to others. You can't go to people and say, 'What should I be? Who should I be?' That's never gonna work. Know who you want to be and tell the world, 'This is who I am.' You cannot go and ask them, 'Tell me who I should be. Should I be the funny, wacky guy?' You can't do that. You have to have confidence, supreme belief in yourself. You have to tell your jokes, whatever persona you take on, whether it's the big brash voice or the small little

ONLY JECKLE LIKES HECKLE

There must be nothing worse for a comic than that stupid drunk sitting five seats away from the stage, yelling at the top of his lungs, "When's the comedian comin' on? Get off the stage, you're lousy!" At some point, every comedian has to deal with that larger-than-life (or drunker-than-a-skunk) member of the audience, the funny wannabe, the irritating heckler.

DAVID ALAN GRIER

"The rule of thumb is this: When a person heckles you, ninety percent of the audience cannot hear what the person said, and if they can hear him it's unintelligible. So for you to stop your act and address that person, you better have something really funny and incredible to say or else you're just wasting time, you're taking yourself out of your act and you've just fucked everything up. So nine times out of ten, just ignore him."

DAVID BRENNER

"I can remember one heckler, I came into Catch a Rising Star one night to get ready for a TV shot, to practice. The comedians said, 'Oh, man, there's a guy up near the front, he's drunk, a visiting businessman, and he has destroyed every comedian. He sent some of them out in tears. He's just nasty.' I said, 'Aw, I can't put up with this. I'm here to practice, to get myself in shape for television and write some material for my stand-up.' So I went out there and he started a little bit with me. I said, 'Hey mister, you've got the wrong guy. You're dealing with a professional here. I'm not one of these young kids that's starting out. You start with me, I'm gonna nail your ass up on the wall over there.' So he starts again. He's with some woman. I lit into him. I'm from the streets with him.

"To deal with hecklers is my nature. I attacked him so much that he was holding up his hands, begging for mercy. I know what it's like to have a set ruined and you don't know if you're gonna get on for a few nights or the owner might never put you on again. After I had destroyed him, I said, 'You know, this is an audience, but in about ten seconds I could turn it into a mob. I could have them lynch you, literally lynch you. Take you out on First Avenue and lynch you,' and the people were cheering. Now he's getting scared. He begs, begs me and I stop. But you know something? It was just nagging at me. Like six minutes later, it was nagging at me that I couldn't get him out of my system. I turned to him and I said, 'You know something mister, when I look at you, all I can think of is what a tragic waste of skin.' He was finished before that. That was the icing on the stupid cake."

NORM CROSBY

"I never had that problem—never, ever, because of the hearing aids. I would run away from them, 'cause I really couldn't hear what they were saying to me so I had no chance to go back and forth; I would avoid them completely. If somebody said something, I would completely ignore it, then it stopped. I don't think I ever had any, but maybe I just didn't hear them.

SUSIE ESSMAN

"Hecklers are always a problem because people are drinking, especially late shows. Late shows tend to attract really young and stupid and drunk people. It was a learning experience when I had to deal with it, I learned how to be really tough. I think that I get fewer hecklers than male comics do because women almost never heckle, it's almost always men who heckle and men are not gonna heckle me because I will make them feel like fuckin' idiots. They don't want to be humiliated by a woman. They don't want me to make them feel like they're this big. Sometimes when they heckle me, it's like, 'Come on honey, you wanna take me on?' First of all, I have the mike. The mike is all power, it's amplification: I have that. Also, I'm gonna be funnier and smarter than them ... they're not gonna be quicker than me.

"Sometimes there will be an area in the audience that is just drunk, and I won't even look at them. I will not talk to them. I give them no attention whatsoever. I give them no energy. That sometimes works and sometimes it doesn't."

RICK NEWMAN

"One of the things about Catch, especially at the beginning, the audience wasn't trained—they're more trained now. In those days, someone would occasionally have a few drinks that didn't know that you don't talk to the comedian unless he's talking to you. That breaks the rhythm and the stride of the comedian. What I would do, I would give the table one warning and then the second time I'd pick up their check and throw them out of the place. Why go to a club? Someone's up there doing their stuff ... it disrupts the evening, it disrupts the comedian, the audience gets angry. Hecklers are a terrible thing. Hecklers should be shot."

RICHARD BELZER

"It's legendary, what I do to them. The problem would become theirs, if they heckled. There are different kinds of hecklers. There are some people who are just a little drunk and they want to be a part of the show. There are some people who are just really mean. There are some people who are just incoherent. There are some people who are really smart and funny and get into it. So every heckler is different, and I would treat each one differently. There was a while there where I didn't mind it, when I was emceeing, 'cause if I was out of material and somebody said something, I had material. There was a point where people would come just to see what I would do to the audience."

PHYLLIS DILLER

"I don't have hecklers. I think it's because of me. I don't want them. I don't handle them. I've never been prepared for them. If they want to be a part of the show, they're gonna have to make an appointment. Either I'm talking or they're laughing, talking, laughing. There's no room for them, there's no dead air."

JEFFREY ROSS

"A buddy of mine booked me to open—I wanna say it was fire-fighters, their Christmas party or their annual fuckin' whatev-er—a private gig for good money. It's a PBA lodge type of place, real low end, private party gig and I'm up there and no one's listening. I'm talking to myself and I'm getting heckled, basi-cally, off the stage. I always pick the biggest, stupidest guy; I start talking to him, goofin' on him. Fuckin' drunk gets up, walks on stage, pulls the mike out of my hand, literally—he's a fireman, what am I gonna do? Raises his fist like he's gonna punch me in the face and I just walked off stage. It's worse than getting the hook. I got this drunk, confused guy—he didn't want to hear a comedian, he wanted to be drinking and talking to his friends. It was just nonsense. I'm not wearing a suit. I'm not even a grown man. I'm just a guy in jeans and a leather jacket talking into a public address system, opening for somebody who's probably gonna juggle or play guitar. I'm just really there to get the crowd's attention."

KEVIN MEANEY

"If somebody does jump in at a good time, it's great as long as it doesn't throw you off or the whole audience off, and you can control it. You can mine a good laugh out of a heckler and it can be a highlight of the show if it's handled right. You're walk-ing a tightrope out there—anything can happen. You have to listen and then you have to react to what you just heard. You have to just use your instinct at being funny to come up with something that's gonna top this guy. Or maybe you don't even have to top him, maybe you just have to acknowledge him and then move on to your next bit. But that could be your biggest laugh of the night because it's so out of the ordinary."

voice, you have to be confident that what you're saying is entertaining and interesting because if you don't feel that, everyone will be bored."

What does Shecky Greene offer to newcomers? "Well, I don't know who a neophyte comedian is, because they do one show on television, one four-, five-, six-minute spot and they can become stars, get their own television shows. We had to work nightclubs and nightclubs, we had to go from a strip club to a fairly decent supper club to the Chez Paris to the Copacabana, and it was very, very tough. These kids today, they think about, 'We need a hunk, we gotta get a hunk.' Well, I never thought 'a hunk.' What the hell is a hunk? But that's important to them, that's important to get on the improvs. They go to the owners and the managers and they say, 'I got a great hunk, I just wanna do it, let me do the hunk,' and they're funny. You listen to the hunk and then they stand there, 'Do another hunk.' 'I don't have another hunk. I'll get the writer and we'll get another hunk.'"

Shecky knows the power of the comedy clubs and the improv joints. "You go ahead down there, 'cause they got some great kids. It's a wonderful, wonderful outlet for these people. I see 'em and I just love their talent. I love great singers, great dancers. I could sit there and not even think I'm in show business. I just admire that person standing on the stage and I wonder what's going through her head, if it's the same thing that went through my head." If it is, then that's one funny new comic up there, that's for damn sure.

Bernie Brillstein might manage your career one day, so hear him out. "First of all, there's no one to write comedy material for a stand-up. When I started, there were a hundred writers doing stand-up material and comedians put them under contract. Buddy Arnold wrote for Milton Berle for years—these guys were great. You don't have anyone to write comedy material any more, so as a comedian you have to write your own material or steal it from somebody else. So what advice I have is that, unless you have a good friend who can write your material or unless you write pretty well, forget it. That's my advice. Everyone's dying for comedians. The fact that no comedian has ever won an Oscar, for Best Actor, it's really sick. Chaplin never won, Gleason never won ... that shows you what the business thinks of comedians.

"When you shoot a movie, you shoot four minutes and stop. When you do a comedy act—Robin Williams will do two hours and just keep going. God, Norm Crosby has, probably, four hours worth of material and he reads *Newsweek* every day, all the magazines and the newspapers, and is constantly thinking of the funny side of it. But where do you go now? You come out and you go to the Improv or you go to The Laugh Factory or you go to Carolines, and you fight to get your five minutes, God knows where and when. God, it's very tough.

"I hate to keep saying 'in the old days,' but in the old days you actually had places to fail in and then you'd learn. You'd go out the next time and if a singer took a liking to you, you could work for forty weeks. Norm went out with Robert Goulet and Tom Jones and worked forty-eight weeks a year with each of them. That was great and you got better and better and better. You worked seven nights a week or six and you get better. Shit, I don't know where people go to get better now." Well not all tips are happy, peppy ones, ya know.

Perhaps Ryan Stiles' tips will be a tad more sugar-coated for you. "Number one, I would say get experience where you are. If you're in the middle of Missouri somewhere and you want to be a stand-up comic, don't come to Hollywood yet. Find a club where you can do it there first and get used to being on stage and get a little experience before you come here. This is a really hard place to learn.

"Do what you want to do. It's really hard to do what you want to do 'cause you're always doing what you think people want to see you do, and that's a real mistake. You're only gonna relax when you do your own thing. You're gonna have more fun and that's the only thing that's gonna keep you in it, 'cause you're not gonna make a ton of money off the top, so unless you enjoy doing it, there's no reason to do it, really.

RED BUTTONS, who started his career in burlesque, is an entertainment staple whose career has covered all mediums: radio, Broadway, film, and television. He earned an Academy Award for Best Supporting Actor as well as a Golden Globe Award for his role alongside Marlon Brando in the 1957 drama *Sayonara.* His other film credits include *The Longest Day, The Poseidon Adventure,* and *They Shoot Horses, Don't They?,* for which he received a Golden Globe Award nomination. He has starred in two of his own television series, *The Red Buttons Show* and *The Double Life of Henry Phyfe* and has been a guest on every major variety show, including Ed Sullivan, Andy Williams, Dinah Shore, Perry Como, Redd Foxx, Eddie Fisher, and the Dean Martin Roasts. Red is also a special favorite at Friars Club Roasts and Testimonial Dinners.

"It's really addictive to be on stage, it's like a drug. Some people, I'm sure, are told by their friends and family that they're really funny, but maybe their friends and family aren't really that funny, I don't know. Some people should not be on stage, period. I know what most of these guys aim for, they want to be on TV or they want their own series, but I wouldn't concentrate on that. I'd just concentrate on being a really good stand-up and doing really fun stuff and those opportunities will come. But if you're going out and your objective is to get a TV show, I don't think it's gonna work for you. If you're not enjoying what you're doing, what's the point of doing it?"

"It used to be you had to be funny as a person to be a comedian. That's no longer true. Now you can be trained. I would say the first thing is, don't do *my* material." Got that? Don't do David Brenner's material. "I had a date years ago in Florida. She said, 'I'll meet you at this club, at the bar, and then we can go out from there.' I parked the car and walked in and went to the bar and I heard a lot of laughter. I didn't realize, 'Oh my God, it's a comedy club.' So I took my drink and I went and stood in the doorway and there was a comedian on and about a hundred people in the club. He was doing an entire chunk of my material. Verbatim. So I called out from the back, 'That's funnier when David Brenner does it.' 'How would you know?' he yelled back. I said, 'Because I'm David Brenner.' He said, 'Yeah, sure you are.' Then someone in the audience turned around, 'It *is* David Brenner,' and they started to applaud.

"So I put down my drink, I walked up, I took the microphone out of his hand, I said, 'Now let me show you how you do that routine.' I completed the next five, seven minutes of the routine, and of course, I destroyed. I handed him back the microphone. He was dead meat. I went back to the bar and met my date. If you want to interpret what I just said about don't do my material, you could extend it. Don't do anyone's material. If you really want to be happy with yourself at the big time, be an original. That way you have a certain kind of good feeling inside.

"Don't listen to any professional in the business tell you anything about yourself or your act or anything. Listen to the audience. They will orchestrate—they will write your act and create your persona by their reaction. Mold yourself according to the audiences. Not to managers, agents, nightclub owners. They don't know what the hell they're doing or they'd be doing stand-up. I mean, they're usually totally ineffective, these people.

"The other thing is take a clock on the stage with you, set it for midnight, no matter what time you go on, so if the owner tells you to do twenty minutes, you don't get up there and look at your watch or forget when you went on.

"I think the best advice I can give a young comedian, and I don't know if they have the wherewithal to do this, is, 'Alright, you have some new ideas. Where do you put them?' Almost every comedian will tell you to put them at the end of the act, when you've got them rolling, or at the middle, when you've got the momentum going. I always test new ideas right up front and the reason for that is, it's the worst place to do it. The beginning of your show is always the slowest part of your show. So, if you get laughs then, you know the material's good. That's the litmus test.

"There are three ingredients to success. They are talent, timing, and tenacity. Now, talent, you can do something about. You can nurture and improve your talent. Tenacity is entirely in your hands, to be tenacious, to never give up. Timing is pure luck. I've met guys on the road, so funny, so brilliant, originals, and they are working comedy clubs for a few hundred bucks a week. Timing is it. I think about my career and what happened from that one *Tonight Show*. Or I think about a guy like Ray Romano, fourteen years on the road, no agent, no manager is getting him anywhere. The guy's ready to go back to being a truck driver. He gets on the Letterman show, David sees him do his routine, invites him to his office and says to him, 'You know, that stuff about your wife and the twins and your other kid, and your brother who's a cop and your parents who are overbearing? I think that would make a great sitcom. Let me make some calls and HBO and blah, blah, and we'll do a pilot.' And now it's the number-one comedy hit in America, because David Letterman, a comedian, saw another comedian do something and said, 'Wow.' Meanwhile, fourteen years of doing it on the road, not one professional working with him came up with the idea. Right? No one said to him, we're gonna do your routine as a sitcom. That's why I say, don't listen to the professionals.

"I saw a guy, not only didn't he get laughs in the beginning of his career, the people booed him and threw things at him, and that was Andy Kaufman. I told him when he came off stage, 'you wanna know something, you're so wild … weird, you're such an original, it's gonna take time for them to understand what the hell you are. You're like a freak up there, but you're one of the funniest freaks I've ever seen.' I was screaming. I was the only one laughing in the whole place. I was standing in the doorway—I was just gone. I got him, you understand. Just like Letterman understood Ray Romano, I understood Andy Kaufman and boy, it took a while, but there he was. You can't judge the first time you appear. You gotta hang in there. That's tenacity. If you believe in yourself.

"A lot of people blame me for the comedy boom because I made it look so easy. All of a sudden guys are sitting in dormitories and they're saying, 'What do you wanna be?' 'I don't know, I'm thinking of being a doctor, maybe, medical.' What about you?' 'Well, I'm more interested in science.' 'And what about you?' 'Well, it's between accounting and comedy. You know, I see David Brenner and it's so easy.'" But now that you've gotten this far in the book, you know better—don't you?

Norm Crosby recognizes changing times for comedians. "It's not just a matter of getting up and being a funny guy, putting on a fright wig or funny jacket and making people laugh. That doesn't work anymore. People are too sophisticated. Television made people much brighter, much more aware. All of a sudden, the people in Spitball, Oklahoma are as sharp and as aware as the people in New York City, because they see all the newest things. They see the news, they see what's going on, they watch Jay Leno, they watch David Letterman, they're just sharp.

"In the early days of the business, they'd say, 'Take an engagement in Dayton, Ohio,' and you break in your material. You can't do that anymore because you go into those places and those people are just as hip and just as aware as the people in San Francisco or Los Angeles or New York. You break in your material in your house. There's no 'sticks' anymore—there's no such thing. Every place you go now there are sharp, intelligent, bright people, which is great, really great if that's the way you work. But if you depend on people picking it up a little slowly, you're in serious trouble."

Ever the optimist, Susie Essman suggests, "Sometimes when you die you do need to get up the next night. If you have talent, you do need to work through it, it's just a matter of technique. Sometimes it's a bad audience, sometimes you're off, sometimes you have your period, sometimes you broke up with your boyfriend, whatever.

"I think that the reason people start to feel really weird and uncomfortable when a bad comic is on stage is that, more than wanting to laugh, people want to be taken care of when they go to a comedy club or a show. When a bad comic gets up there, it changes the expectation. All of a sudden the audience member has to take care of him—'Oh no, I feel so sorry for this person, I feel so bad.' Now, all of a sudden the audience is taking care of the comic instead of relaxing, having a drink, laughing, enjoying the fact that they're in good hands. I want the audience to know what I'm doing. I'm gonna take care of you, you can relax. That's the job of the performer—to take care of the audience.

"Stage time is everything. You gotta get on stage everywhere, anywhere ... just get on stage, get on stage, get on stage. 'Cause there's no way to develop those senses and instincts without having the experience. I didn't have that when I first started. You are not too good for any venue, every venue, you will learn from. Oh, these Jersey gigs I used to do, standing on a bar with some shitty microphone and sound system.

"Knowing who you are on stage takes a really long time. It's years and years and years before you understand your own persona on stage. You always have to be true to yourself, but it's harder in the beginning 'cause you have no idea of who you are. I think that the mistake that I see most young comedians make is, they don't connect to an audience. They talk in some of kind of voice, like a comic cadence, that they picked up somewhere, and it's not who they are, it's who they're pretending to be. Talk in your own voice. Talk to the audience, don't use the audience. Actually listen. I mean, don't stand up there like you're reading a cue card and just recite material—tell them the material, connect with them. Have a reason why you're telling them the material. Don't go for the laughs, go for the connection, go for the emotional connection with the audience. Go for the experience of it, as opposed for waiting for your applause break, waiting for your laugh, 'cause then it's all result-oriented, and you're not in it. Be in the moment, be Zen."

Howie Mandel is succinct in his advice, "It's NIKE's tip and I say it to everybody—just do it. Just do it. No matter how crazy it seems, no matter where you are in your life, no matter what you're doing. I was six months into my engagement to be married to the woman who is now my wife and I was doing well in retail. If I never did it, if I didn't take that dare, I wouldn't be here today, and I'm very happy with where I am. I would've been unhappy saying 'I shoulda ... I coulda....' Life's too short, you just gotta go for it and be true to yourself.

"Don't do what you think should be done. Do what entertains you. There's room for so many different, unique things—there are so many different people on this planet. If you have it in you, go for it and don't be discouraged. Don't be discouraged by one night, don't be discouraged by two weeks. If you have the strength and the stamina, keep going at it even if it doesn't work out. I think people get discouraged too easy.

"I know people who are still at The Comedy Store today that were there in 1979 when I went on stage. You don't know them and you may never know them, but there is something that drives them onto that stage every night or a few times a week. They're not getting the television shows, they're not getting the club dates, they're barely scraping by, and they've been there for twenty years. I don't begrudge them, I say, 'Man, there is something in them, the need to do what they're doing, and they're going for it.' I respect that a lot more than somebody who comes up to me and says, 'Oh, I would really love to do that. How do you get started?' My answer is, just do it. If you don't do it then nothing will come of it. If you do it, maybe nothing will come of it, but you're giving yourself a chance."

There you have it, the comedians have spoken. Now, do you think you have the cojones to pull this off? Your road to stand-up comedy may not necessarily be paved with gold, but barring stomach ailments and possibly a drug or alcohol dependency, the potholes are certainly maneuverable. Those in-the-know have shared their first time and their worst time, their style, tricks, and tips—if these don't get you on stage, nothing will.

Perhaps David Mishevitz, who is still just getting started in his stand-up career, said it best when he shared, "It's cool. You write stuff that you think about and you tell it to strangers and they react and people pay you. Who does that? I did a lot of writing and short story stuff and I'd send it out and have to wait weeks for a rejection letter. I write a joke—I might know tonight whether it's got any kind of grasp to it." Maybe it doesn't, but in any case, he's finding out.

Maybe, these personal reflections and recollections from some of the most successful comedians in the business have better informed you about the craft of stand-up comedy. You may never set foot on a stage in your life, but if you do, feel secure in the knowledge that you're taking one small step for man and a giant leap onto that banana peel of laughter.